# THE RELUCTANT SUPERPOWER

# THE
# RELUCTANT
# SUPERPOWER

*A History of America's*
*Global Economic Reach*

# RICHARD
# HOLT

KODANSHA INTERNATIONAL
*New York • Tokyo • London*

Kodansha America, Inc.

114 Fifth Avenue, New York, New York 10011, U.S.A.

Kodansha International Ltd.

17-14 Otowa 1-chome, Bunkyo-ku, Tokyo 112, Japan

Published in 1995 by Kodansha America, Inc.

Library of Congress Cataloging-in-Publication Data

Holt, Richard D.

The reluctant superpower : a history of America's global economic reach / by Richard Holt.

P.    CM.

Includes bibliographical references and index.

ISBN 1-56836-038-X

1. United States—Foreign economic relations—history.
2. United States—Economic conditions.   3. United States—Economic policy.   4. Free enterprise—United States—History.
5. Keynesian economics—History.   I. Title.

HF1455.H55    1995

337.73—DC20                                                      94-46382

Book design by Kathy Kikkert

Printed in the United States of America

95  96  97  98  99  Q/FF  10  9  8  7  6  5  4  3  2  1

*To Nigel Whitham*

# CONTENTS

# PREFACE

It is a common perception that Americans, by shouldering a large burden of responsibility for the security and prosperity of other nations, have constrained their own ability to flourish over the last fifty years. It is another common perception that, thanks to America's global leadership, many of the world's countries have now attained living standards and economic opportunities at least comparable with those of the United States. As a result, and because the Cold War is over, it seems reasonable that the United States should retreat a little from its global obligations and focus instead on domestic issues. In doing so, Americans may even wish to adopt some of the mercantilist tactics that other nations have used to promote their own interests—policies that perhaps worked in the past at Americans' expense, and that Americans may now wish to use to the possible detriment of Japan, say, or the European Union, Korea, or Taiwan.

This appears to be the thinking of the Clinton administration. The willingness of at least some Clinton staffers, such as Laura Tyson (Chairman of the Council of Economic Advisors), to consider using restrictive trade policies as part of an interventionist industrial strategy signifies an economic philosophy geared to reclaiming jobs that many Americans believe have been lost to foreigners. Much more subtle but no less striking is Labor Secretary Robert Reich's belief that the same result can be achieved if Americans simply raise their educational standards. Meanwhile, it is so obvious that the American government will not launch a Marshall Plan for Eastern Europe that nobody even bothers to suggest such a thing, despite the many crises apparent throughout almost all the former Soviet empire.

The United States, it seems, has become reluctant to continue carrying the burden of being the world's preeminent economic superpower—perhaps because doing so is no longer necessary, or appreciated, or even possible. Fifty years after Bretton Woods and the landings on the Normandy beaches, Americans seem to be changing their priorities.

If this is true, and if indeed a decisive change is occurring in the pattern of global economic and political leadership, then it will have profound implications in Japan, in Europe, and also in the United States itself. Part of the subject of this book is a consideration of what the options for world leaders may now be, at least within the sphere of economic policymaking. However, the discussion is set within an economic history that suggests that, in the economic field, Americans have always been reluctant fully to embrace their nation's superpower status. Thus the years through which we are now living are perhaps not as distinctive as many people claim, and the future may not be quite as unfamiliar as is often supposed.

One basic point is that the United States first became an economic superpower not during World War II but much earlier. A century ago, after decades of strong growth, American output moved ahead of production in both Germany and Britain. The United States thus acquired the largest economy in the world, with average incomes exceeding those in any other major nation.

Part of this book is concerned with demonstrating how long it took for American governments to accept even a shared responsibility for the management of the global economy. The possible reasons for this reluctance are numerous. Before World War I they included the low level of American dependence on foreign trade, and the substantial role that Britain still seemed to play, apparently leaving American governments little to contribute. After that war, though, the world's need for American leadership became very considerable: hitherto, Britain had provided the world with finance for investment and an open market in which to sell, and had thereby fostered world economic expansion; now only the United States was in a position to do the same.

American unwillingness to provide that leadership, and the retreat into isolationism, contributed significantly to the nation's problems in the Great Depression. Meanwhile, a faulty diagnosis of the cause of the Depression persuaded Americans to introduce anti-big-business regulations that undermined the very basis of the nation's rapid economic growth. The United States saddled itself with an extreme free-market economy in which investment and long-term growth were sacrificed to considerations of immediate gratification. In contrast, other nations, most obviously Japan, retained big business empires that closely resembled those of the old American robber barons, and that pursued starkly different strategies to those now favored by American firms. Despite the temporary boost provided to the United States by World War II, the groundwork for the country's relative decline had already been laid.

It was thus ironic that although the war made Americans realize that their own interests were best served by the promotion of a vibrant world economy, their ability to lead the world forward was already in doubt. Moreover, the leadership that the United States offered in the postwar period was itself less certain than is often realized. Many American initiatives such as the Bretton Woods exchange rate pact either failed or were ineffective, often because of a prevalent but flawed belief that market forces rather than government policies could be left to make all the necessary decisions. In that as in other senses, the lessons that Keynes attempted to teach in the thirties remained substantially unlearned.

In consequence, the world economy as it developed over the subsequent five decades probably owed less to American initiatives than is commonly supposed. Partly for that reason, it is unlikely that the burden of leadership has in fact been as heavy as many Americans claim. Nevertheless, it is certainly true that the world economy cannot easily prosper unless the governments of one or more major nations identify global economic policymaking as a legitimate matter for concern. Accordingly, Japan, the United States, and other nations may do themselves more harm than good if they now all focus on domestic policies to the total exclusion of any sense of international responsibility.

This, in part, makes for a hefty degree of suspicion about many of the Japan-emulating trade and industrial policies that are periodically canvassed in the United States, whether by politicians such as Richard Gephardt or by economists such as Robert Kuttner. And even those such as Robert Reich who argue that the United States will prosper if it simply raises its skills, its knowledge, and its educational attainments are seriously deluded. Tougher competition —by fair means as well as foul—in an economically stagnant world is a recipe for severe global conflict. The United States, Japan, and the rest of the world all need international economic policies that take their inspiration from Keynes's twenty-year quest to move beyond the economics of nationalism and toward a more cooperative policy approach.

# ACKNOWLEDGMENTS

This book draws on the published work of many historians, economists, and political commentators. I have attempted to acknowledge all of my sources through footnotes and the book's bibliography, but I apologize for any omissions or misrepresentations of which I might be guilty.

Many friends and colleagues have encouraged and supported me in the writing of this book. I hope that they will accept my thanks and forgive me if I do not mention them all personally. Paul De Angelis and John Urda of Kodansha America have been far more tolerant than I deserved, and I am grateful for that, and for their continuing enthusiasm. This book is dedicated to Nigel Whitham as a small recompense for all that I owe him.

# THE
# RELUCTANT
# SUPERPOWER

*Chapter One*

# BUILDING THE AMERICAN ECONOMY

## *Toward Prosperity*

In the nineteenth century, American business leaders built the most successful economy in the world. They created a new economic system, managerial capitalism, quite unlike that envisaged either by the nation's early-eighteenth-century colonial masters, or by most of the new nation's founding fathers.

In the eighteenth century, the great issue of American political economy had been land. In the mid-eighteenth century the British government could see little advantage in allowing the nation's North American colonies to expand westward across the continent. More land would mean a longer border to defend, and it was not the colonists who bore the costs of defending the border but the British taxpayer.[1] In 1763 the British government told the colonists by royal proclamation to stop pushing the frontier westward; by ignoring the proclamation, the colonists took a critical step toward revolution.

When independence came, the American government forced the British to surrender not only the original colonies but all the rest of the land bordered by Florida, Canada, and the Mississippi. For the time being, though, Americans no longer needed more land: in 1790 the population of the United States was only four million—just a fraction of the population of Britain—with most living on or near the Atlantic seaboard. The territory above Kentucky was almost devoid of white settlements, as was the disputed territory below Tennessee. The population could easily grow rapidly within its own borders; there seemed little need for further expansion.

However, the Louisiana Purchase changed matters. The purchase may have been an accidental by-product of the government's wish to buy Mississippi transit rights through New Orleans, but it unleashed a powerful lust for land and a series of more deliberate expansions. Politicians in Washington succumbed to talk of "manifest destiny" and went to war for the Spanish territories to the south. Further expansion followed the 1845 annexation of Texas.

Clearly the British were wrong: territorial expansion was a massive economic success. Mining and the exploitation of resources such as timber provided much of the basis for American prosperity, while American farms provided both food for a rapidly expanding population and spare produce for export to Europe. Farms dominated American exports from colonial times until the twentieth century, and turned the United States into the world's third largest trading nation by the time of World War I.

There were probably other, less tangible benefits from the nation's great expansion. Frederick Jackson Turner famously claimed that the frontier spirit gave the nation its resourcefulness and vigor. More generally, many Americans attribute their native individualism to the nation's particular history, and they see this individualism as the true source of American economic achievements. Although such attempts to identify American specialness are ultimately futile, the nation's natural advantages have clearly been among its greatest assets. In the nineteenth century, cheap and plentiful minerals, fuels, and food underpinned the phenomenal rise of American industry.

Great geographical scale was nearly the ruin of the American nation, not its making. At the very least it is true, as nations such as Britain and Japan have shown, that it is perfectly possible to thrive by importing food and raw materials in exchange for manufactured exports. Theoretically, the American economy could have prospered in the nineteenth century without agriculture, mining, and the vast lands of the West, but not without the manufacturing industries of the East.[2] More than that, however: the extensive and rapid development adopted by the United States was fraught with problems. In the eighteenth and nineteenth centuries most people still regarded land as the source of all wealth; sometimes, however, that amounted to little more than a rationale for speculation. New states such as Mississippi and Alabama were founded on little else. Their land values did in fact spiral upward for many years, but the bubble was always liable to burst, as it did in the 1840s.

Other basic problems impeded rural economic progress—for example, it took a month for a midwestern farmer to clear an acre of virgin land. Often it was years before a farm would feed those who lived on it, let alone repay their efforts or make them rich. Meanwhile farmers took other jobs or borrowed heavily. As a result, debt-ridden small holders, poor tenants, and overworked laborers populated the American Midwest. By the mid-nineteenth century, incomes in the Midwest were still half the level in the Northeast. Even southerners earned more on average, despite the prevalence there of slavery.

Further west and later on, the prairies became easier to work. However, prairie farmers had to invest heavily in livestock, draught animals, and materials for buildings and fencing. Only people who were already well off could consider the venture. There was also a serious labor shortage on the prairies; for crop growers this meant problems at harvest time, and a consequent risk of financial ruin.

Still, land was cheap. In the first half of the nineteenth century, official auction prices were little more than a dollar an acre, compared with perhaps fifty dollars for a horse or twenty dollars for a cow—and farmers often bought land for much less than the official price. Those who wanted to put their wealth into land could buy an awful lot, and many did. Settlers thought that through their efforts land prices would one day soar and they would become rich; they bought, and they toiled, and mostly they stayed poor.

Real agricultural prosperity could only come from the introduction of methods to increase productivity. In 1834 Cyrus McCormick brought farmers his mechanical harvester, which offered dramatic improvements in productivity and, therefore, in profits. However, the introduction of the reapers required other changes, which delayed their widespread adoption by a couple of decades. Farms had to be big enough to use the giant new machines, and farmers had to be wealthy enough to buy them or sufficiently well organized to lease the equipment. Agricultural success thus depended on the emergence of large, highly commercial farming operations. Such farms were mostly financed by, and even owned by, urban banks and corporations.

In 1862 Congress passed the Homestead Act, legislation offering individuals 160 acres, almost for free, to help them become yeoman farmers. It was a last defense of a way of life already in decline as the nation became more prosperous. Farming was still tough, but it required a dwindling number of workers. The first generation had struggled to win the West; the second generation found that thanks to mechanization, fertilizers, and modern farming methods, there was insufficient farm work for them to do. Large commercial organizations already overshadowed the tiny homesteads of popular mythology. So, instead of moving yet further west to their own farms, young people migrated back east. There they found well-paid and secure office or factory jobs in the newly industrialized cities, alongside millions of European migrants.

The innovation that most turned the great American landmass from a liability into an asset was the railroad. Had it not been for the railroad, history might easily have proved the eighteenth-century British, who opposed American geographical expansion, right and the new nation builders wrong. It is difficult to see how, without the railroads, the United States could have developed into the nation we recognize today. In the early nineteenth century, the only easy American transport was by sea or on the Mississippi—and in the latter case, only downstream. There were roads and there were wagon trails, but they were hardly ideal for carrying heavy or perishable cargoes.[3] So the American nation clung to the Atlantic seaboard. In 1807, however, Robert Fulton's steam powered *Clermont* made its first voyage on the Hudson. Within a few years steamboats were carrying cargoes both up and down the Mississippi. Canal building followed: by 1855 there were seven hundred steamboats working the Mississippi and nearly four thousand miles of canals, including the most famous, the Erie. One effect of canal building was to make New York the most important American port, accounting for half the nation's shipping by midcentury. However, canals had a more general impact: they helped Americans to edge away from their coastal origins and create a national economy.

Indeed, there have been various attempts by economists and historians to argue that the canals and fledgling road network were so good that the United States could have developed just as it did, even without the railroads.[4] More canals and horses would probably have met the transport needs, but the expansion of the railroad had a larger significance beyond the provision of cheap transport: the railroads meant new technology, dynamism, and innovation. The experience of building, repairing, and running the railroads taught Americans skills that they could apply in other spheres. Local workshops, set up to mend locomotives and carriages, gave Americans practical engineering skills that were both new and open ended: Not only could they repair other forms of machinery but the men who repaired often started to build, and then to design, machines that might never have existed had the railroads not given them a push.

The transformation wrought by the railroads began in 1828

when work started on the thirteen-mile Baltimore-Ohio railroad. By 1860 there were 31,000 miles of track, and by 1890 nearly 170,000 miles, with expansion still continuing.[5] Railroads brought western and midwestern produce to the factories of the East, and to the Atlantic for export to Europe. They also carried westward the goods that the farmers and small-town people wanted to buy. The railroad companies integrated the United States into a single economy, and they integrated that economy into the wider global system.

Many railroad companies were quite clear about their nation-building role. They advertised for people in the East and in Europe to settle in the West, offering to pay their fares, house them, and teach them the ways of Great Plains farming.[6] The companies' motives were, of course, no more altruistic than their marketing pitches were honest: they wanted to create a demand for their own services, and they wanted to find buyers for the huge tracts of land which they themselves owned. It was nation building, and often it was very successful, but business set the pace, not individual pioneers—and technology made progress possible.

At least as much as anything else, investment and innovation were critical to American economic success. From the colonial period onward, Americans searched for ways to reduce their costs and compete with European, primarily British, imports. Right from the start, American industry invested in new technology while the British, then the world's industrial leaders, did not.[7]

In the eighteenth and early nineteenth centuries, Americans lacked access to good fossil fuels and thus found it difficult to produce high-quality iron for use in making machinery. However, many Americans simply built machines out of wood. Eli Terry, for example, made clocks from wood and employed the first Yankee peddlers to hawk them round the nation.[8] The British found such American wooden machinery hugely amusing: after a year or two's work, they said, flimsy American machines fell apart, whereas solid British iron machines kept on running for decades. However, every time the Americans replaced their machines, they updated and improved them. As the Americans became ever more competitive,

British machines did not go bust, but British companies eventually did.

Gradually, Americans gained better access to the resources such as iron and coal that their continent offered, and they were able to make more use of the technology Europe had to offer, a process clearly helped by the migration of Europeans to the United States. However, Americans also had their own contributions to make: Robert Fulton's *Clermont*, for example, used not James Watt's low-pressure steam engine but a revolutionary high-pressure engine developed by Oliver Evans, and Eli Whitney's 1793 cotton gin was one of the greatest innovations of the Industrial Revolution.

More important then either, however, was the development by Whitney and others of new manufacturing methods.[9] In 1798 Whitney applied a novel approach to the manufacture of firearms for the American army by developing machines to make gun parts with great exactness.[10] His aim, later taken up and improved upon by the U.S. Ordnance Department, was to produce weapons whose parts would be interchangeable, allowing soldiers to repair them almost in the midst of battle, simply by swapping the parts of one gun for another. There are doubts about the military significance of this innovation, but the new production technology had profound commercial importance. By removing the need to smooth and file components before assembling them, Whitney speeded up the production process enormously, reducing the number of workers needed in each workshop and so cutting costs. Workshops grew into factories. By the middle of the nineteenth century what had become known as the American system of manufactures had spread to such items as sewing machines, clocks, and bicycles. Of these, the first was perhaps the most important, since it contributed to the development of a widespread but small-scale clothing and footwear industry, with wide-ranging social and economic consequences.[11]

Back in Britain, though, ancient craft-guild methods still dominated much of industry.[12] For the rest of the century people would still call Britain the "workshop" of the world, not its factory. British industry would remain labor intensive and make little use of new technology, in contrast to its innovation-driven American rival.

In the 1850s about two thousand American patents were recorded each year; by the 1890s the annual number had climbed to twenty-one thousand. The American telegraph system, which already spanned the nation, grew and became highly sophisticated in the post–Civil War period. Its network rivaled that of the railroads (the two were of course mutually reinforcing). In 1876 Alexander Graham Bell sent the first telephone message; a decade and a half later there would be almost a million users. Such developments encouraged commercial life, as did the introduction of typewriters, cash registers, and adding machines. Agriculture, meanwhile, felt the effects of canning techniques and then refrigeration; although neither of these was an especially American innovation, they made it possible to transport fruits and vegetables far across the continent and abroad, allowing isolated farmers to reach markets hitherto too far away.

In the 1880s American companies such as Westinghouse also developed new methods of generating, transmitting, and using electricity. As a result, electrically powered factories, mines, and locomotives became possible, freeing American industry from the resource and location constraints that had impeded its growth. The development of high-quality steel allowed Americans to produce more precise tools, and in 1889 the first electric elevator was installed in an American building. Americans developed the technique of making steel-framed buildings, and the cost of steel plummeted thanks to new open-hearth production processes. The skyscraper was on its way. And not only skyscrapers: by the century's end locomotives, bridges, ships, tracks, factories, and machinery could all be manufactured in the United States, often in larger volume, at higher speed and at less cost than anywhere in Europe.

American innovation was an "unbound Prometheus" and a "lever of riches," as the titles of two famous books on the subject have put it. The United States in the nineteenth century was transformed by technology like no other nation. In the eighteenth century, land and natural resources had given Americans a higher living standard than any nation in Europe; in the nineteenth century, in contrast, it was industry that generated rapid growth. By the century's end the American economy was the largest in the world, and by the time of World War I, the total output of the United States exceeded that of Germany, Britain, Russia, and France combined.

In contrast with the roles played by domestic expansion, investment, and innovation, little direct contribution to the nineteenth-century growth of the American economy was made by international trade. Even so, the growth of American trade through the century was pretty impressive. Initially the United States mainly exported food and raw materials: cotton was the major export crop but tobacco, wheat, and other items were important too. Export values grew from $67 million in 1825 to $334 million in 1860. In part this stemmed from the expansion of American industry, for manufactured goods began to swell the nation's export earnings. However, European demand for food and raw materials also soared, thanks to industrialization and Europe's population explosion. Helped by an emerging business selling to Asia and Latin America, the net effect was that, at the outbreak of World War I, American exports were valued at $2.4 billion. The United States was beginning to rival Germany and even Britain as an exporting nation. Much of Europe bought food and some raw materials from the United States, while the British (to their embarrassment, no doubt) also bought large amounts of American machinery.[13]

However, because imports into the United States also grew rapidly, in the first half of the nineteenth century the American trade account was almost constantly in deficit. (Fortunately there was no International Monetary Fund to chide the seemingly profligate nation!) Living standards were rising, and Americans were keen to buy European manufactured goods. Yet, as the quality of American products improved, and as their prices fell, so trading patterns began to change. In 1860 there was still a modest trade deficit of about $20 million, but over the next half century import growth comfortably lagged behind export growth; by World War I, American imports were valued at $1.9 billion, giving the country a substantial trade surplus.

Although American trade grew rapidly in the nineteenth century, the domestic American economy grew faster still. By the end of the nineteenth century trade had declined in importance to the American economy, even though American trade had grown in importance to the rest of the world. That divergence shaped American attitudes toward international trade policy into the twentieth century. Trade restrictions such as the Morrill Tariff Act of 1861 and McKinley's 1890 tariff implied that, if push came to shove, the United States might just stand aside from international trade and go it alone.

Such attitudes, misguided even in the nineteenth century, would be severely dangerous in the twentieth century. Although the direct contribution of international trade to nineteenth-century American growth was modest, the importance of international capital flows was immense.

In the nineteenth century the United States enjoyed an almost continuous inflow of financial capital. Much of the capital came from banks and institutions in London. Barings, the city's most august bank, lent Jefferson the money for the Louisiana Purchase, and followed that with loans to several state governments. Many other institutions did the same, partly on the assumption that Barings knew what it was doing. It seemed a good idea at the time, except that the governments in question were not always very good at raising the taxes to repay the loans. When Maryland and Pennsylvania defaulted in 1842, the indignation was immense. Rothschilds in Paris said that never again would they lend Americans "a dollar, not a dollar." A prominent London clergyman declared that "there really should be lunatic asylums for nations as well as individuals."[14]

The danger to the American nation was very real. Fortunately, Barings kept their nerve: they discreetly bankrolled candidates in state elections who favored repayment and organized public agitations on the side of probity. Their money was repaid, but there were other defaults. Despite that, British and other European institutions remained remarkably keen to invest in the United States, particularly in its canals and railroads. When in 1848 revolutions seemed to threaten half the governments of continental Europe, the City of London put even more of its eggs in the American basket, investing heavily in mines. Scottish investors, whose assets were then quite large, tended toward cattle ranches. Allowing for investment from other European countries, it seems likely that the United States was the largest single recipient of international investment through most of the nineteenth century.

Americans thus did very well by the international financial system—even though many foreign-funded railroads and other projects failed commercially. The creation of a national infrastructure served to improve the returns made on other projects, in agriculture and in industry. Had it not been for international capital flows, the American economy might have stumbled in the nineteenth century; instead, the investments boosted the economy, contributing to the trade account's gradual swing into surplus.

As the trade account went into surplus, so Americans began to lend abroad. Indeed, well before the end of the nineteenth century the United States was a net exporter of financial capital to the rest of the world. That cut by a third the debts accumulated during the century's first half. Financial muscle now added to the nation's existing strengths in industry, infrastructure, agriculture, minerals, and people. The nation's first full century could hardly have been better planned.

## The Government's Role

In 1791 Alexander Hamilton, secretary of the treasury, declared that the role of the government was to support, not constrain, private enterprise. Hamilton's *Report on Manufactures* argued that the federal government should promote the industrialization of the United States. Hamilton advocated industrial policies resembling those favored by some commentators today. Although subsequent administrations did not entirely agree with or follow Hamilton's argument, they accepted his ambitions.

Hamilton and Adam Smith both agreed that the United States was primarily an agricultural nation, and Britain was primarily a manufacturing nation. Trade between the two would benefit both American agriculture and British manufacturing. Hamilton, however, had a deeper insight: free trade would make it very difficult for the United States to industrialize. And because he wanted the United States to become a manufacturing nation, he saw that this presented a problem. Hamilton rejected Adam Smith's assumption that there was a natural, fixed, and immutable division of labor between nations and denied that Britain had a natural advantage in manufacturing and the United States a natural advantage in agriculture; on the contrary, he argued that the division of labor was a mere historical accident, and that governments could use active policies to shift comparative advantages. Hamilton thus repudiated laissez-faire policies. He wanted the United States to attract capital and skilled labor from Britain and the rest of Europe, and to develop a domestic banking system geared toward financing industry; yet he also believed that the state should help to finance American industrialization. Finally, he advocated a tariff to make imported goods more expensive, believing that such a measure would help domestic manufacturers to compete against their established British rivals.

Hamilton's *Report on Manufactures* daunted Congress, which only agreed to a modest tariff in order to raise some revenues for the federal government. Congress did accept Hamilton's view that governments could and should involve themselves in the economy, but it lacked his eagerness to shift the economic balance away from agriculture and into industry, and away from consumer spending and into investment. Hamilton wanted both profits made on the land and the revenues from tariffs to be invested in factories. Opposition to Hamilton was bound to develop from those who would inevitably lose in the short term: Thomas Jefferson wrote that "were we directed from Washington when to sow, and when to reap, we should soon want bread."[15] This, more or less, *was* the point—Hamilton was willing to sacrifice some bread now for more bread later. He saw that the existing American economic system would not create an industrial revolution, so he wanted to intervene in order to make it happen.

Whether the precise interventions Hamilton favored would have worked, we cannot know. They might simply have provoked retaliation, risking both exports and capital inflows. However, we *do* know that even Jefferson, when he won the presidency and especially in his second term of office, espoused active government. He wanted the government to finance the nation's infrastructure —its roads, canals, and schools. Jefferson was not in as much hurry to see industrialization as was Hamilton, nor did he share Hamilton's enthusiasm for private financial markets: he remained determined not to hurt the farmer, and he was probably unwilling for the government to go into debt to fund industrialization. However, Jefferson nevertheless showed himself to be in favor of affirmative action by the government to support long-term economic growth —as is demonstrated by his request to the Treasury to draw up a ten-year construction program for roads and canals.

Unfortunately, the War of 1812 with Britain asserted a prior claim on the public purse, and Congress dropped the plan. After the war, aspirations grew bolder. President James Monroe devised a more ambitious scheme incorporating investment in the nation's infrastructure, tariff protection, financial reform, and land legislation. Monroe did not implement his scheme, but John Quincy Adams—who also advocated a comprehensive approach to economic management—picked up the baton. He said that the objective of government was to improve the conditions "of those who are party to the social compact," and advocated government initiatives for "the advancement of literature, and the progress of the sciences."[16] But it all came to nothing: Adams was patrician, isolated, and unable to get his policies through Congress.

Without any government coordination, the construction and management of roads, canals, and especially railroads was random, corrupt, and sometimes ridiculous. Many state and local governments suffered financially from subsidizing loss-making canals; they did not want to do the same with the railroads, nor did they want to be the only area without a track or a terminus. Thus they went ahead despite their misgivings subsidizing private investments, exempting railroad companies from taxes, guaranteeing their local monopoly positions, and generally doing everything possible to ensure that tracks ran through their land.

Inevitably the railroad companies built too many tracks; further, safety standards were poor, tracks of several different gauges were run, and time zones varied unpredictably. Companies accumulated crushing debts and fell victim to ruinous price wars. The railroads may have been the making of the American economy, but they were very nearly its ruin as well: corrupt owners issued more stock than they had assets, and they flouted laws and bribed officials, journalists, and politicians alike. In one spectacular escapade the notorious Jay Gould, owner of the Erie Railroad, used a trainload of eight hundred hired thugs in an attempt to wrest control of a rival company from its owners; Gould's rivals simply loaded another train with 450 thugs of their own, and the two trains crashed head on in a tunnel. The takeover bid failed.[17]

The glory of the railroad network was supposed to be the 1862 project to build a great transcontinental railroad. Congress chartered Union Pacific to build the eastern section and Central Pacific the western section. The federal government lent them capital, and the two companies raced to complete their sections first, disregarding safety and quality—so that barely was the project completed than it had to be rebuilt and resited. The company directors subcontracted the construction to other companies that they themselves owned. By vastly overcharging, the subcontractors were able to make huge profits for their owners while the railroad companies staggered under the resultant debts.

Eventually the federal government realized that it had to do something about the railroads, so it provided generous grants of land, giving away a total area of land greater than that of either France or Germany. This provided the companies with the means to raise new capital to build new railroads and repay existing loans.

Even the Union Pacific and Central Pacific paid off their debts to the government.

On the other hand, the new railroads raised the value of land still owned by the government, which boosted federal finances but annoyed those who wished to buy and settle government land. It was bad enough that the railroad companies gained vast amounts of free land, without the added annoyance that everybody else's land costs increased in consequence. Furthermore, the railroad companies were distinctly shady, and the passage of the land grant legislation depended on extensive vote buying, so it is hardly surprising that the land grants have been much criticized. Nevertheless, their contribution to the nation's development was immense. Five transcontinental railroads eventually traversed the nation, and vast networks developed in both the West and the area east of the Mississippi. In sum, the land grants were a pragmatic way to achieve the building of the nation's transport infrastructure.[18]

No more obvious case for government intervention could exist than the need to reconstruct the southern economy after the Civil War. Both North and South suffered during the conflict, but the South clearly bore the brunt of the economic loss.[19] The death of a quarter of a million southerners and the destruction of homes, farms, factories, and railways were the tangible manifestations; meanwhile, defeat rendered Confederate bonds and currency worthless. Bankruptcies were widespread, and the slave owners lost the very thing they were fighting for—the $2 billion of wealth embodied in the slaves. Freedom may have been priceless to the liberated slaves, but they also needed jobs and homes and prospects of advancement. They needed a viable southern economy.

In 1866 the Freedmen's Bureau Bill offered former slaves forty acres and a mule. It was not a very realistic offer: if four million ex-slaves were to acquire family farms, then the government would have to arrange vast land redistributions and huge capital investments. Troops would have to remain to keep the peace, and the federal government would also have to address the problems of white southerners. The government, to be sure, had no stomach for such a scheme. It provided some temporary shelter for the needy, plus limited educational and medical facilities, and a few people settled on confiscated or abandoned land. Generally, however, the government did little. The Treasury even seized $30 million in reparations and a number of private estates, including that of General Robert Lee's family at Arlington. That aside, the South was mostly left to languish.

A new society did, of course, develop, but the new tenurial and credit systems failed to utilize or enhance the skills of the labor force. The southern economy was hampered by low rates of investment, confining southerners to industries such as textiles, coal, and mineral extraction, which required large numbers of poorly paid, unskilled workers and made little use of new technologies. Because there was limited innovation and hence little chance of rapid productivity gains, income levels were destined to lag behind those in the North.

Could matters have been different? Could the government have done more? Perhaps the necessary intellectual arguments were not then available. Perhaps southerners just had to wait for new ways of thinking—hence for the New Deal—before their economic reconstruction could occur. However, the examples of Hamilton and others warn us not to dismiss pre-twentieth-century thinking about economic policy issues. The problem was lack of will, not lack of understanding: after the Civil War, the federal government and Congress were simply more concerned about the development of the northern economy. The war had destroyed the slave-owning aristocrats of the South and had absorbed the attention of northern radicals, which gave free rein to northern business interests. With the war won and their opponents distracted, northern businessmen demanded and got tariff protection, "sound" money, low taxes, and minimal business regulation.[20]

One positive effect of the Civil War was that it destroyed much of the nation's opposition to banking and finance. Before the war, Jeffersonians and Jacksonians twice closed down the Bank of the

United States. There was a prevalent belief that finance was a private matter with which state legislatures, but not the national government, might perhaps concern themselves. Some states allowed anybody to open a bank and run it as they pleased and issue as much currency as they wanted, heedless of the economic consequences; other states primly declared banking illegal. As a result of such inconsistencies there were frequent financial crises, and financial transactions were hard to conduct. Although this chaotic system did not prevent economic progress, it posed a long-term threat. The nation had to cope with the ever-increasing complexities of economic life and, without an efficient banking system, it was bound to encounter problems.

The Civil War forced the federal government to borrow on a scale never before seen: war debts were twice those incurred by the nation in building the prewar railroads.[21] To make such borrowing possible, Congress sponsored in 1863 and 1864 the creation of new national banks which agreed to buy American government bonds in return for the right to issue currency, and in return for exemption from taxes imposed on other state banks. People had faith in the new government bonds and, by extension, in the banks that held them. Such banks prospered and became more professional. The whole banking system came under regulation for the first time, which further improved public confidence. The experience of selling government debt proved invaluable, and banks transferred their new expertise to corporate lending.

Admittedly there were problems. There was no central bank, and so no lender of last resort. Further, banks were forbidden from opening up branches, in the belief that the banks would syphon money away from local communities to their head offices in such cities as Boston and New York—a confused and parochial view that would create severe problems in the twentieth century. Despite that, however, Americans were now in possession of a better banking system than they had hitherto enjoyed, and one that would help their nation to continue to expand in the rest of the nineteenth century.

## Recession and Economic Management

With the Civil War behind them, Americans resumed the strong economic growth of the antebellum years. Inevitably, however, there were some periods of economic difficulty—and when they occurred, the clamor for government action was as loud then as it is today. The difference is that, today, people usually complain about too much unemployment or too much inflation. In the late nineteenth century the main gripe was not too much unemployment or inflation but too *little* inflation: agriculture, in particular, seemed to be hard hit by falling prices, both before the Civil War and especially in the 1870s. Wheat fell from $1.45 a bushel in 1866 to 44 cents by 1894, and corn prices slipped a similar amount; cotton prices fell even faster. Farmers, not surprisingly, protested.

The facts did not completely justify their protests, though. On average, farmers' costs fell too, by more than the prices of the produce they sold, leaving the average farmer better off. However, many farmers were far from average, particularly those in debt. For farmers to buy the machinery they needed, they had to borrow— but to service their debts, they had to sell their produce into an ever weakening market. Many did not own their own land, even if they had done so formerly, and so had no security to fall back on. Only a minority were directly imperiled by falling prices, rather than indirectly through their debt problems, but most farmers saw themselves as the innocent victims of falling prices.[22]

The problem was, however, partly of the farmers' own making. Individually, they could do nothing about falling prices except increase their output to bring in more revenue, a response that could only push prices down further. As the century progressed a global crisis of agricultural overproduction developed. Farm sizes and numbers rose. Fertilizers and mechanization raised yields, as did the introduction of cheaper, better tools and new food-preservation technologies; railroads, too, facilitated the spread of agriculture. This situation was exacerbated by developments abroad, for similar increases in production were recorded in Argentina, Australia, Canada, and the Russian Ukraine.

Farmers did not relate their difficulties to their own overproduction but preferred to blame the railroad companies, the banks, and the manufacturers. Though all of these were indeed carriers of American economic progress, and all indirectly supported the farming sector, farmers accused railroad companies of charging monopoly prices, alleged that the banks' commission charges, levied on top of interest rates fixed by law, were usurious, and that manufacturers used bulk buying power to impose ever lower prices for farm produce.

In February 1892 various farming groups got together to form the People's Party in order to champion their cause. They wanted, among other policies, the nationalization of the railroads, the telegraphs, and the telephone system. The new party's candidate, James Weaver, did poorly in that year's presidential election; Grover Cleveland, dull though he was, retained the White House for the Democrats. Populism might have died then, had the economy not slid into recession in 1893. Within the course of a few months, thousands of firms closed and two and a half million people lost their jobs; prices, including farm prices, slid further.

As the decade progressed the economy recovered, but the experience kept the populist flame alight. President Cleveland's conservatism and his unwillingness to act cost him his job: he who once had said, "though the people support the government, the government should not support the people," was replaced as the Democratic candidate in 1896 by the charismatic populist, William Bryan. By promising unlimited minting of silver currency, Bryan offered to bring the wonders of inflation to the American nation.[23] He also promised to cut tariffs, which he believed impeded American farm exports.

Although many expected Bryan to win the presidential election, he failed by a large margin. Perhaps he repelled voters with his demagogic excess, but there were other reasons for resisting him. Bryan's promises of higher farm prices and an end to the tariff that apparently protected industry from foreign competition were not likely to win many votes in the industrial cities. Since the United States had become an increasingly urban industrial economy, the party that won the support of the urban industrial worker was the party that won the election.

The 1896 election taught another lesson. Although Bryan lost by advocating government policies that would have damaged the economy, Cleveland lost his party's nomination by failing to have *any* policies. Americans were beginning to see the government's unwillingness to intervene in the economy as a weakness. Their views about the kind of intervention needed were muddled and dangerous, but the desire for intervention was becoming abundantly clear.

A century has passed since the Bryan-Cleveland dispute over the government's role in the economy, but the arguments have not changed. Ronald Reagan famously said, not long ago, that government is the problem, not the solution, and many Americans evidently still agree. George Bush may have had a similar experience to President Cleveland, although Bill Clinton is not as interventionist as William Jennings Bryan or Franklin Roosevelt. So who is right? Some of the themes that emerge from nineteenth-century American history may shed light on subsequent experience.

It is clear, for example, that despite the absence of grand planning, the federal government did make some important contributions to the development of the American economy. The U.S. Ordnance Department's sponsorship in the nineteenth century of research into ways of manufacturing guns from interchangeable parts had huge ramifications. The guns that Eli Whitney and others developed were more expensive and took longer to make than those produced by traditional methods, but the Ordnance Department did not care: it wanted weapons that soldiers could repair in the battlefield regardless of cost. American firms then applied the lessons that they had learned to the production of other things— for example, sewing machines to be used in the critically important textiles industry. Thus the federal government financed a crucial area of industrial research and development, and so played the role now advocated by modern supporters of government intervention.

The genesis of the American system of manufactures illustrates one problem that government may be able to remedy. Firms or individuals may be unwilling to invest in innovation. Typically, problems occur if the returns lie too far into the future, or are too uncertain or too easily appropriated by other companies. Governments can subsidize the investment, or they can protect innovators via patent or similar laws, or they can pay inventors for their ideas—as the government of South Carolina did when it awarded Eli Whitney fifty thousand dollars for his cotton gin. Since innovation is crucial to economic growth, that represents a key role that government might perform.[24]

In this example, the government acts on behalf of future potential beneficiaries of innovation in order to make sure that the process actually happens. This role has a close analogy with something else that governments often do—represent the interests of people who are too poor to pay the market price. That in turn is reminiscent of some of Hamilton's arguments, when he said that the infant American industries of the late eighteenth century needed protection from existing industries in other countries, especially Britain. In this view free trade, the market mechanism made global, was not completely desirable if national inequalities were sufficiently large.

There is another case for government activism, one that does not rely on inequalities between generations, people, firms, or nations. As noted, in the late nineteenth century farmers expanded their output, depressing farm prices. In this situation, the market became profoundly unstable as farmers tried to defend their cash incomes by producing even more—yet there was nothing that *individual* farmers could do to solve the problem. This created a case for government intervention, to bring order to a disorderly market, and it was in that direction that American farmers were edging when they tried to persuade the federal authorities to halt the deflationary prices.

Other Americans did more than edge, though. Intense competition was as likely to produce price collapses in the railroad business as in farming; the same was true, if less clearly so, in other markets. To a handful of business leaders, the implication was clear. Men like Andrew Carnegie and John Rockefeller realized that they had to control the markets in which they operated. By creating monopolies, they sought to impose order and security where there had been instability and danger. Such men hated the uncertainties created by free competitive markets; by taking control over markets, they achieved the orderly conduct of affairs that government was unwilling to offer. The result was an economy run not by government, nor entirely by markets, but by corporations.

## Big Business

Early in the nineteenth century most American companies were creatures of government. State governments awarded charters to companies, giving them rights to provide certain services such as constructing turnpikes or canals; states frequently held shares in the companies, blurring the boundary between the public and the private. In 1811, however, New York became the first state to pass a general incorporation law permitting individuals to set up corporations and obtain a degree of limited liability without a specific legislative grant. Limited liability gave corporations their own legal existence, and protected owners from the full impact of financial failure. The change encouraged investment and greater risk taking, boosting growth. By 1860 most industrial states had such laws on their books.

Still, most corporations were small. Single cotton mills were among the largest business operations in the first half of the nineteenth century: following a pattern established by Francis Lowell in Boston in 1814, they integrated spinning and weaving under one roof. Such operations probably seemed huge at the time, but few had more than $1 million of capital and none more than $10 million.[25] In the century's second half, however, new industries such as iron and steel, transcontinental railroads, and power generation developed—and with them came the development of the first giant companies, driven by economies of scale. By the century's end, three hundred American companies each had capital of at least $10 million.

Often, growth came through merger. Between 1894 and 1905 three thousand American firms merged.[26] By 1904 seventy-eight different American industries were each dominated by only a few companies. The story of American Tobacco is typical: in 1880 in North Carolina, James Buchanan Duke took over his family's pipe tobacco business. The firm was small, with a tiny market share, and was going nowhere; Duke diversified into cigarettes, a fast-growing market, but the business was still tiny. That was the way it seemed likely to stay.

Then, in 1884, a Virginian named James Bonsack perfected a machine for rolling cigarettes. The Bonsack machine could make one hundred thousand cigarettes per day, compared with the two thousand an individual worker could make. Machine-made cigarettes were cheap and easy to sell, so Duke bought the new machinery; most of his competitors did not. Within a year, Duke had 10 percent of the cigarette market and soon bought other tobacco firms, merging them into his own. By 1890 "Buck" Duke's American Tobacco dominated the cigarette market; by 1908 it made three quarters of all the cigarettes in the United States—from just two factories. "I resolved from the time I was a mere boy to do a big business," Duke said shortly before he died.[27] He succeeded, and in a way that has come to seem characteristically American.

Duke's American Tobacco was big, but the Carnegie Company was bigger—it was the largest firm in the American steel industry, making it about the largest company in the world. At the center of the business were the Pittsburgh steel mills, but the firm also mined for iron ore and for coal, ran railroads, and built steel suspension bridges. Carnegie had rivals but no equal: the firm looked as permanent as the structures it built.

Suddenly in 1901 Andrew Carnegie sold the Carnegie Company for $447 million. Carnegie forsook the life of a robber baron and turned to philanthropy. His firm became part of U.S. Steel, a behemoth that incorporated both the Carnegie Company and most of its former rivals—Federal Steel, National Steel, National Tube, and many others. Among them they sold half the nation's steel. The merger created a firm with a capital base of $1.4 billion and a workforce of one hundred thousand people. Nothing quite like it had been seen before. Whose idea was the merger? Probably not Carnegie's, despite the fortune he made from the sale of his company; instead, the initiative came from the banker involved, John Pierpont Morgan.[28] Federal Steel and National Steel were both Morgan creations, but they were much smaller than the Carnegie Company. Morgan feared that a price war might destroy his companies, so he masterminded the grand consolidation of the steel industry.

Morgan was the most powerful banker in the United States, and his creation of U.S. Steel repeated his previous tactics with railroad companies. Many railroad companies had fallen into ruinous price wars, destroying themselves and hurting those who had lent them funds. Morgan used his financial muscle to take over one railroad company after another, reducing competition and thereby restoring profits. By the turn of the century, he had forced one third of all American railroad companies to merge. Not only did Morgan safeguard his bank's investments, but he earned huge fees in the process. Even so, railroad mergers were puny compared with the creation of U.S. Steel. The House of Morgan and its syndicate earned $50 million in fees from arranging and underwriting the U.S. Steel merger.

Behind every successful corporation stood a powerful investment bank. J. P. Morgan topped a pyramid that included Kuhn Loeb and Company, Kidder Peabody, the First National Bank, the National City Bank, and others. All of them, but Morgan especially, went beyond the mere making of deals. In the terminology of the day, companies were "Morganized": Pierpont forced companies to improve their procedures and finances. He reorganized whole industries, and he reorganized the companies themselves, strengthening their finances and their managements.

One firm that felt the impact of Morgan was the McCormick firm that made the famous reaper. Late in the nineteenth century, McCormick had fallen victim to fierce competition from the Deering Harvester Company. So Morgan arranged a marriage, and created International Harvester. However, the new firm's performance was disappointing, so Morgan sacked almost all of the original managers, moved in his own men, and International Harvester began to prosper.[29]

Aggressive tactics such as Morganization were magnificent in their way, but they provoked strong antagonisms. Mention has already been made of the unhappiness of American farmers whose transport costs rose because of railroad Morganization. Without restructuring, many of the railroads might have closed down, but that was not how the farmers saw matters. As far as they were concerned, Morgan was a villain.

In 1878 Louis Brandeis left Harvard Law School and went into legal practice. After a year in St. Louis, Brandeis returned to his native Boston where he made a niche for himself by providing advice to small firms. Many were being exploited and cheated by the big companies that dominated Boston's commercial life. The experienced galvanized Brandeis: in the 1890s he committed himself to reducing the power of big business.[30]

Brandeis was one of many. Henry George's *Progress and Poverty*, published in 1879, was probably the first public attack on the corporations. In 1894 a retired Chicago journalist, Henry Demarist Lloyd, published another tract, *Wealth against Commonwealth*, in which he attacked John Rockefeller's Standard Oil as a threat to democracy. Though it was emotional and exaggerated, his work nevertheless impressed Brandeis and others, and it made a point that has a parallel in today's world of multinational corporations, which are able to relocate around the world: whenever state governments tried to legislate against big business, the companies, Standard Oil among them, simply transferred their registered offices to other states.

Brandeis, Lloyd, and others believed that giant firms were themselves undesirable: they represented conspiracies both against consumers, to raise prices on Main Street, and against farmers, to lower produce prices. Long before, Adam Smith had written, "People of the same trade seldom meet together, even for merriment and diversion, but the conversation ends in a conspiracy against the public, or some contrivance to raise prices."[31] In the late nineteenth century, Smith's words seemed increasingly apposite.

Lloyd wanted to see monopolies nationalized, but others drew a more limited conclusion: any action against trusts had to come from the federal government, not from the states. In 1890 Congress passed the Sherman Antitrust Act, which ostensibly outlawed any "combination" or "conspiracy in restraint of trade or commerce." The time had come, said Brandeis, Lloyd, and their fellows, for government to act. In 1895 came the test case. E. C. Knight was a firm of sugar refiners who monopolized no less than 98 percent of their market. The restraint to trade that they exercised was clearly nearly total: the Sherman Act seemed destined to be their nemesis. Knight argued, however, that since *manufacturing* was neither trade nor commerce, the Sherman Act did not apply to sugar refining. The judges seemed even minded, but the prosecuting attorney general's presentation of his rebuttal was so incompetent that the court sided with the firm. The company won its case.

Subsequently, though, other decisions went the other way. The basic point remained clear: those who argued against big business were failing to convince the public, the politicians, and the judges. Like the farmers, the critics of big business were swimming against the tide. The 1896 election of the probusiness William McKinley, and then his reelection in 1900, only confirmed the point.

In 1899 a minor Wisconsin academic shot to public prominence with the publication of *The Theory of the Leisure Class*. Thorstein Veblen chastised bankers and industrialists not for their energy but for their indolence. He disparaged their "conspicuous consumption," calling them the "leisure class": people like the Rockefellers and the Vanderbilts abhorred competition and cared only about boosting their social status.

Veblen probably had a point: at the turn of the century New

York's Fifth Avenue was laden down with *seven* mansions of the Vanderbilt family alone, and Newport, Rhode Island, was even more overburdened with opulence. Furthermore, many rich American families made mutually advantageous alliances with impoverished European aristocrats.[32] Those industrialists who were not refinancing Europe's aristocracy gave away large chunks of wealth to charity. That too provoked scorn from Veblen, who soon became the leading American social critic of his day.

However, Veblen said something else, much more important, but less noticed, and much less antagonistic toward big business: he argued that those firms which try to maximize their profits in the short term are unlikely to invest in new and innovative technology. Innovation frequently fails to generate immediate increases in profits, and so will be eschewed by profit maximizers. However, Veblen remarked that American economic prosperity clearly was rising, thanks to technological innovation, and his conclusion was clear: American firms could not, then, be seeking to maximize their short-term profits. Furthermore, Veblen knew from his readings in economics that in highly competitive markets firms need to be ruthless profit maximizers if they are to survive. From this he deduced that such fierce competition was not present in the commanding heights of the American economy. And this was indeed what the evidence showed: Pierpont Morgan and others were doing their best to *reduce* competition, and the economy was apparently benefiting from the process.

What Veblen recognized was that the great driving force of business life, the quest for market power, was the driving force behind the economy. Economic theory and business experience taught the same lesson: it is hard to make much profit when you have many competitors. Each firm drives down the prices and the profits of the others. The solution is to take over your rivals, reduce the competition, raise prices, and use the proceeds to take over even more competitors.

That was still only half the story, though. Many American firms at the turn of the century succeeded first by taking over their suppliers, distributors, and retailers. They integrated both backward, to control the source of raw materials, and forward, to control the distribution and retailing of their product. A manufacturer might take on distribution because it could not find a company sophisticated enough to perform the work; this was especially likely when goods had to be refrigerated, or when the speedy delivery of perishable goods was vital. Sophisticated machinery like reaping machines or sewing machines needed equally sophisticated selling and after-sales support. Manufacturers who took on these tasks prospered at the expense of those who did not, which gave them the chance to take over those rivals. As a result, expansion occurred in every direction.

The classic case is Standard Oil. During the late nineteenth century under Rockefeller's direction, Standard Oil built its own pipelines, ran its own refining plants, controlled its own distribution, and systematically tried to buy or bankrupt all its rivals. Between 1882 and 1885, the company concentrated production in twenty-two of its fifty-three refineries. The company closed its other refineries, thereby cutting costs by two thirds. When the great boom in oil demand came early in the twentieth century, Standard Oil had already cornered much of the market.

The Rockefeller recipe did not always work, however. Standard Oil prospered, but Standard Rope and Twine did not.[33] Great size was sometimes a handicap, not a strength, and many would-be giant corporations simply collapsed. Partly, to be sure, it was a matter of being in the right industry: in sectors that used lots of capital to produce a continuous flow of output, whether of steel, gasoline, or biscuits, size clearly helped. This was important, too, in the extraction and distribution sectors. However, in labor-intensive activities such as construction, size seemed to be a disadvantage, especially if there were no nice neat continuous flows of work; size often brings inflexibility and often unnecessary bureaucracy, and confers no benefits.

However, success or failure was not just a matter of the industry concerned; those who succeeded did so ultimately because of proper organization. Americans were uniquely quick to realize that in business, organization matters. Again, the railroads were crucial to the story: by its very nature, a railroad company is far flung. Because of this, railroad owners and managers found themselves obliged to exercise control over employees, many of whom were hundreds of miles away. In order to do that, they had to think for the first time about the nature of management in a big, diverse organization.[34] As in other nations, the railroad companies started by copying the ways of the military, but in the United States that was only the beginning. In 1881 the Wharton Business School was established, committed to a new science of management—that of managerial capitalism, the Visible Hand.

Every new production manager, new cost accountant, or sales supervisor in every big new American corporation testified to the power of the organization in contrast to the vagaries of the free market. That, no less than technological innovation, was critical to American success.[35] Politicians stayed in the background, accepting bribes and maneuvering to make sure that railroads passed through their states, and that prosperity came to their localities. Salaried managers kept the system going, and workers were just thankful to have jobs. They disregarded the inevitable cases of corruption in high places and rejoiced as their nation grew in prosperity and self-confidence.

## Chapter Two

# THE GLOBAL BACKGROUND TO AMERICAN EXPANSION

## The Beginnings of a Global Economy

In looking back at the United States' economic past, the greatest mistake is to see only the domestic economic events described in chapter 1 and to miss the wider global economic context that made those events possible. For the prodigious rise of the American economy in the century after independence is only part of the story of how the United States came to be, briefly and reluctantly, the global economic superpower of the twentieth century. Such a development required a global economy available to be led, which in turn required that other nations lay the groundwork.

The seventeenth-century Dutch Republic gave the global economy its first major injection of energy. Dutch traders already dominated the coastal shipping business of Europe—three quarters of all the vessels carrying cargoes long-distance around the coasts of Europe were Dutch—but in the seventeenth century the Dutch moved far beyond European waters to the rest of the world. They traded with Brazil, the Caribbean, and across the Indian Ocean; they settled in North America; and for two centuries they maintained a trading post on the Japanese island of Deshima in Nagasaki, despite the severance of all other links between Japan and the West. Carrying timber, grain, and other produce around Europe was probably more lucrative, but the rapid expansion of Dutch oceanic trade added greatly to the young republic's prosperity.

The wealth and sophistication of the seventeenth-century Dutch surpassed that of any other people.[1] A contemporary writer, Melchior Fokkens, wrote in 1665 that although Amsterdam was not actually overflowing with milk and honey it *was* overflowing with milk and cheese, as well as with other foods, fine silks and taffeta, books, maps, scientific instruments, fine porcelain, tapestries, and great houses with alabaster columns and—perhaps an exaggeration here—floors inlaid with gold.[2] By the end of the seventeenth century incomes per head in the Netherlands were half as high again as those of any other nation in the world. The Dutch had by far the largest share of world trade, and had by their efforts greatly increased the amount of trade occurring in the world. Although often under military or naval threat, they were financially and politically independent and felt able to capture any trade they coveted.

In the eighteenth century, however, Dutch international trade began to decline while that of Britain, a small but aggressive rival, rose fourfold.[3] Both nations lived under the creed of mercantilism: trade like mad and stop your rivals from doing the same, since their gain is always your loss. European mercantilist nations traded with each other and with their own colonies, but not with one another's colonies. Force of arms maintained the arrangement. Merchants assumed that trade conducted by the merchants of other nations meant a loss to themselves, and it was a government's task to exclude other nations from as much international trade as possible. The extreme manifestation of that was war.

All of eighteenth-century Europe was mercantilist, but until the American Revolution, the British were undoubtedly the most successful.[4] As early as 1651 Cromwell's Parliament passed the first of the infamous Navigation Acts, intended to prevent the Dutch from either trading or fishing in British waters. In a succession of wars the Dutch proved unable to force the British to abandon the Navigation Acts; indeed, the latter gradually toughened the acts so that by the eighteenth century the laws seriously threatened the Dutch. The acts stipulated that British colonies could no longer export to Dutch or other foreign ports, as they had, but instead must send their produce exclusively to Britain, from where it could be reexported to the rest of Europe. The law also required that imports into Britain could travel only on ships owned and crewed by British residents, British colonists, or nationals of the exporting country. This largely restricted Dutch entry to British ports. The law further required that the ships sail directly to Britain and not via other nations—which meant a further loss of business to the Dutch— and that the ships had to be British built.

The British had more than trade barriers in their armory of weapons to use against the Dutch.[5] To back up the Navigation Acts the British government spent heavily on building up the Royal Navy. Since the Dutch, unlike the British, faced war on land too, they could not match the latter's naval buildup. A diminution of Dutch power became all but inevitable: as the Dutch navy waned and the Royal Navy waxed, leadership of global trade switched in the eighteenth century away from the Netherlands to Britain. Henceforth, the Royal Navy patrolled the world's seas.

As the eighteenth century progressed, however, Dutch political and business leaders largely ignored the speed at which Britain was growing. Because they had acquired large holdings of overseas assets, and could more or less live off the proceeds, Dutch merchants' lifestyles remained very comfortable. During the seventeenth century successful merchants had abandoned life in congested towns

such as Haarlem in search of more elegant lifestyles in the coun-
tryside; by the third quarter of the century a British traveler, William Aglionby, said of the village of Leiderdorp near Leiden that it
had "more palaces than country people's houses."[6] A century later
another British traveler, Joseph Marshall, said "I know hardly any
country where they spend their money more freely to pace their
time agreeably."[7]

The Dutch had discovered the joys of consumption, despite
their rather parsimonious reputation. For a long time, wealth cush-
ioned the merchants from the slow growth in their basic trading
activities. The cushion, though, could not last forever, and still less
could it protect the Dutch from the naked aggression of the British.

Dutch merchants knew that their manufacturing base was declining, but they blamed that on the high level of Dutch wages.
What they did not recognize was that their industry was uncompetitive, not just because of high wage costs but also because of the
high value of the Dutch currency.[8] For Dutch business leaders, a
strong exchange rate was necessary to maintain the value of their
overseas investments; they seemed not to notice the resultant damage to Dutch manufacturing competitiveness.

By the middle of the eighteenth century British territories in
North America, the Caribbean, India, Africa, and the East Indies
formed a colonial network without equal. To the British, international trade was initially just a by-product of domestic trade; as
a small island economy, it was hardly surprising that commerce
often involved some trade beyond the nation's boundaries. British
shops in the mid-eighteenth century typically sold products sent to
them from all around the world: sugar and tobacco, spices such as
turmeric and cinnamon, and drinks such as brandy.[9] In sharp contrast to the imperatives behind Portuguese, Spanish, and later,
French global expansion, British merchants thus took to international trade as an extension of what they did at home. The British
had few ambitions of imperial glory: even when the British economy became the strongest in Europe, the government continued
to avoid direct military rivalry with the great European powers. For
almost two centuries, Britain would wage war in Europe mainly

by proxy, paying other nations to fight its battles—as some people claim Japan did in the 1991 Gulf War.

## The Rise of Great Britain

The success of the British in replacing the Dutch as the world's leading economic power had a deep irony. The Civil War, the republican Commonwealth, the Stuart restoration, and the Glorious Revolution of 1688 all forced the English to rethink how they ran their nation—and they looked to the Netherlands as a model. By consciously copying the Dutch the English government made itself strong; in the Glorious Revolution, the English even took a Dutch prince as their king.[10]

A lesson that the British learned from the Dutch, and one that would have profound importance for Britain's role in the world economy, was how to manage public finances. When in 1688 Parliament gave the throne jointly to William and Mary, it stipulated that they renounce any claims to revenue-making powers; instead, Parliament assumed the right to tax. With the monarchy stripped of power, Parliament was the servant of the farmers, who created most of the nation's output, and of the merchant classes, who sold that output.[11] Parliament thus sought to reduce the absolute amount of finance drawn out of the private sector, both for its own sake and to prevent the monarchy from risking the nation's security in continental adventures.

Parliament appointed professional civil servants to run the new Excise Commission according to well-developed rules and procedures. They largely replaced the old "tax farming" system, under which private individuals had acted as tax collectors in return for a share of the receipts. In their place, government excisemen now toured the country, assessing the extent of trade and how much tax the nation's shops and workshops should pay. In the late seventeenth century Ralph Lawton, a "dissolute gentleman," transformed himself from a rake and a gambler into a "sober and sedulous man" by working his way up the excise department's strict hierarchy.[12] Men like Lawton were efficient, unyielding, but largely incorruptible, and they brought in handsome revenues.

Old-fashioned patronage did not disappear in this "financial revolution," and indeed it became a hot political issue in the nineteenth century. Even so, its significance was for a century much less than that of financial reform. Thanks in large part to the foundation laid by men such as Lawton, eighteenth-century excise tax revenues increased sixfold—far ahead of any increases achieved by Britain's rivals. This had two implications. First, the British government was not reliant on tariffs for revenue. That contributed to Britain's leadership of international trade. Second, by modernizing the methods of raising finance, and by conferring democratic legitimacy on those methods, Parliament could raise much larger amounts than before. Of course, some people still avoided taxes, but by earlier standards there was little resistance; the increased legitimacy of the British government was one reason—especially after 1688, when the monarchy became constitutional rather than absolute—and the lack of powerful oppositional institutions was another. The Church was under the government's thumb, and there were no provincial princes or assemblies with any power to challenge the center—not even in Wales or Scotland. More important, though, the government was sensible about not annoying people unduly: the legal system was not especially corrupt, the tax system was not especially unfair (since almost everybody paid taxes), and by the standards of the time there were few conspicuously idle or corrupt government officials causing resentment. Best of all, perhaps, there was no rowdy standing army demanding food, bed, and entertainment.

The eighteenth-century British government's increased ability to tax extended its ability to borrow. The government often announced a new tax when it issued a new stock of debt. By doing so, it simultaneously created more debt *and* more capacity to settle debt. As confidence grew, borrowing rose faster than the underlying taxes. Indeed, so highly desired was government debt that the authorities were able to reduce the dividend they paid on the borrowing, which prevented debt-servicing costs from getting out of hand, despite the rising stock of outstanding debt. The government also began to issue debt with several years to maturity; this practice made the management of a large stock of debt much easier, though only because private sector financial markets felt confident that the British government would always settle its debts.

At first the market in government debt was managed, and often manipulated, by a few key players. These included the Bank of England, the East India Company, the Sword Blade Company, and, after 1711, the South Sea Company, all of which fought for the opportunity to buy government debt, since it provided them with a regular stream of dividends and raised the quality of their asset portfolios. As a result a market in secondhand debt developed, which made government bonds even more desirable, boosting still further the willingness of the public to buy new debt.

Other institutional developments occurred, and eighteenth-century Britain acquired within the City of London a set of financial institutions that were far more sophisticated than those of rivals such as France. People made increasing use of bills of exchange (a precursor of modern paper money), the stock exchange developed, and insurance companies grew in importance. Although there were often crises—most notably the collapse of the South Sea Company in 1720—the City of London always found ways to reform and improve itself. In doing so, it gained from and added to the financial stability of the nation as a whole, and helped to elevate Britain to the leadership of the emerging global economy.

In the eighteenth century Britain generally exported more goods and primary products than it imported. For British companies selling their goods abroad, there were inevitable problems getting paid; so, to make life easier, eighteenth-century London banks provided loans to companies engaged in trade. They lent to the buyers of British goods, who could thus pay promptly and, in return for taking the risk, the banks earned a profit.

Dutch, French, and Italian banks all did the same, of course, but the British banks were special: the scale of Britain's trading alone, both in imports and exports, meant that Britain was bound to be the world's biggest source of finance. However, traders often used British banks in international trade deals, even when neither party was a British company or person. The British government pledged that the Bank of England would always be ready to swap on demand paper for gold bullion from the British government's reserves, and this helped to reassure the financial markets. Fundamentally, however, it was the obvious strength of the British economy that gave the world confidence in British assets; and since British banks held British government debt, they were more secure than any other nation's banks. Indeed, foreign banks and even foreign governments proved their own financial respectability by holding British financial assets, often on deposit at the Bank of England.

Companies were happy to be paid in British pounds sterling, partly because they were safer to hold than the currency of other nations, and partly because everybody else did so—making sterling into an international medium of exchange. Previously, gold or silver bullion had been the normal medium of international exchange, but with British currency, people had the best of both worlds: they avoided the inconvenience of bullion as well as the inconvenience of repeatedly switching currencies when conducting a series of international transactions.

Against that background came the Industrial Revolution. In 1709 Abraham Darby of Staffordshire in the British Midlands found a way to strip the impurities out of coal and thus to produce a fuel, coke, that was almost pure carbon. The production of iron became much more efficient in comparison with prevailing charcoal-burning methods. Six years later Thomas Newcomen developed the first pump capable of safely ridding deep mines of water.[13] Thanks to developments such as these, in the early eighteenth century the British were already able to exploit the earth's deep mineral wealth.

In the second half of the century innovations such as Henry Cort's iron puddling and rolling process appeared. The pace of technological change quickened, helped by the development of precision machine tools, allowing a whole range of other machines to emerge. New tools that could make cylinders and condensers with great accuracy allowed James Watt to improve on Newcomen's steam pump, reducing its prodigious appetite for fuel. More than that, by finding ways to regulate its motion, he turned the pump into an engine suitable for flour milling and, crucially, for spinning cotton. The eighteenth century saw the production in Britain of perhaps twenty-five hundred steam engines. About a third were Watt's, while a similar proportion were used in coal mining.[14] In New England, by contrast, water power still dominated.[15]

Textiles were already a large, but mostly home-based, British industry.[16] People needed clothes as much as they needed food. Cloth making was bound to be an important part of any early industrial economy. In 1733 John Kay of Lancashire invented the flying or self-returning shuttle, which allowed one weaver to do the work of two. It was a start, but it was not until 1764 when James Hargreaves invented a spinning wheel with many spindles— the spinning Jenny—that an equivalent increase in spinning productivity became possible.[17] Then in 1769 Richard Arkright unveiled a spinning machine (not necessarily of his own invention) that, driven initially by water power and later by steam, promised much greater productivity improvements. (Arkright's machine also pulled workers together into small factories for the first time.) A few years later Samuel Crompton introduced his "mule," a better spinning machine than Arkright's; the machine could twist yarn into a thinner, stronger thread of a quality suitable for a cloth's warp as well as its weft. In 1785 Edmund Cartight developed a weaving machine that, although not immediately introduced, offered productivity gains in weaving to match those already achieved in spinning.

As these inventions became widespread, British production of textiles soared. At the start of the eighteenth century Britain imported just five hundred tons of cotton per year; by the beginning of the nineteenth, though, cotton imports had reached twenty-five *thousand* tons annually, and by the middle of the century, British demand for cotton was approaching one half million tons per year—a staggering increase and one that conferred huge benefits on the United States, thanks to Eli Whitney's 1793 cotton gin.

Because of such growth, cotton textiles unambiguously became Britain's leading industry in the nineteenth century, something that was possible only through innovation and new technology. Great progress occurred in other sectors too, much of it also technologically based. Although engineering has received most popular attention, important innovations also occurred in other industries; often the underlying innovation was not British in origin, but the critical application occurred most successfully in Britain. For example, in 1798 a Frenchman, Nicholas Louis Robert, produced the first machine for making continuous sheets of paper, but it was a British engineer Bryan Donkin who made it workable; similarly, another Frenchman, Nicholas Leblanc, developed chlorine bleaching, but it was British industry that put the technique into mass usage between 1820 and 1850. One possible reason is that British science was largely empirical and focused on the resolution of practical problems, whereas continental European science tended to be more mathematical and speculative. Less charitably, Daniel Defoe said in 1728 that the English mainly perfected other people's ideas.[18] The same is often said of modern Japan.

French scientists like Antoine Lavoisier and Nicholas Leblanc had few British equivalents. (Michael Faraday was one striking exception, and he too built upon the ideas of others.) Nevertheless, British industrialists such as John Roebuck and Samuel Garbett did much in the eighteenth century to put the new science of chemistry to commercial use. Thus industries like dyeing, paper making, glass making, and pottery all experienced their own eighteenth-century industrial revolutions. Those revolutions were all rooted firmly in Britain, even if they had first germinated elsewhere.

## Britain: An Uneasy Global Leader

Despite all these obvious achievements, there was no shortage of gainsayers. In 1776 Adam Smith denounced mercantilism in *The Wealth of Nations*. As others joined him, and their views found new credibility after Britain's defeat in North America, a series of moves by the British government away from mercantilism and toward free trade ensued. Although the British embarked on a frantic and largely successful search for new territories to replace those they had lost, the territories the British acquired in their search for a new empire were, with the glaring exception of India, very different from the great continental landmass of the United States; they were deliberately kept small, to act as garrisons, naval bases, and trading ports, but not to be developed into colonies.

With trade restored, Britain's prosperity increased and with it Britain's international influence. (In contrast, French support for the American rebels seriously damaged French finances, which greatly weakened France's global influence after the war, strengthening Britain's position.) Meanwhile, the British opened negotiations on trade liberalization with France, the Netherlands, Portugal, Prussia, and Spain. In 1786 the British and French governments signed the so-called Eden Treaty, which opened up France's market to British cotton and Britain's market to French wine. It seemed to represent a decisive break away from mercantilism and toward free trade, and it symbolized a more general perception that the government ought to intervene less in the affairs of the economy, including its trade relations.[19]

Before long, however, war interrupted this development. In the Napoleonic wars between Britain and France free trade retreated in the face of embargoes and severe trade restrictions; not until 1817 did it win another hearing, when a Scottish economist, David Ricardo, reworked and improved Adam Smith's arguments against mercantilism and in favor of free trade.[20] With peace in Europe, the tide of sentiment began to flow against mercantilism.

As the century progressed it became apparent that railroads and steamships, by removing the major natural obstacles to significant long-distance transport, were conferring great economic benefits on the world. World trade volumes increased some twenty-fivefold thanks largely to the revolution in transport, and people began to wonder whether the removal or reduction of tariff barriers might produce similar benefits.

Among the few who expected to lose from free trade were Britain's still powerful farmers and landowners, who held out against the new ideas. They benefited from shortages of food and other produce, since such shortages kept land values artificially high. Thus the landowners and the farmers gained from barriers to trade, as did their counterparts in other countries. However, the pace of Britain's industrialization was such that these vested interests had come to exercise less power than they once had. By the middle of the nineteenth century, agriculture was beginning to give way in economic importance to manufacturing industry. The repeal of the Corn Laws, which split the Tory party, symbolized this shift and Britain's consequent conversion to free trade.[21] The Corn Laws had imposed tariffs on imported grains used in baking bread, which raised the cost of food for the bulk of the population. Manufacturers lobbied government through the Anti–Corn Law League to end the tariffs and to use free trade as a vehicle for opening new markets to British products. The prime minister, Sir Robert Peel, was already intent on abolishing the Corn Laws when in 1845 an epidemic of potato blight caused widespread starvation in Ireland and Scotland. In defiance of his own party and with the support of the opposition Whigs, Peel persuaded Parliament to remove the laws in January 1846, both in order to cut food costs and to stimulate trade and hence create jobs. Three years later, in 1849, Parliament finally repealed the Navigation Acts. More liberalization followed, and by 1860 Britain set almost no tariffs against the imports of any other nation. By doing so the British gained access to cheap food and raw materials, especially since the whole world now competed hungrily for the British market. Even if British manufactured exports did not benefit from lower tariffs in other markets, they would gain from lower costs—so the British were as happy to see lower tariffs on their imports as on their exports, and they reduced tariffs against nations even when the other nation did not reciprocate.

In the mid- to late nineteenth century many other nations reduced or abolished tariffs, encouraging faster trade growth. On the other hand, because trade grew rapidly in the middle of the nineteenth century, governments found it easy to agree to tariff cuts.

Furthermore, although the British pioneered free trade, they were not very successful at persuading other nations to adopt the policy: they had made their tariff cuts unilaterally, naively believing that other nations would do the same. When this did not happen, though, in frustration the British threatened to raise barriers again. It was a potent threat, since for most countries Britain was the largest export market, whereas for Britain no single nation was on its own an important export market. Even so, other countries were inclined to push their luck, knowing that the British would not throw away lightly their ideological investment in free trade.

Fortunately the French were also committed to promoting open markets, and it was they who did most to put Europe and hence the world on the path to free trade.[22] In 1860 France negotiated the Cobden-Chevalier Treaty with Britain, in which the French agreed to eliminate tariffs on British textiles and to reduce other tariffs on British goods; in return, the British removed all tariffs on imports from France other than wine and brandy. Such tariff cuts were important, but even more so was the treaty's provision known as the "most favored nation" clause. If either nation subsequently negotiated a better deal with a third country, then the terms of that new deal would apply to both of the original signatories. The French went all round Europe, negotiating tariff cuts, and in each treaty they inserted a most favored nation clause. The resultant network of most favored nation clauses gave rise to a bias in favor of successive reductions in tariffs all around the world. By the 1870s, European trade was almost as free of tariffs as it is today. Russia was the only major nation to resist the change.

The speedy growth in world trade in the eighteenth and nineteenth centuries was possible only because finance was available to fund the growth. Behind this movement was the City of London, the center of the global financial system: by lending abroad a larger value of sterling than the nation could possibly back with gold bullion, the City, as it was popularly known, provided the world with more financial liquidity than had ever before been possible.

Such a position appeared to confer major benefits on the British economy. By the middle of the nineteenth century Britain no longer exported more goods than it imported, yet it benefited handsomely from the interest on the money that it lent abroad, as well as from earnings on related activities such as shipping and insurance. This kept the current account in surplus, which permitted Britain to lend even more abroad thereby keeping London at the center of global financial affairs.

Furthermore, because a large share of global lending was channeled through London, Britain's financial institutions had a significant influence over nineteenth-century patterns of international finance, and hence over the relative prosperity of different nations. London banks such as Rothschilds and Barings were to the world what the IMF and the World Bank are today. Having provided much of the finance for the 1803 Louisiana Purchase, Barings bailed out the Bank of England in 1839, when the latter was in trouble; Barings also funded much of the railroad building in North and South America. When Maryland and Pennsylvania defaulted, it was to Barings that American bankers such as J. P. Morgan went, cap in hand, for help. Unlike the IMF and the World Bank, however, the City's banks and other institutions had no political axes to grind: they were private companies, and they each pursued their commercial interests without much regard to the overall interests of Britain, and without any sense that they were responsible for the management of the global financial system.

The same is true of the British government and the Bank of England, which showed little concern for the role that history had conferred upon them as managers of the nineteenth-century global economy. After the Napoleonic Wars the British authorities restored their prewar commitment to sell sterling in exchange for gold at a fixed price. Since sterling was so widely used, that commitment may well have conferred a degree of financial stability on the world economy. However, it was not the British authorities who encouraged other nations to peg their currencies either to sterling or to gold. As far as the British government was concerned, other countries were free to do as they wished—either peg their currencies to silver or commit themselves to exchange their currencies into either silver or gold at a given rate as needed. The pressure for stability came from companies in other nations that borrowed sterling or used it in their international trading. In order to spend it they still had to convert the sterling back into their own currencies—thus borrowers abroad pressured their governments to make sure that their currencies did not fall, relative to sterling. This exerted a stabilizing influence on currencies across the world, and that perhaps helped the world to grow as rapidly as it did during much of the nineteenth century.

Nor did the British government show much concern about using the leverage that it gained from sterling's pivotal world role. So long as sterling dominated international finance, the world's governments and financial markets had to take their policy leads from London. If the British raised interest rates, causing an international switch into sterling, then other countries had to follow. The British authorities alone could decide, for domestic policy reasons, to raise or lower interest rates, since Britain alone was the major source of global lending. Governments in other countries could not do so unilaterally; any such attempt would either provoke massive outflows of gold (in the case of interest rate cuts) or would generate retaliatory rate hikes by the British (in the case of interest rate increases). When the British did raise interest rates, however, everybody else followed, and when the British reduced, so did the rest of the world. The Bank of England, people said, could raise interest rates high enough to draw gold from the moon.[23]

In practice, the British government sacrificed domestic industrial interests to keep the international financial system stable and hence to keep the City of London sweet. Through much of the nineteenth century the deterioration in Britain's trade balance and the investment problems of British industry suggested that interest rates should have been cut and sterling should have fallen in value.[24] In a pattern that recalled the behavior of the eighteenth-century Dutch and that would be replicated in the United States in the 1960s and the 1970s, international selling pressure on the currency ought to have signaled that sterling could not remain permanently strong while the nation's industrial base was under threat. However, since the Bank of England was determined to protect the City's earnings, and since it took only a short-term view, sterling remained high. When in the last quarter of the century sterling came under heavy selling pressure, the Bank raised interest rates to prop up the pound; further, it led resistance to a proposal, backed by many industrialists, to adopt a joint silver and gold currency standard that would have introduced greater currency flexibility.[25]

Just as the British flirted with "bimetallism," so other nations moved onto the gold standard. In 1871 the German government created a central bank along the lines of the Bank of England and pegged its currency to gold, and later in the same decade the United States government also pegged the dollar to gold; both, like the British, now believed that they could attract generous amounts of gold into their financial systems.[26] Regular current account surpluses and rising international confidence in their economies made the Americans and the Germans the equal of the dominant but beleaguered British and transformed the international monetary system into a competition for gold in which Britain was no longer the only player of note. Other countries joined in and pegged their currencies to gold too, giving rise to a global system that can properly be called the "gold standard." But it was a symbol of Britain's new relative weakness, not Britain's relative strength.

In 1890 came decisive evidence of Britain's financial decline. With the world in recession, South American railroads in difficulties, and Argentina gripped by a corrupt government, Barings found itself holding securities of collapsing value. The bank almost went bust, and to its great shame, the consortium of banks that rescued Barings included an American firm: J. P. Morgan. Worse still for the prestige of London's banks, the same firm also raised money for the British government during the 1899–1902 Boer War, a conflict in which Britain fought for control over southern Africa.

Britain's problems were not purely financial, for no nation as entangled in the larger global economy as was Britain could expect to keep its industrial revolution to itself. Early in the nineteenth century the new industries spread to Belgium, where there was a long tradition of clothmaking on which to expand, plentiful coal, and ready access to the markets, people, and ideas of adjacent countries—including, across the North Sea, Britain. Indeed, several people such as William Cockerill of Leeds migrated from Britain to Belgium in order to set up business there. Other nations industrialized according to their own pattern. France experienced an early industrial revolution, but one that was repeatedly impeded by political and social problems—the French Revolution, the Napoleonic Wars, a declining population, and the 1871 loss to Germany of Alsace-Lorraine.

Another major nation to industrialize early was Germany, although the Germans also had to wait, both for political union and for the exploitation of the Ruhr coalfield, which occurred only in the second half of the nineteenth century with the help of British, Belgian, and French machinery and expertise. Most important of all, the United States too gradually industrialized during the course of the nineteenth century.

Despite these and other developments, Britain in the middle of the nineteenth century still accounted for about 15 percent of world manufacturing production, more than double the share of France and three times that of Germany. Furthermore, Britain by then probably produced half the world's iron and used half its cotton in the manufacture of textiles. In several such sectors, Britain was exceptional, and overall the British economy looked like that of a superpower. However, in the final quarter of the nineteenth century, the German and American economies accelerated; in contrast, Britain's growth rate slowed. As a result, Britain's industrial leadership was really rather short lasting. Indeed, although at the end of the nineteenth century Britain was still by far the largest exporter of manufactured goods in the world, for much of the Victorian period Britain's share of world output was in decline, even if in absolute terms Britain was stronger than ever before.

The relative decline of Britain was not just the result of younger industrial powers catching up to the leader. Toward the end of the nineteenth century a cluster of innovations occurred in science-based sectors such as the chemicals industry and electrical engineering.[27] Although these innovations promised the world new possibilities for economic growth, almost amounting to a second industrial revolution, they went largely unnoticed in Britain. The British continued with the Bessemer steel-making process even when the better open-hearth method was available. Although British scientists such as William Perkin pioneered research into chemistry, British firms showed little interest in their work. In chemicals and electrical engineering British industry failed to adopt the new technologies.[28] German and American companies introduced in-house research and pioneered the new products and processes that were reshaping the world. Electricity was left mainly to the Americans. And so on: as other countries embraced innovation, their manufacturing productivity leapt.[29] Economic and industrial leadership was not wrenched away but fell from Britain's grasp.[30]

In a narrow sense the British were being quite rational, even if not desperately entrepreneurial.[31] Britain boasted plentiful cheap, unskilled labor and bountiful supplies of coal and iron—implying that Britain's comparative advantage rested with old-fashioned industries and methods. Britain also had easy access to supplies of cotton and other staples, the foundations on which Britain had first built the industrial revolution. It was always easier and cheaper to stick with existing products, methods, and markets than to respond to, let alone initiate, new market opportunities.

However, because in the late nineteenth century most British exports came from a few low-level technologies, dependency on low-value-added products severely constrained the nation's economic options. British companies could only sell their products to the world's poorer and more slowly growing nations. In Britain itself wages barely increased, so the domestic market failed to grow. Foreign manufactured goods were widely sought after, much as Japanese goods are in the United States today. Meanwhile, in the lucrative European and American markets, British firms were losing ground.

British companies hardly knew what was happening to them.

Mostly they were small: in 1834, Britain's twelve hundred textile factories were mostly independent of one another, owned by the men who ran them.[32] Small scale meant little investment in sales and marketing networks, which allowed—or forced—British managers to live in a state of ignorance.[33] They thought that what they supplied was what the markets wanted, but it was a delusion. American and German industry invested heavily in new technologies, products, production methods, and in the techniques of mass marketing. Had the British embraced new production methods and new technologies as the Germans and the Americans did, then British productivity might well have accelerated in the second half of the nineteenth century.

In Victorian Britain the government was neither able nor willing to defend British industry. Instead it concentrated on maintaining the prosperity of the City of London as a financial center. The City was both the fastest growing part of the economy, and the most closely integrated into the policymaking process in Whitehall and Westminster, but London's banks had no commitment to industry. Although they still called themselves "merchant banks," the City's great financial houses were primarily concerned in the late nineteenth century with lending to governments at home and abroad, and lending to other banks; their directors spent much of their time courting politicians and one another, while neglecting industry.[34]

One manifestation of this was Britain's commitment to free trade. The City's banks, commodity traders, shipping companies, and insurance companies reasoned that if free trade meant more trade, then that would mean more business for them. When the end of the Napoleonic Wars came, promising a sharp cut in government borrowing, the City was anxious that its lucrative earnings from trading public sector debt were in danger; a larger global role would fill the gap nicely—especially if, as seemed possible, more trade would lead to more investment opportunities in the colonies and in places such as South America. Since the City's leaders were substantially closer to government than to industrialists, in terms of background, lifestyle, and location, it was their commitment to free trade which did most to swing the argument.[35]

Faced with such indifference, many companies did not bother to seek bank loans at all, but relied instead on their own profits to fund investment. Those that did go to banks encountered a reluctance to take risks or make long-term commitments via equity ownership.[36] Despite their willingness to invest in long-term projects abroad, such as railroads, the banks, in their domestic lending, were committed to earning high returns over short periods and knew little about the use that companies made of their money.

Lack of commitment on the part of bankers meant a short-term bias on the part of corporate borrowers, which in turn meant a reluctance to innovate. That had implications going beyond industry: it affected both the kind of education that the nation gave its young people and the willingness of the government to finance education. Since Britain's economy was concerned with immediate prospects the nation barely invested in education, and showed little interest in the systematic development of technical and managerial skills.[37] British managers of the late nineteenth century had poor qualifications by German standards, as did British skilled and unskilled workers.

At the higher levels, formal education made little contribution to the spread of new scientific thinking.[38] Public lectures were almost the main means for promoting scientific and technical knowledge. Learned societies such as the Manchester Literary and Philosophical Society also contributed, as did journals, but they could hardly compensate for the lack of proper teaching. The British cult of the amateur had worked well enough in the late eighteenth century, when single individuals provided the source of innovation; however, it left British industry quite unable to compete in the more scientific and technological world of the late nineteenth century.[39]

## Protectionism Returns, War Threatens

The great danger for the world at the end of the nineteenth century was that the problems of Britain's industry would push the British government to return toward protectionism.

Others had already moved in that direction—indeed, scarcely had free trade arrived than it was in retreat. A primary reason was the power in most countries, including France, of landowners whose prosperity was contingent on high agricultural prices. Sharp declines in prices during the 1870s, partly precipitated by the expansion of American farm exporting, provoked a global recession in output and so raised a clamor for a return to protectionism.[40] War between France and Germany also severely damaged the network of liberal cooperation on which free trade had been built, and in 1879 German Chancellor Bismarck approved a new German tariff, intended to protect German agriculture *and* industry from foreign competition; the French responded in 1881 with a rather milder tariff designed to protect only industry. Then in 1892 came the Meline Tariff, which signaled a much more thorough return to old French protectionist ways; a tariff war with Italy followed. The Austro-Hungarian empire also raised tariffs, and the Russians, who had never lowered tariffs in the first place, raised them to levels that made trade all but pointless.

In 1890 the Americans joined in, becoming one of the world's most protectionist nations. That year's McKinley Tariff Act raised existing duties to prohibitive levels and extended tariffs to hitherto untouched items. Since many goods became either unavailable or hugely expensive, the tariff was widely disliked, even by farmers, and it contributed to the Republican Party's growing crisis and to the agrarian revolt, as well as to the growing crisis in the global economy. Even so, there was no immediate prospect of the tariff being revoked, and indeed American trade policy remained severely protectionist for many decades to come.

All that was needed for the global trading system to collapse was for Britain to join the retreat into protectionism. Had Britain abandoned free trade and opted for protectionism (as the United

States would do in the 1930s) then global recession would probably have followed, with possibly catastrophic consequences. Instead, Britain stood firm, though not from altruism: since British exports were less geared toward Europe than were those of other nations, and more toward the underdeveloped nations of its empire and South America, British exports were less harmed by tariffs than those of other major nations. From the British perspective, what mattered was keeping import prices down in order to keep British products competitive, and so the British eschewed tariffs.

For the world economy British policy was nevertheless highly beneficial: the tariffs that other nations erected simply redirected trade toward Britain, which became the export market of first and last resort. Thanks to British trade policy, world trade continued to grow, despite the return to protectionism elsewhere, and despite the resultant catastrophic deterioration in Britain's trading deficit. Britain's continuing commitment to free trade thus acted as a powerful stabilizing influence on the world economy—but its roots lay in the weakness of the nation's manufacturing sector, not in its strength.

Despite the persistence of British free trade, there was deep anxiety in Europe about world growth drying up. Companies pressed governments to pursue mercantilist international policies and pleaded with governments to secure control over lands in Africa and Asia which would offer new sources of cheap raw materials. Britain had a head start in this respect, whereas Germany, only recently unified, was a latecomer.

British government policy had long been to allow other countries to benefit from the growth of the open global economy. Late-nineteenth-century Germany clearly benefited from the integration of the world economy into a single financial and trading system. As part of that integration, the British gave other nations trading access to the British Empire, so German industry had access to all the raw materials it needed. Within continental Europe, though, Germany took its own initiatives, gradually establishing production bases in other parts of Europe, not least in France. The Germans increasingly financed, and so controlled, much of the Italian economy; indeed, like their modern Japanese counterparts, many German diplomats and politicians saw commerce as an effective way to engage in national rivalries without taking recourse to war.

For military reasons, too, the German government, like the British, was genuinely keen to avoid war. In Berlin the authorities knew that a titanic struggle between the two nations might leave both in ruins, giving effective victory to an uninvolved third party—as indeed did happen. In any case, the German authorities had little desire to destroy the international system, particularly its economic component, under which their nation, like others, prospered.[41]

Despite this, German manufacturers felt that their inefficient British rivals gained advantages from what looked like British global hegemony, and they complained that the British ran the world economy to their own advantage and to the disadvantage of all others. Whether or not that was correct, the future of British policy was uncertain, and German industry was vulnerable to the possibility that one day the British would exclude it from access to world markets. To Germany's business leaders, the nation's interdependence with the rest of the world often felt like dependence: booms and slumps seemed to originate abroad, unsettle the German economy, and defy German control. In the event of a return by Britain to mercantilism, Germany would be vulnerable. In the slump of 1908–1909, British politics did indeed become openly anti-German, and a tariff looked a real threat.[42]

Britain's residual strength was its undisputed naval mastery. From the Battle of Trafalgar until World War I, the Royal Navy dominated the seas as effectively as the United States Navy has in our own time. The British government never relaxed its old policy of having a fleet larger than the next two combined, and sometimes the Royal Navy may have been larger than the next three of four fleets together.[43] On land, however, Britain was much weaker, with a small army by European standards, most of which was deployed far away, in India and elsewhere. It should not be forgotten how vast a possession India was, and only one of many; Britain expanded its nineteenth-century empire, almost without challenge. Furthermore, British finance was still constantly available to friendly governments in Europe and elsewhere which did have large armies, and in that sense the British exerted more influence in Europe than is obvious on the surface. Britain did that while spending an historically low proportion of the nation's income on the navy and army.

In 1911, however, Britain finally became involved in an arms race with Germany. For the latter, rearmament was made easier to finance by the introduction of progressive income taxes, which had been advocated throughout Europe by socialist politicians keen to finance improvements in housing, welfare, and education, but which were instead or as well used for financing battleships and other weapons.

Yet the fact remained that it was neither the German nor the British government but that of the Austro-Hungarian Empire which precipitated hostilities. From about 1870 until the outbreak of war, the old Habsburg Empire was one of the largest and fastest-growing economies in the world, yet within the empire regional variations in income and growth were huge and reflected deep ethnic divisions. The sort of market-driven development that had occurred especially in Britain, but also in France, Germany, and of course the United States, had passed the Austro-Hungarians by: the empire shared out its wealth and income in ways that seemed unfair to many of the fifteen or more distinct ethnic elements. There was always a risk that small but assertive neighbors like Serbia would attempt to annex parts of the empire, in the hope of building new nation states on clearer ethnic lines—and that was precisely what the Austro-Hungarians believed was happening in the early summer of 1914.

In June 1914 the imperial armies conducted maneuvers in Bosnia, on the borders of Serbia in order to intimidate or to infuriate both the independent-minded Bosnians and their Serbian friends. It succeeded rather too well: on 28 June 1914 the Archduke Franz Ferdinand, on his way to inspect troop maneuvers in Bosnia on the borders of Serbia, was assassinated in the Bosnian capital of Sarajevo, together with his wife Sophie, Duchess of Hohenberg. The Austro-

Hungarian emperor, Franz Joseph, did not seem to mind too much the death of his unloved nephew, but the assassination of an heir was politically embarrassing, and the excuse to attack Serbia too good to miss. The Austro-Hungarian government declared war on Serbia. Since Germany was allied to the former and Russia and France indirectly to the latter, a major European conflict was thus precipitated. Britain felt obliged to join in, fearing that whoever won the war would thereby be strengthened in comparison with Britain. Whether that was the right decision is very doubtful, though Ferdinand's assassin, a nineteen-year-old boy called Gavrilo Princip may have been right when he said, "If I had not done it, the Germans would have found another excuse."[44] Germany's naval buildup did pose a grave threat to Britain, and perhaps a war between the two was inevitable; but the coming catastrophe was set to destroy Europe, and open the door for another nation, far away, to grasp leadership from the embattled European rivals.

## Chapter Three

# FROM THE GREAT WAR TO THE GREAT CRASH

## *The Reluctant Belligerent*

By 1900 the American economy was by far the largest in the world. American factories accounted for over half the world's manufacturing production and almost twice as much as the next two largest economies, Germany and Britain, combined.[1] The United States was also beginning to assume a significant role in global politics. In 1823 the Monroe Doctrine was little more than idle rhetoric, but by 1895 the United States was close to declaring war on Britain in its defense. In 1898 the United States did go to war, at first to liberate Cuba from Spain but later to annex the Philippines and other Spanish colonies.

However, Americans moved only slowly toward the assumption of a large global role. They were already a great power but, in Paul Kennedy's words, were not yet part of the Great Power system.[2] Since the people of the Philippines showed no great desire to become American subjects, the United States found itself caught up in a three-year campaign to subjugate them, and, unlike Hong Kong and Singapore, the Philippines never became a major Far Eastern trading station. Cuba did become an offshore production facility for American sugar and tobacco companies, but that was largely accidental. In 1889 economic considerations clearly persuaded John Hay, McKinley's secretary of state, to warn the Europeans against trying to exclude the United States from access to China's markets, but the Open Door policy was never tested in adversity, and it is doubtful whether the American people would have gone to war to enforce it. In 1905 Theodore Roosevelt implicitly compromised the Open Door policy when he mediated a settlement that gave Japan control over southern Manchuria (as well as Korea and part of Sakhalin). Although Taft later attempted to minimize the impact of Roosevelt's deal by actively encouraging American companies to invest in China, especially in its railroads, the private sector showed little enthusiasm for such dollar diplomacy, and under Wilson the policy collapsed.

Theodore Roosevelt, in addition to mediating in the war between Russia and Japan, sought to intervene in some of the major infra-European tensions of the day, such as the 1905 Moroccan Crisis. His interventions were purely diplomatic, and although the United States already had the world's third-largest navy as well as its largest economy, Roosevelt never threatened to use force in Europe. Subsequent presidents eschewed even diplomatic interventions, and as European antagonisms rose inexorably, American neutrality came to seem more like indifference to Europe's fate.

There are many explanations for American isolationism, and there is no reason to rehearse them here, except to note a widespread belief that conflict within Europe might be *beneficial* to American interests. Americans such as Willard Straight, a former consul general in Manchuria, hoped that in the event of hostilities

American firms would be able to continue trading with the bellig-
erents on both sides, and that they would gain hugely by doing so.
Indeed, a great war between Britain and Germany might even crip-
ple the economies of either or both, and hence create significant
opportunities for American companies.

The accuracy of such cynicism became apparent in 1914, when
war finally broke out. American ships continued to trade freely with
Britain and Germany alike, as well as with third parties, whereas
British ships were vulnerable to German attack and vice versa. Even
when Britain blockaded Germany, the American position remained
strong. Although the British mined the North Sea and Royal Navy
warships intercepted neutral ships and confiscated their cargoes,
they initially exempted American cotton from the blockade. Furthermore, the British paid compensation for cargoes they seized, so
that little hardship accrued to American companies from the barriers
to trade.

Gradually the British became less accommodating and by 1916
they had made it almost impossible for the Americans to trade with
Germany. Although the Americans protested against Britain's clear
violations of international law, their anger was diluted by the wealth
of orders that the British placed with American firms. In 1914 the
British government had appointed J. P. Morgan to be its American
purchasing agent. Morgan bought almost every type of good that
American industry could produce, from locomotives to barbed
wire, spending $10 million a day, and also arranged much of the
financing.[3]

British orders helped to keep the American economy out of
recession, and supplying the allied war effort soon became one of
the biggest American businesses. In addition, the United States developed a dyestuff industry to replace the German imports that the
British blockaded. Oil refining doubled during the war, the production of rubber goods increased threefold, and the output of the
American motor industry quadrupled. Beyond manufacturing,
farmers prospered thanks to a booming domestic economy and
plenty of demand from war-ravaged Europe. American shipping
also prospered as it moved into markets that British vessels could

no longer serve; in 1917 when German submarines and ships were badly mauling British convoys and Britain's fate depended on the flow of supplies from the United States, American freighters and naval vessels shifted away from the North Atlantic, so that they could capture the lucrative Latin American trade that the British could no longer serve.[4]

Others nations also benefited from the war. The Japanese declined a British request for troops to use in Europe, and instead busied themselves with picking up the East Asian export markets that the British were temporarily unable to serve. India gained, too, as it created a modern textiles industry and became an important source of manufactured products in the Middle East and Asia. Canada and to a lesser extent Australia expanded their industries, agriculture, and mineral extraction. It was the United States, however, that was the main beneficiary of European problems—particularly because, in addition to the boost to American output and the boost to American trade from supplying Britain, there were also financial advantages that flowed from the war.

Britain financed much of its war effort from higher taxation, but to pay for American food, materials, and munitions and to compensate for the loss of normal export earnings, the British also sold much of their American assets and borrowed heavily from American banks, most notably, J. P. Morgan. Britain also borrowed from the United States on behalf of its European allies, especially France and pre-revolutionary Russia. The $3.7 billion of American loans that allowed Britain to keep fighting also meant that when the war ended the United States would no longer be just the world's leading industrial power—it would also be the world's financial leader.

So long as hostilities posed only a small threat to American ships and nationals, the American government was in no hurry to see a speedy end to the Anglo-German fighting. American neutrality was, however, a long-term threat to Germany: although the Germans were militarily a match for Britain, and in isolation economically stronger than Britain, they were severely hampered by the fact that Britain could obtain all the resources from the United States that it could pay for, whereas Germany could not.[5] Accordingly, in February 1915 the German government decided to redress the balance by launching unrestricted submarine attacks on all British merchant vessels, with the addendum that any American vessels found in the war zone might also be sunk "by accident."

The Germans knew that such a policy risked bringing the United States into the war, but they felt that they had no alternative. At first their gamble paid off—President Wilson protested to Germany about submarine attacks and threatened retaliation if American lives were lost, but he clearly wanted to avoid involvement if at all possible. The sinking of the *Lusitania*, with the loss of over a hundred American lives and more than a thousand others, provoked only a formal diplomatic protest; even that was too much for William Jennings Bryan, who resigned from his post as secretary of state. After the *Lusitania*, German submarines sunk more ships, at a cost of more American lives, but in Washington the government remained resolutely inactive. Wilson made a number of diplomatic protests and initiatives, but refrained from any physical entanglement with Germany—even when, in 1915, evidence emerged of German sabotage and espionage in the United States. In his presidential election campaign he warned voters not to vote Republican if they wanted to stay out of the war.

During 1916 several considerations caused Wilson to shift his opinion. The president had begun to believe that if German submarines gained control of the Atlantic, then they could threaten American interests almost as effectively as they could threaten Britain's. After the *Lusitania* sinking the German ambassador had promised that no more passenger ships would be sunk, but Wilson was well aware that the promise could easily be revoked; indeed, so long as the Germans confined themselves to attacking only some British vessels, their chances of winning the war were much constrained. It thus came as no surprise when, on January 31, 1917, the German government warned the Americans that it was about to resume unrestricted submarine warfare. A month later, two

Americans were among those who died when the Germans sunk a British liner, the *Laconia*; in mid-March, German submarines sunk several American merchant vessels. On April 2, President Wilson at last asked Congress to declare war on Germany.

However, it was not only the German naval threat that altered the president's thinking. By 1917 Britain was massively in debt to the United States, and American financiers were worried about the security of their loans; although the Americans held collateral, the true wartime value of the assets was quite uncertain, and even their peacetime value would depend to a degree on the kind of peace settlement that followed the war. That point was even more true with respect to trade: the war had turned Britain into a major export market for American businesses. However, in 1916 Britain and its European allies had signed the so-called Paris Agreements, in which they pledged themselves to restrictions on postwar German trade; and the American government was worried that it too might be excluded from access to British and other markets. It thus became important for the United States that any postwar settlement should include American access to the British and wider European and colonial markets—and for that reason it made sense for the United States to involve itself in the war, in order that it could help to shape the peace. It was that essentially economic concern that motivated Wilson's demand for a liberal postwar order.[6]

Nevertheless, many Americans saw the situation differently. Senators Robert La Follette and George Norris, of Wisconsin and Nebraska respectively, questioned whether propping up Britain's empire was really consistent with Wilson's promise of a world "safe for democracy." They claimed that the real reason for going to war was so that bankers and armaments makers could profit from the adventure. According to Norris, President Wilson was sending the United States "into war upon the command of gold."[7] However, it was not to make new profits that the United States went to war; the only economic reasons were to safeguard and exploit the advantages that the war had already brought.

Even so, there was a further delay between the American declaration of war and the arrival in Europe of the first American troops. To some extent this was the fault of the British, who diverted ships from troop transport to trade in an attempt both to stem the loss of markets to the United States and to reduce the American military contribution to the defeat of Germany.[8] However, such a policy if anything played into the hands of the American government, which in 1918 kept its forces stationed in France out of action, while French and British troops suffered heavily from that year's great German offensive; the Americans believed that if they gave Germany the chance to weaken Britain further, and then themselves crushed the German army, American postwar diplomatic and economic strength would be all the greater. In 1917 Wilson wrote of Britain and France, "when the war is over we can force them to our way of thinking, because by that time they will, among other things, be financially in our hands."[9] Wilson was right, but whether the American government was ready to put its advantage to use was a different matter.

## The Age of Mass Production

The end of the war meant problems for the American economy. Major cuts in armament production followed the armistice, depressing activity in the United States, and with Europe almost in ruins there was little growth in overseas markets. For a time, business confidence was low, and in 1921 and 1922 the American economy experienced a deep recession.

The problems were temporary, however. Gradually, the American economy returned to normal. Better than that, giant new factories and high levels of consumer spending testified to a regeneration of American confidence; strong growth in consumer spending reflected both high wages and the impact of the newly invented consumer credit.[10] Spending created demand and hence jobs and output. The economy grew at prewar rates.

As before, American economic growth was closely associated with two phenomena—the growth of big business and the development and diffusion of new technology. The latter included the development of chemicals and synthetic textiles, electricity generation and distribution, and the growth of radio and the movies. However, most important was the development of production technology. The basis of that had been laid down in the nineteenth century with the emergence of the American system of manufactures; now the time had come to take the next step, toward mass production.

One of the companies that had first developed and exploited the American system of manufactures was the Singer Manufacturing Company, makers of the famous sewing machine. One of Singer's employees was Walter Flanders, a mechanic with a strong commitment to modern production methods; in 1906 Henry Ford persuaded Flanders to leave Singer and enter the automobile industry.

Ford was already a car manufacturer, though not very successful—his firm had gone bust once. Ford reckoned that if he was ever going to be successful he would have to sell cars in very large quantities at low prices. (Earlier users of interchangeable parts like Singer had used the system to achieve high margins rather than low prices.) To achieve this, though, he needed Flanders's expertise. Helped by another mechanic, Max Wollering, Flanders created for Ford a highly efficient method of using interchangeable parts in the assembly of cars; Ford's productivity rose to a level that no other motor manufacturer could match.

Wollering and Flanders designed and built their own machine tools. They rearranged the Ford factory, locating the machines in a logical order, according to the sequence in which the cars were made. They arranged for parts to be brought to the assembly workers in order to cut down on the amount of time the latter spent away from their work stands. Today these pre–assembly line innovations sound rather modest, but they meant that for the first time the mass production of cars was a possibility. In 1908 the firm sold six thousand Model T Fords, a car with the advantage that it was genuinely popular—as one of Ford's agents enthused, "the greatest creation in automobiles ever placed before a people . . ."

To raise productivity further the Ford team soon decided that each individual worker should specialize in one very specific assembly task, walking from bench to bench to perform that task on each car in turn. Partly as a result of this specialization, by 1911 Ford sales were above forty thousand. However, the system of moving the workers around served to draw attention to the sharp differences in the work rates of individual workers. Slow workers were a problem, but particularly fast workers were no great asset, since they had to hang around and wait for slower workers to do their jobs. Accordingly, on April 1, 1913, Ford adapted a device already widely used in the Chicago food industry—the production line, in which workers remained at their machines while the cars moved steadily past.[11] Production soared, and in 1916 sales exceeded one half million. By then, Ford was selling as many cars as all the other American manufacturers combined.

This profusion of cars had a number of ramifications. More cars meant more demand for roads, hence a construction boom, as well as new opportunities for travel and tourism, hence the opening up of states like Florida and California, which hitherto had seemed remote and marginal. The success of the motor industry also meant heavy demand for steel, revitalizing the steel companies, which expanded into many other new markets.

The desire of companies such as Ford to introduce production lines depended on a reliable source of continuous energy—electricity. The construction of power stations and supply grids to provide the new assembly plants encouraged the supply of electricity to other business and domestic users, pushing the United States yet further onto an industrial rather than agrarian footing.

Even so, much of the early demand for the Model T Ford came from American farmers who wanted to use the car on their farms, mainly as transport but sometimes even as tractors. The use of proper tractors also began to spread, largely because, by dispensing with horses and other pack animals, farmers could eliminate the need to grow fodder. Hitherto, two out of every five American fields had been devoted to feeding working animals; almost overnight, the acreage of American farmland available for cash crops increased by a quarter. Output increased sharply and prices fell. The automobile, along with the growth of chemical fertilizers (a German invention available again in the United States after the war had ended) transformed American agriculture.

The impact of "The Machine That Changed the World" was thus as dramatic as the British agricultural revolution of the eighteenth century. Farm workers, displaced by mechanization, found themselves at work in factories where new production and process techniques allowed them to achieve higher productivity levels, and hence higher real wage levels, than ever before thought possible. As the United States developed new industries, products, and manufacturing processes, other countries were left to move into older manufacturing sectors where profit margins were narrow, the potential for product development was limited, and there were few opportunities for developing new markets. Thus the United States set about the mass production of motor cars, household appliances, and chemicals while India, for example, developed its textile industry until it began to rival that of Britain.

Mass production brought with it high wages, which in turn meant the emergence of the mass market without which the mass production would itself have been pointless. Ford repeatedly reduced the price of the Model T and, as a result, sales increased to a staggering two million in 1921. The increased sales themselves reduced Ford's unit costs which, at least for the first few years, justified the price cuts. For a while, it all seemed very easy.

Ford had done something revolutionary. Although the American system of manufactures, interchangeable parts, and even assembly lines had all been seen before, Henry Ford understood the value of selling large quantities of a product at a cheap price. It was for that purpose that he used mass production and for that reason that he was slow to see the merits of modern marketing techniques and of the organizational reforms that others introduced. To keep costs low, Ford eschewed product variety. He ignored those who doubted how many identical black Model T Fords Americans would really buy; yet the more that the company sold, the stronger became the doubts of his critics.

Ford's problem was its inflexibility. When it replaced the Model T with the Model A, it took over a year for the factory to get up to speed. Although this inflexibility was partly a reflection of the firm's dominance by a single founding figure, a similar organizational inflexibility pervaded the company. In order to maintain quality Ford had gradually taken on the manufacture of all its own components, thus applying mass production techniques to the whole manufacturing process, not just final assembly. This vertical integration greatly increased the complexity of the Ford business—but since one man ran the company, and since he was autocratic and unwilling to share control, the firm inevitably fossilized. As the company ignored innovation, its market share slipped, from over half in 1921 to less than a third in 1926.[12]

If Ford faced a problem, it was another American company, General Motors, that had a solution. General Motors, a marketing-led firm, had developed flexible production techniques so that it could respond to customer demand—and it realized that an annual model change would provide a great marketing opportunity. Ford stood in relation to General Motors as British craft manufacturers had once stood in relation to American factory manufacturers: inflexible, unable to change, and committed to the past.

Alfred Sloan's innovations at General Motors, like those of his rival, Henry Ford, built on a long, evolving American tradition, that of the very large company made successful by attention to management methods. Sloan was made president of General Motors after Pierre Du Pont moved there from the chemicals company that bore his name. Du Pont was one of the first American firms to engage in extensive diversification, and hence one of the first to tackle the management problems that such diversification engendered. Hitherto, most firms produced only a few items for a few markets. During the consumer-driven twenties, however, Du Pont and a number of other big American firms diversified. Single firms began to produce many ranges of new goods—radio, cars, refrigerators. Yet firms that adopted such diversification strategies had to introduce the appropriate structures if they wished to prosper—and that meant decentralization, which also helped with the development of financial procedures and market forecasting.

In contrast General Motors under its founder William Durrant had grown by a process of acquisition, and in 1920 it contained a variety of subsidiaries, often competing with each other and badly managed, in whose affairs Durrant erratically intervened. Du Pont and Sloan kept General Motors split into five independent divisions and set them clear targets, allocating them the resources they needed, but otherwise they did not intervene in the running of those divisions, thereby avoiding the organizational logjams that bedeviled Ford. Through people like Du Pont and even more so Sloan, management rather than science transformed American society in the early twentieth century; intensifying efforts by Americans to invent a science of management only served to emphasize the fact.[13]

More than anything else, the new methods meant the further rise of big business. The big companies got yet bigger: at the start of the decade there were already nearly three hundred firms in the United States capitalized at $20 million or more. Then in the twenties the United States experienced its second wave of merger mania: there were nearly six thousand mergers between 1925 and 1931. Most of the new giant firms were manufacturers, and many, such as Nabisco and General Electric, are still with us today. They were vertically integrated: a single company mined for, quarried, or farmed its raw materials, assembled them, shipped them, and retailed them to the final customers. Instead of a chain of firms there was just one, and middle managers ran the company from day to day while senior managers monitored the performance of the middle managers and allocated resources, especially finance, where it seemed they would be most useful. Financial accounting developed as a tool of management.[14] Within the boundaries of these giant integrated companies, there were no prices, no competition: bureaucracy did the work of the market.

Many small companies remained, of course, and in some sectors they still dominated. In the distribution sector and in those parts of manufacturing where the production process was very simple and skill levels low, firms remained small—examples are timber and clothing. In most sectors of the American economy in the twenties, however, the largest firms were very large.

American companies knew the merits of being big: not only did size permit the introduction of expensive new production technology, it also reduced vulnerability to competition. Ford's vertical integration, Sloan's marketing and organizational innovations, and above all Rockefeller's long-established exploitation of monopoly power all provided better guarantees of corporate prosperity than did price wars and laissez-faire capitalism.

This pattern reflects the successful modernization of the American economy and the shift in the nation's industrial structure.[15] However, while many industries such as oil and motor manufacturing prospered, others such as shipbuilding, railways, cotton textiles, and coal did badly in the decade. The net effect was that job security declined—even as employers renewed prewar efforts to reduce the power of trades unions and even to outlaw them if possible. Not surprisingly, therefore, the revolution in American industry was not universally popular, despite its evident success at delivering the economic goods. The United States changed, but without making any arrangements for cushioning the impact on the losers.

Faced with a series of fundamental transformations in the industrial structure of the nation, the federal government was unsure what, if anything, it should do. Many politicians distrusted big business on principle: progressivism had dominated American politics before the war, and it still exerted a pull on the nation's sympathies. Two events had particularly defined the Progressive Era. The first was the prosecution, from 1906 until 1911, of Rockefeller's Standard Oil for breaching the Sherman Antitrust Act. President Roosevelt called the company's directors "the biggest criminals in history," and his Democratic rival, William Jennings Bryan, called for Rockefeller's imprisonment.[16] The courts examined Standard Oil's business practices over the preceding forty years and concluded that Rockefeller's "very genius for commercial development and organization . . . soon began an intent and purpose to exclude others."[17] The company was given six months in which to dissolve itself.

A year later the House Banking and Currency Committee launched an inquiry into the power of Wall Street. Called the "Pujo committee," its investigations laid bare the extent of cross-holdings and cross directorship that linked banks such as J. P. Morgan to industrial concerns, insurance and savings institutions, and to one another. It seemed that, beneath an outward show of competition and independence, a closed cabal of bankers ran not just the financial system but, via their links to the trusts, virtually the entire nation's economy. Morgan's bank was sufficiently worried that it attempted to buy a multitude of newspapers, including the *Washington Post*, to represent its case.[18]

Fortunately for the banks, although the committee identified a "community of interests," it could not prove any law breaking. Wilson used this to help his project for creating the Federal Reserve, which, although initially attacked by most bankers, did nothing to prevent the banks from continuing with their practices. The Federal Reserve Act came into being in 1913; a year later World War I began, and with it the return to favor of big business and the banks. That year the Clayton Act supposedly outlawed price discrimination and interlocking directorships when the consequences reduced competition, but in practice the legislation was toothless and ineffective.

In 1917 the War Industries Board, under the financier Bernard Baruch, and other organizations such as the Fuel Administration and the Food Administration mobilized all of American business for the war effort. In military terms it was not a great success, and the Americans fought mainly with French artillery and British- and French-made airplanes, but the new regime had one important effect: it rehabilitated some of the most vilified of bosses—even Rockefeller. In the winter of that year the United States encountered an energy crisis. Britain was buying as much American oil as it could, and the American economy was running at full tilt. In these circumstances, the nation virtually ran out of coal; factories closed down, and homes went unheated in the depths of winter. So the government turned to the oil industry, asking for a coordinated plan, a centralized policy on production and buying; Rockefeller, the champion of order over disorder and the enemy of laissez faire, was back in favor.

The lesson of the War Industries Board survived the war. In the twenties American governments tolerated associations and trusts between companies. Herbert Hoover, a former head of the Food Administration and commerce secretary under President Coolidge, went further still, resolving that he would cartelize those American industries that had not been reorganized by Morgan, Rockefeller, and their like. In forestry, for example, Hoover believed that pure competition was leading to widespread deforestation as timber firms chased prices ever downward, so he encouraged firms in the industry to get together and agree on rules for proper forest management. Hoover helped the aviation industry to establish navigational aids and safety standards, and he helped the movie industry to establish both distribution agreements and supposed nationwide moral standards.

Motivating Hoover was his anxiety about the most obvious policy problem of the decade—the effects of falling prices. Hoover's reasoning was that American business was failing the nation because it was producing too much, so it was necessary to reduce output in order to raise prices. Restrictions on competition had to be introduced, and production had to be regulated to avoid any undesirable downward pressure on prices. Hoover encouraged trade associations to set forth output quotas and so to maintain prices and profits. He also argued that to avoid overproduction it was essential to maintain strong demand, and he urged companies to pay higher wages to stimulate more spending.

Others disagreed with Hoover's diagnosis of the causes of falling prices, though. The Progressives, although weakened, had never completely disappeared. Indeed, in 1924 La Follette had made an almost plausible bid for the presidency, winning a little under five million votes; he died in 1925, taking the Progressive

Party with him, but the old principles hung around. To the Progressives, American prosperity was uniquely based on individual enterprise. They believed, however, that the juggernaut of big business was threatening the free enterprise system, and that Hoover was compounding the problem.

According to the Progressives, big businesses did not mind falling prices; rather, big companies simply made sure that they grabbed ever larger shares of ever larger markets. Thus the rising size of American companies in the early twentieth century meant increasing work and high wages for many industrial workers and for the new managerial classes. In contrast, however, farmers and small manufacturers had no such protection. Factory gate and farm gate prices fell in the twenties more than did the prices of materials and fodder, squeezing the incomes of farmers and small businesses. As a result, farmers, small businesses, and those in regions of the country which experienced industrial decline all faced severe difficulties. It was these constituencies that the Progressives represented.[19]

However, with La Follette gone, and the vast bulk of the American economy growing strongly, Progressive concerns provoked little interest in Washington. So it would remain, for just as long as the American economy continued on its path of rapid growth.

## Europe in Trouble

The duration of the American business boom was bound to depend on a variety of factors. One that seemed to provoke little interest in the United States was the extent to which the American economy could persistently follow a very different path than that of Europe. If the two economies were quite separate, then the prospects for the United States looked favorable; if, however, the American economy was in some way entangled with that of Europe, then the latter's economic problems might easily spread to the United States.

World War I devastated much of Europe. British industry survived relatively unscathed, but that was scant comfort for a nation that was now dependent on exporting services such as shipping and on the earnings of overseas investments to pay its heavy import bill. The United States had taken over a large chunk of global trade in services, and Britain's American assets had been turned into debt. At least Britain was spared invasion. Those nations who suffered most were the ones in which the bulk of the fighting took place. Transport and communication systems ceased to exist, and the institutions of both government and commerce had become unusable. Workers lost their jobs, their homes, and the means of feeding themselves. In France, the war laid waste six thousand square miles of land, and one quarter of a million French buildings were destroyed. In the nation's agricultural heartland, half the livestock were killed. Elsewhere in Europe the devastation was as bad—half of Poland's river bridges were blown up, and roughly one and three-quarters million Polish buildings were flattened.

In 1917 the Russian people became so embittered by the war that they submitted to the Bolshevik coup. The Bolsheviks promised to withdraw from the war, as indeed they did, but they also cut all financial and trading links with the rest of the world. At home, the new communist government began to replace the market mechanism with a bureaucratic command economy. Russia thus withdrew from the world economy, which in the twentieth century was coming together as never before, and Germany lost its most vital export market, while Britain lost a loan of £2.5 billion it had provided to the tsarist government and that the communists refused to repay. The United States, now the world's leading creditor nation, lost a possible investment market that might have eclipsed all others.

Other countries had other problems. The collapse of the Austro-Hungarian and Ottoman empires created difficulties similar to those that have recently emerged in Eastern Europe and the former Soviet Union. Many new nations were created in the wake of hostilities without much consideration being given to their economic viability. National economic systems were broken up and formerly integrated industries suddenly split by redrawn national boundaries. Nations found themselves with two or more railway systems using different gauges, or without a proper postal system, or no civil service, or too many stock markets, or no access to coal to supply their iron foundries; many newly created nations lacked even their own laws or tax systems. Thus many nations which gained land or industries or people in the postwar settlements were unable to make efficient use of them. European output as a whole was almost certainly reduced, in comparison with what it might otherwise have been, by the division of the empires.

The end of war provoked a widespread European slump, triggered by cuts in military and naval spending and mass demobilization. Businesses that had been hoarding raw materials dumped them, with a resulting tumble in prices. Unemployment increased, and hungry people weakened by years of conflict fell victim to influenza and other epidemics; as a result, more lives were lost in the peace than in the war. The death toll, including those who died from the famines or epidemics which followed the war, was probably about forty million people, half of them in Russia.[20]

The end of the war thus presented the American government with the problem of what, if anything, it should do to generate a recovery in the European economy. Europe's own governments spent heavily after the war, mainly on unemployment benefits and military reequipment, and by doing so they probably prevented the postwar recession from becoming even worse. Despite this, Europe's immediate need was for humanitarian aid, and in 1919 the American government lent money to the governments of Europe, with which the latter could buy food and raw materials; that same year the Washington government set up the American Relief Administration to provide famine relief for Europe. However, both initiatives were tiny in relation to Europe's problems.

Still less was there any official American commitment to reconstruct Europe's ravaged economies. Having gone to the trouble of fighting the war, Wilson's government was determined to ensure that postwar Europe would provide a market for American exports and investments alike. However, Wilson believed that the only mechanism by which that could happen would be the free market. Since market forces require a favorable environment in which to flourish, the American government decided that its role in 1919 would be the promotion of financial stability and good government in Europe.

One of the obstacles to a stable peace was that the war had been politically and militarily inconclusive: it had ended with an armistice and a negotiated truce, not an unconditional surrender. Thus when in 1919 President Wilson traveled to Versailles to meet other allied leaders, he sought to get them to agree to a postwar settlement for Europe that would justify his nation's entry into the war two years earlier. The great issue that confronted him, which confounded his famous Fourteen Points, was the French and British demands that Germany should pay heavy financial reparations for the war. Lloyd George, elected prime minister of Britain on a promise to create an early welfare state, wanted to finance his ambition by exacting German reparations so high that they would make "the pips squeak." Similarly, the French government under Clemenceau was determined that reparations should be set high enough to destroy the German economy.

Both Britain and France were heavily in debt to the United States, and their governments claimed that they would never be able to repay the debts unless the Germans first paid them reparations. Although the Americans doubted whether the Germans were in a position to pay reparations on any significant scale, and suspected that the British grossly underrepresented their own remaining wealth, they knew that some agreement had to be struck if American private enterprise was to have enough confidence to send its capital and goods flowing across the sea to Europe.

Wilson asked how, if Germany was to be kept in a state of financial and industrial ruin, it would pay the reparations that the French and British wanted. The German economy was already devastated, with much of the population close to starvation. Germany had no hidden reserves of gold or foreign currency; the best it could hope for would be to pay reparations gradually from export earnings—which could hardly happen if the reparations payments were set punitively high. The French and British policies thus seemed to be self-contradictory.

The most prominent skeptic at Versailles was not Wilson himself but a precocious young economist, John Maynard Keynes, attending the conference as part of the official British delegation. Keynes believed that it was vital to scale down French and British demands in line with Germany's ability to pay the reparations. Indeed, more than that, Keynes's goal was a prosperous Germany, and the sooner the better. In a world in which countries trade with one another, one country's bankruptcy is another country's lost export market. Given how depressed Germany already was, resources had to be transferred *into*, not out of, Germany.

In making such arguments, Keynes was beginning to think through the complex interrelationships of an international market economy.[21] Later, he would refine his thinking and make other contributions to the study and the practice of economic affairs. In 1919, however, he had a simple proposal: the Americans should abandon or at least scale down their demand for loan repayments from Britain and France, which in turn would reduce to a minimum their demands for reparations. Debts would be forgiven and forgotten. Only by that means, Keynes believed, would the world economy revive and catastrophe be averted.

Keynes managed to secure grudging agreement to his idea from both the British and the French governments. However, as the conference progressed the American president, fearful of growing isolationism at home and realizing that he had alienated those Republicans on whom he depended for support, began to shift his position. President Wilson, who went to Versailles scornful of Anglo-French reparations demands, now insisted on the repayment of American war loans. Worse still, he told the French and British that they could set almost any reparations level they liked in return for their commitments to join his proposed League of Nations.

The American refusal to cancel war debts was motivated by more than kneejerk isolationism. The Americans reasoned that if Britain and France repaid their debts, this would help to finance growth in the American economy and raise the financial standing of New York's banks. Thus global financial leadership would shift more decisively toward New York—the "American economic invasion" would get underway.[22] Wilson justified the refusal on the grounds that the world needed a new, stable financial order, and that tolerating financial delinquency would provide a rather unpromising start; however, the main effect was that Britain and France reaffirmed their insistence on receiving reparations from Germany, and withdrew their support for Keynes. Despairing of "the evil round me," Keynes walked out. He wrote to Lloyd George: "I am slipping away from the scene of the nightmare . . . I leave the twins [Clemenceau and Wilson] to gloat over the devastation of Europe . . ."[23] The expression was apt: the Senate rejected the Versailles Treaty, and in 1923 at a conference in Washington the American government insisted that Britain begin to settle its war debts in full. Keynes himself was publicly villified when, on his return to Britain, he published a scathing account of the proceedings at Versailles. Meanwhile Germany, deprived of one third of its iron and steel capacity, and through shifts in its borders, of seven million members of its population, could not and did not pay reparations. That year France invaded the Ruhr in order to extract tribute of another sort. Versailles proved to be as much a preliminary to World War II as a conclusion of World War I.

## Errors of Judgment

To the American government in the twenties, international trade and payments were a small part of their national economy. In contrast to the situation in nineteenth-century Britain, and in a rejection of the principles that President Wilson had espoused, domestic policy issues dominated international ones. The American economy prospered in the twenties, and that was all that mattered.

By 1925 world trade was only just above its level of 1914, while European trade had barely recovered from the war. The same was true for European output, which was on average no higher than it had been before the war. European unemployment was a cause as well as a consequence of the problem: it depressed real spending power and so harmed output, which in turn prevented employment from rising. Unemployment also harmed the political stability of many countries, and that, together with rapid inflation, added to the difficulties of recreating proper economic and market relationships within and between nations.

One reason for Europe's problems was tariff barriers: many European nations, led by Britain, used tariffs in a foolish attempt to offset the problems bequeathed by the war and by Versailles. Meanwhile, those countries whose manufacturing industries had gained from the wartime absence of European competition decided to extend their advantage into the peace by erecting tariff barriers against Europe. Australia, for example, erected barriers to protect its new iron and steel and chemicals industries, while India used tariffs to protect textiles.

The United States was among the chief culprits. In 1921 Congress introduced a tariff to protect the infant American dye industry, which had grown during the period when it faced no German competition, and in 1922 the Fordney McCumber Act set widespread tariffs at record levels. Such protectionism ensured that Europe struggled to share American prosperity.

The American refusal to cancel war debts had been partly intended to strengthen American financial institutions at the expense of those of Britain and the rest of Europe.[24] The same result was supposed to arise from a second, no less dangerous, American policy: the restoration of the prewar gold standard. The war had caused a large shift in the world's gold stock to the United States, and the American government believed that the restoration of the gold standard would allow Americans to capitalize on their newly enhanced holdings. Washington believed that if all currencies were tied to gold, and if the dollar had the strongest gold-backing by an overwhelming margin, then the world would tend to use dollars in its international transactions as the most stable currency. Accordingly, business would flow away from London's banks and toward those of New York.

The dollar returned to the gold standard in 1919, but none of

Europe's currencies followed. Lloyd George allowed the value of sterling to depreciate against the dollar and other currencies, much to the alarm of the City, which saw the value of its remaining overseas loans declining. However, the governments of Britain and the other countries of Europe knew that currency levels that had been sustainable before 1914, when Europe was economically strong, looked far too high after the war when Europe was weak and its economies prone to inflation and to balance of payments deficits. Those deficits could be avoided, of course, by governments reducing imports, but that would imply either a global trade war, or domestic policies that cut private spending by raising taxes and reducing welfare payments. Given the degree of social unrest across Europe in the early twenties, policies of that sort were hardly appealing.

Accordingly, in 1922 at a conference in Genoa the British government revealed a scheme to create a new global financial system, the gold exchange standard, which would allow Europe to run balance of payments deficits for several years—perhaps even decades.[25] However, to avert any consequent financial panics, the British proposed that Europe's fledgling central banks should maintain stocks of dollars and British pounds in addition to gold in their reserves. This system would give the world more liquidity and allow American dollars and exports to flow to Europe, while at the same time restoring the old fixed exchange rates that had seemed so important before 1914. Finally, the British also offered to coordinate an international loan to the Soviet Union in return for the latter's willingness to relax its isolation.

The gold exchange standard was intended to allow the world economy to recover and prosper much faster than would the traditional gold standard, which the United States still favored. The British proposal, however, was undeniably self-serving, and the United States rejected it.[26] Had the gold exchange standard been accepted, the influence of Britain in international financial affairs would have been much greater than under a traditional gold standard, in which only those nations with lots of gold would have any clout. The only nation that had sufficient gold to maintain pre-

eminence under the old system was the United States, so its opposition to the British proposals hardly came as a surprise.

The failure of the Genoa proposal for a gold exchange standard
left various possibilities: the restoration of the old gold standard in
its original guise, the restoration of the gold standard but at lower
parities for the European currencies, or no system at all. At the
time, the last of these seemed unthinkable (although today it would
not be). The idea of restoring the gold standard at rates that made
European firms more competitive relative to their American rivals
faced almost the same problems as the gold exchange standard: it
favored Europe at the expense of the United States. Thus the
American authorities insisted on the most conservative of the options. The European governments refused, and no deal followed.

By 1924, Europe was in crisis. The French invasion of Germany the previous year had misfired financially, since confidence
in the franc had collapsed. The Germans, still unable to pay reparations, were unable to obtain the international loans that they desperately needed. So the British persuaded the Americans to offer a
deal, the Dawes Plan, comprising a huge loan from the United
States to Germany, a cut in the reparations bill, and an extension
of the repayment period; in return, the German government agreed
to peg the price of the Reichsmark to gold.

Although the Dawes Plan was partly instigated by the British
government, it nevertheless placed pressure on Britain and France:
if the Germans fixed their currency to gold then they might become the recipients of almost all of the capital likely to flow out
of the United States toward Europe—including not just cash, but
also factories for cars, electrical appliances, detergents, paints, and
all the other modern goods that American industry offered. Because
Berlin might also become Europe's financial capital if it alone had
a currency pegged to gold, Germany's return to gold would oblige
Britain and France to do likewise. Thus in 1925 the British government pegged sterling to gold at its prewar rate and in 1928
France too pegged its currency to gold, although at a much less
demanding rate than Britain's. The gold standard was back.

Thanks to the Dawes Plan, the crisis that threatened the world economy faded. Inflation, which had been rampant throughout Europe, fell, and Europe's economies grew at respectable rates. However, they did so only so long as the United States provided them with both finance for investment and markets for their exports. With sterling and the mark pegged at very high rates, competition with American producers was not easy, and any shift by the United States toward protectionism might be potentially disastrous. Equally, with Germany now struggling to pay its reparations and Britain struggling to repay its war debts, any withdrawal of American funds could be very damaging.

For a while such events elsewhere hardly seemed to matter to Americans. Their own economy was strong. When President Coolidge left office in 1928 he made a point of reassuring the nation that he was leaving it in good shape: the economy was sound, stocks were cheap. By the following March, however, the American economy had slipped into recession. Automobile sales peaked in March 1929; by September they were one third down.

After several years of making large profits, American companies were half expecting to see a recession. If they were right, there were few reasons to invest heavily in extra plant and equipment: trading margins were bound to fall. The potential return on new capital expenditure would be slight compared with returns in the recent past.

So, instead, companies bought stocks—their own and one another's—or placed their profits in banks, which did the buying for them. Despite the common perceptions of the time (and popular usage today) this was not *investment* in the real sense, even though it was very lucrative. Those who buy financial assets are simply deciding where to put their savings; it cannot be assumed that the recipients of the cash will invest it in new machinery, buildings, or some other durable asset. On the contrary, in the twenties companies were explicitly choosing not to invest.

The stock market was rising, and for a while companies made large financial gains that boosted their total profits, masking from shareholders the deterioration in their underlying trading performance. Shareholders saw profits rising, so they felt justified in continuing to buy equities, pushing the stock market up still further. Companies felt vindicated in their behavior, bought more equities, and sent the spiral twisting on its way. However, American companies bought stocks, not because the underlying economy was strong but, perversely, because they thought it was weakening.

Plenty of people were worried: in February 1929 Roy Young, chairman of the Federal Reserve Board, criticized the banks for lending money to customers to use in speculating on the stock market. In August he decided to slow the stock market's ascent by raising interest rates. The policy backfired, though: because of the higher interest rates, companies cut their plans to invest in plant and machinery, and consumers reined in their spending still further, preferring to save rather than to borrow at high interest rates. People took their savings to the banks and put them on deposit, but since companies showed no interest in borrowing to finance new investment, the banks were forced to find something else to do with the funds flowing into them—so they bought equities. A cut in interest rates might have solved the problem by encouraging investment and discouraging saving, but the Fed had *raised* interest rates, which only made the problem worse.

Still, the New York Stock Exchange saw no problem. It sold more seats so that more brokers could trade on behalf of more clients and thus boost activity and price levels even further. Then, on September 19, the market fell. It had happened before, and the market had always rallied, but this time it did not: prices moved sideways for a few days, neither rising nor falling. Then on October 3, the market fell again, and began to drift downward. On October 24, Black Thursday, panic gripped the market, which fell sharply; five days later came Black Tuesday, when over sixteen million shares were sold.[27]

Much of the market's rapid precrash rise had resulted, directly or indirectly, from stock purchases by industrial and commercial companies. Then, as profits forecasts were slashed, companies sold equities. The consequent decline in stock prices reduced the prospective profits of every firm that had been buying stocks instead of buying plant and equipment; to remain viable, firms had to get out of the market faster than everybody else—hence the panic to sell and the Great Crash.[28] By the middle of November the value of the market, and thus the value placed on American industry, had been almost halved.

Another factor contributed to the rise of Wall Street and to its subsequent crash. In the early twenties, the American government had justified its insistence on the restoration of the gold standard in terms of the need to impose stability onto the international financial system. However, by fixing currencies at rates that seemed dangerously high given the problems of Europe's economies, the effect had been that American banks preferred to keep their funds at home, and European funds preferred to flow to the United States.

Had the dollar been able to float upward, this mobility would have absorbed much of the pressure and reduced the inflow; alternatively, had American interest rates been able to float downward, that might also have done the same trick, partly by stimulating the corporate sector into investing in more plant and machinery, and partly by encouraging consumers to spend more. High dollar interest rates encouraged foreigners to sell either their domestic currencies or gold and put the proceeds into dollar deposits in New York banks, which used the deposits to buy stocks. In that sense too, the Fed's decision in August to raise interest rates compounded rather than reduced the problem of an overvalued stock market.

By 1928 the United States was awash with finance, with savers looking for more places to put their funds than really existed. The funds flowed onto the stock market, which rose beyond all reason, drawing even more funds from abroad.

Faced with such outflows, most of Europe's currencies came under severe pressure. The governor of the Bank of England raised the possibility that European central banks would have to borrow back from the American markets the funds that were flowing to them out of Europe. Governments all over Europe raised interest rates in 1929 in order to stem their capital outflows. Since their economies were not very strong, this was not easy for them to do; nor would it necessarily succeed, if the financial markets were to conclude that higher interest rates would merely generate greater economic problems and so more risk. However, the only alternative for Europe was to abandon the gold standard.

The gold standard was supposed to provide reassurance to American banks that they could lend to Europe without worrying about currency risks. So long as the gold standard seemed to work that was fine—but if the whole system collapsed, then all the risks would suddenly become real simultaneously. Furthermore, American banks had another form of reassurance, but one that was equally flawed: they made loans in the form of bonds, which they issued and then immediately sold to others, supposedly passing on the risks. The purchasers were happy to hold the bonds, because each individual reckoned that he or she could in turn sell the assets if it looked likely that the borrower would default on the loan. So, by using bond finance, the banks felt that they did not need to be too concerned about either the quality of their lending or the ability of borrowers to repay the loans. The markets would take care of the risks.

Keynes was later to criticize this form of behavior as "the fetish of liquidity." In his *General Theory of Employment, Interest, and Money* Keynes denied that "it is a positive virtue on the part of investment institutions to concentrate their resources upon the holding of 'liquid' securities," arguing that instead "there is no such thing as liquidity of investment for the community as a whole."[29] Keynes's point is that an individual bond is only a low-risk asset when it can be easily sold, and if everybody else also wants to sell, then the liquidity of the individual bond disappears. This is what happened in 1928 when the first American banks started to withdraw their funds to spend them on the New York stock market. An international financial system that looked pretty liquid in the early twenties began to look dangerously illiquid by the end of the decade. The panic of banks to get out of Europe helped to drive Wall Street to the point where it too crashed in 1929. Already, Americans were paying a price for their government's reluctance to constructively intervene in the affairs of the global economy. And the real crisis was yet to occur.

*Chapter Four*

# THE WORLD
# IN DANGER

## The Great Depression

On October 29, 1929, the day of the Wall Street Crash, the Federal Reserve board met. The questions that the board had to consider were quite simple: If the collapse of the stock market had halved the value of American industry, did that imply that on average the wealth of Americans had halved too? If so, what would happen to spending, and hence to output and employment?

Some members of the Fed's board believed that spending would fall and thus that a recession would follow. Others disagreed, but the evidence seemed to be against them: American industrial production fell by almost 5 percent in October and by about the same amount in November, largely because of falling demand for cars. House prices and commodity prices also fell: the disease seemed contagious. Business confidence evaporated, banks called in loans, and the stock market started to slide once again; companies sacked workers and cut the wages of those they kept; consumer spending spiraled downward; and unemployment doubled, then doubled again, and again. By the summer of 1932, one quarter of the American workforce was unemployed, including over one third of nonfarm workers. Industrial production was cut in half, and the stock market had almost disappeared: its value was a mere one tenth of its peak level. Homeless Americans took to living in cardboard shanties, or "Hoovervilles."

The Wall Street Crash still has a strong symbolic pull. To many people it is a blot on the copybook of capitalism. The collapse of the stock market showed that the financial markets were a casino. Even if the Wall Street Crash did not actually cause the Great Depression, the events of October 1929 suggested that people could not trust the market economy to honor their most basic needs. Long years of unemployment and poverty followed; confidence had shattered, business optimism had evaporated, the way forward seemed unclear or even nonexistent to politicians and to industrialists.

At the time there were some Pollyannas. The day after Black Thursday, the *Wall Street Journal* carried the headline BANKERS HALT STOCK DEBACLE. Had that been true, the ghosts of those who had quit the windowledges the previous afternoon would have been mightily aggrieved. More pertinently, President Hoover said that the "fundamental business of the economy, that is production and distribution of commodities, is on a sound and prosperous basis." The president's words, supposedly reassuring (even if, as we now know, untrue) carried a deeper implication that did not go unnoticed: the *superficial* business of the economy, trading in stocks and shares, was unsound and unwise. Wall Street took the hint, and when the market reopened it resumed its fall. A New Jersey senator said, "there is something about too much prosperity that ruins the fiber of the people," which was one way of seeing the silver lining around the cloud. Others hoped that after a decade of decadence Americans would see sense, and begin to work harder and stop dancing to jazz records. Times were going to be tough— and, some said, the tougher the better.

Almost the entire nation suffered in the Great Depression. Admittedly, the millionaire who lost everything in the Great Crash and lived out the Depression in poverty was more a myth than a reality. Jack Morgan, head of the J. P. Morgan bank, decided to put his yacht *Corsair IV* into mothballs, not in order to save money but to save embarrassment about his continued huge wealth.[1] However, for the first time in American memory the middle classes suffered along with the working classes—even if not quite so severely—and urban workers suffered with rural workers. The government cut its spending on schools; malnutrition became widespread though schools often provided children with free food in term and out. In 1940 when the government introduced conscription, many draft boards turned away half their would-be conscripts as too malnourished to be suitable for active service.[2]

The birth rate fell in the thirties: people turned to religion, but they turned to contraception in even greater numbers. Predictably, mass migration from Europe dwindled, and not just because of steps such as the National Origins Act, which took effect in 1929, severely tightening American immigration control. There was even some modest outmigration: in 1931 in one famous episode, one hundred thousand workless Americans applied for six thousand skilled jobs on offer in the Soviet Union. People continued to quit the farms in a futile belief that they would find work in the cities; many simply joined the vast nomadic population of five or six million people—half the unemployed—who lived in shantytowns and stole rides on freight trains.

Past experience suggested that the economic downturn of 1929 would persist through much of 1930, but that by the end of that year or in early 1931 recovery would get underway. In anticipation of such a recovery, business confidence did indeed improve during 1930. The Great Crash began to fade from memory, and companies started to look forward to the usual cyclical upturn. However, farm incomes fell sharply that year and, partly in consequence, consumer spending fell too. The government worsened the situation by running a budget surplus, which suppressed demand in the economy; as a result, the modest interest rate cuts that the Federal Reserve had made after the October Crash had little impact. Neither businesses nor consumers increased their spending. When the net effect of all these factors became apparent, business confidence slipped sharply, and so too did investment and output. The recession deepened and began to look like a permanent state of affairs. By 1933, the American GNP was only two thirds of its precrash level, and fixed investment was just one tenth of what it was before the onset of the recession.

One reason the 1929 recession turned into the long-lasting Great Depression is that the problems of the stock market quickly worked their way back to the banks. In the twenties, the banks had developed a habit of lending money to companies and individuals to use in speculation on the stock market; often, customers borrowed just enough to cover a percentage or "margin" of the price of the stock they were buying. Firms and individuals borrowed a dollar to put down as a deposit on a stock, confident that before they had to pay the rest of the price, they would have sold the stock for a generous profit.

While the stock market was booming this was good business for the banks, but when the market crashed the banks found themselves heavy with bad debt. This, of course, exacerbated the usual bad-debt problems faced by banks during any economic recession. Some banks had enough capital to cover themselves, but many did not: unable to pay back all the people who had deposited their savings with them, they faced stampedes of depositors desperate to withdraw funds. The banks then responded by halting new loans and asking for the return of funds already lent out, leaving companies, farmers, and householders unable to pay their bills. Such problems fed back into the banking system, setting the spiral twisting round again. Production slowed, and that threw people out of work. What had started as a mild downturn in the American economy turned into a major and sustained depression.

Many researchers have harshly criticized the Federal Reserve for not doing more during the recession to help the banks. During the thirties a University of Chicago economist, Jacob Viner, accused the Fed of keeping interest rates higher than they needed to be; in the sixties Milton Friedman, also from Chicago, repeated the charge, arguing that during the Great Depression the Federal Reserve repeatedly kept the banking system short of reserves and as a result, the banks were unable to cope with financial panics, let alone expand their activities and keep the economy liquid.[3] Although subsequent research has largely overturned Friedman's analysis, the Fed's lack of sophistication was real enough:[4] its managers and directors failed to understand the impact of their actions on the banks, still less did they understand the links between the banks and the wider economy.[5] By the time that the Federal Reserve had switched its approach toward more accommodating policies, the banking system was so lacking in confidence that it could barely respond to the help that the central bank tried to provide.

A more important reason for the persistence of the recession, though, was the failure of the federal government to act. President Hoover, having shrugged off the interventionist mantle that he wore as commerce secretary, committed himself to a doctrine of benign neglect.[6] Hoover refused to set up a system of federal unemployment relief, insisting that it would deprive people of their sense of individual personal responsibility. Even if that were true, Hoover's critics argued, it was still a rather precious view to hold: unemployment benefits would have put demand back into the economy and helped to lift it out of recession, as well as helping people to lift themselves out of poverty. Although Hoover may have been "a sensitive soul who cared deeply about people's sufferings," he still managed to care more about balancing the budget than about reducing the suffering that he witnessed from the White House.[7]

Despite his refusal to help ordinary Americans, Hoover was quite willing to consider measures to help banks and companies. In 1931 he announced a one-year moratorium on the requirement for foreign governments to repay debts to the American Treasury.

Hoover hoped that this measure would help boost exports and make it easier for American banks to recover their private sector debts from foreign borrowers. Neither hope was very realistic, though. The president also encouraged legislation to release gold to support the dollar at a time when it was struggling in the foreign exchange markets—but since a weaker dollar might have helped the American economy by making it easier to export and making imports less competitive, the release of gold was probably counterproductive.

In 1932 Hoover announced the formation of the Reconstruction Finance Corporation (RFC) to provide funds to ailing banks, railroad companies, and insurance firms, and later for various forms of public works. However, the RFC soon began to look like a welfare program for the rich. Oris and Mantis Van Sweringen, railway magnates who had been worth $100 million before the crash, lost their fortune in 1929, borrowed $40 million from J. P. Morgan, lost that too, and so went to the RFC for help, which they promptly got, borrowing $75 million from the RFC almost on the day that it opened.[8] This hardly seemed a sensible use of public funds, and it sat oddly with Hoover's professed belief that government assistance reduced people's sense of individual responsibility. The president suffered a further decline in credibility.

Hoover lacked a convincing diagnosis of what was wrong with the American economy—although not for lack of advice. American economists debated endlessly what policies, if any, would best restore economic growth and full employment to the American economy. While Jacob Viner and others claimed that the real problem was high interest rates, Wesley Mitchell, a leader in business cycle research, argued that, since the American economy appeared to be vulnerable to extreme fluctuations, a high level of government planning and intervention was needed.[9] Meanwhile, Harvard's Alvin Hansen suggested that the problems were structural not cyclical. According to him, the United States had grown in the nineteenth century through the expansion of its land and population, generating jobs; for the last two decades, though, growth had come from investment in machines, which tended to reduce employment.

Hansen doubted whether the unemployed would ever get jobs except through government makework schemes.[10]

An alternative view was that the government should cut taxes or increase spending in order to stimulate demand. The great advocate of this idea was Keynes, who had left the employment of the British government after Versailles, but who nevertheless continued to comment on British government policy, sometimes from a remote Cambridge vantage point, but often through his deepening participation in the British establishment.[11] Keynes was convinced that politicians suffered not just from their own foolishness but also from the foolishness of the economics that his fellow academics urged on them. The implication was that the economic theories needed to be overturned, and that he, Keynes, had to do it.

In 1931 Keynes visited the United States for the first time since the furor occasioned by his Versailles book, *The Economic Consequences of the Peace.* He had been invited to participate in a symposium on unemployment, but mainly he wanted to study the deepening Depression firsthand.

Keynes left the United States despairing of Hoover. The Federal Reserve had impressed him with its efforts to use monetary relaxation to stimulate the economy, but he doubted whether those efforts would succeed, fearing instead that, in the extreme circumstances afflicting the United States in 1931, cuts in the interest rate might fail to revive activity. As he saw it, with ample spare capacity and the confidence of investors shattered, there might be no cut in interest rates that would succeed in persuading companies to invest—hence the government needed to act as well, by increasing spending or reducing taxes. Equally, however, Keynes believed that with federal government spending only about 2 or 3 percent of gross domestic product, there was a limit to how much could be achieved in the short term. Accordingly, he argued that interest rate cuts had to be *part* of the policy response to the recession: they would not work on their own, but combined with action from the federal government, they might have an effect.

Whereas to many Hoover represented defeatism, his 1932 presidential rival promised a "New Deal for the American people."

When Franklin Roosevelt won the election, Keynes saw a glimmer of hope: Roosevelt offered a political equivalent to his own nascent attempt to construct a new approach to economic theorizing. Keynes immediately set about trying to advise the new president on what policies to pursue. He sent Roosevelt a copy of his pamphlet "The Means to Prosperity," and followed that with an open letter to the president, published in the *New York Times* on December 31, 1933, but seen by the president a few days before. Keynes advocated "expanding loan expenditure [and a] reduction of long term interest rates."[12] He said that although the president was right to want both recovery and reform, the former should be the priority: "speed and quick results are essential," he wrote. "[I]f you succeed . . . we may date the first chapter of a new economic era from your accession to office."

The following year Keynes again set sail to the United States, and on May 28, 1934, he took tea at the White House. Roosevelt proved largely impervious to Keynes's lobbying, however, and the latter came away disappointed, both by the president's grasp of economics, which he thought poor, and by the president's hands, which he thought "firm and fairly strong, but not clever or with finesse, shortish round nails like those at the end of a businessman's fingers."[13]

## The Three New Deals

Despite what is commonly assumed, Roosevelt was initially no more willing than Hoover to use government borrowing to spend the American economy out of recession. On the contrary, he said that he wanted to balance the budget and reduce government spending, and he criticized Hoover for being insufficiently conservative. In that sense, Roosevelt campaigned on a policy that was as Hooverian as Hoover's.[14] "Let us have the courage to stop borrowing to meet continuing deficits," said Roosevelt, and in his first budget, introduced on March 30, 1933, he proposed to balance government finances, helped by cuts in veterans' pensions and pay cuts for federal employees.[15] Even Roosevelt's famous inauguration assertion that "the only thing we have to fear is fear itself" echoed Hoover, who had claimed that the Great Depression was the result of psychological problems rather than poor government.

However, Roosevelt did recognize that a key element in changing psychology would be a restoration of confidence in the banking system, and on that he was prepared to act: immediately upon assuming office, he placed all American banks under federal control. "The money changers have fled from the temple," declared the president.[16] Congress passed the requisite legislation, the Emergency Banking Act, in just ten hours. Previously, two thirds of the nation's states had responded to repeated bank runs by closing banks: Roosevelt's innovation was to close all American banks, weed out the insolvent from the solvent, and allow the latter to reopen. His aim was to restore confidence and therefore protect deposits; the legislation's speedy passage was testimony to years of pent-up frustration during the Hoover presidency, but also testimony to the pervasive belief that restoring the health of the financial system was central to the recovery process. When former Louisiana governor Huey Long tried to amend the bill, other senators shouted him down.

Within its own limited terms, Roosevelt's policy worked. When the best of the banks reopened, there was no resumption of the compulsive withdrawals of funds. People even began to trust the banks with their savings once again. Thanks in part to the first of Roosevelt's famous fireside chats, confidence returned. The United States had a meaningful banking system once more, able to perform ordinary day-to-day functions such as financing commercial transactions. It was a decisive improvement.

Roosevelt's next step was to increase the role of economic planning in the American economy. In the twenties, often under Hoover's tutelage, trade associations had reorganized the structures of many industries. Although those reorganizations had failed to generate higher output, Roosevelt hoped that some form of planning could nevertheless help to get the American economy moving. Ray Moley, assistant secretary of state, said that the antitrust laws represented "anarchy" and that laissez-faire was "gone forever."[17] "Fear of big business has become unnecessary" said Rexford Tugwell, a member of Roosevelt's so-called Brain Trust.[18]

Many business leaders supported Roosevelt in his ambitions. They were afraid that Congress and the wider public, frustrated by Hoover's inaction, would become dangerously radical unless something was done, and tended to blame the Depression on cutthroat competition, which reduced prices. They wanted to increase their own control over the economy and the fate of American business, and so they offered Roosevelt their planning and management skills to help get the economy moving again. Since federal government officials were distinctly feeble, Roosevelt was glad of the opportunity to pass responsibility for economic policy over to business planners. Thus, an important part of the First New Deal was born.[19]

Several measures designed to implement that approach followed in quick succession. On May 18 Congress approved the creation of the Tennessee Valley Authority (TVA), charged with building dams to control flooding and generate electricity, and with attracting new industry to the Tennessee Valley area. A month later, on June 16, 1933, Congress passed Roosevelt's National Industrial Recovery Act (NIRA), which suspended the main antitrust laws and created the National Recovery Administration (NRA) as a device for achieving the recovery of business activity. The NIRA also provided for the establishment of the Public Works Administration (PWA) to create jobs in the construction industry. On the same day, Congress also passed the Railroad Coordination Act which suspended antitrust legislation with respect to railways. The act allowed a newly created federal coordinator of transportation to rationalize railway services hitherto operated by competing companies.

Drawing on the advice of the Brain Trust, Roosevelt's government attempted to use central planning to reform significant chunks of American industry. In particular, NRA staff were supposed to obtain agreements within industries on output, price, and wage levels. Although unions and consumer representatives participated in the negotiations, in practice they were normally too weak to have much impact, and the NRA thus gave significant power to corporate planners.

Once the negotiators had reached agreement, the NRA sent the plans and codes to the president. Roosevelt's signature would make them binding on all companies in the respective industries, whether or not they had been involved in the negotiating process. The theory was that the agreements would stop prices from spiraling downward; real wages would also increase (it was not quite clear how) and so, in consequence, would consumer spending, ending overproduction and raising company profits.

Another New Deal measure was the Agricultural Adjustment Act of 1933, which aimed to reduce farm production and so to raise food prices. By imposing levies on some farm products, Roosevelt funded subsidies to other farmers who reduced their own activities, often by culling: six million pigs met early deaths so that their fellows could fetch higher prices at market. Unfortunately, as often happens with agricultural price support schemes, larger farmers gained at the expense of smallholders, tenant farmers, and sharecroppers; they also gained at the expense of consumers, many of whom were poor or unemployed or both, but who nevertheless had to pay higher prices for their food.[20]

Such was the First New Deal—a collection of measures, each designed to raise the incomes of particular groups, but without anything that directly addressed the need to raise the income of the nation as a whole. Instead, Roosevelt's policies were aimed at making people feel happier and more confident, and thus more willing to spend.[21] That was the theory, at least. The NRA turned out to be very effective at promoting pay increases for people working in the industries protected by the NRA, and it promoted profit rises for the companies concerned. However, the increases came at the expense of the unemployed and people working in sectors excluded from the cozy price-fixing agreements. Many people's real incomes declined, especially the very poor, and that diminished overall demand in the economy. As a result, although the First New Deal *accidentally* meant an increase in government spending and borrowing, it had a negligible impact on the economy and failed to generate significant increases in either total output or total employment. Although the American economy started to recover slightly in March 1933, the month of Roosevelt's inauguration, by the summer when the NRA and the other agencies were just getting underway, the recovery was beginning to fizzle out. From then on, neither the NRA nor Roosevelt's other policies did much to rekindle the economy; although economic growth resumed in 1934, few people were willing to attribute it to the New Deal.

Furthermore, since it left some people such as poor farmers and small business owners worse off, Roosevelt's First New Deal left the president vulnerable to attacks from rabblerousers such as the broadcaster Father Coughlin and Senator Huey Long. To make matters worse, big business leaders also lost faith in Roosevelt and the New Deal, not least because they resented having to share with the trade unions decisions about wages, prices, and output.

Roosevelt and his planners were equally disillusioned with the corporations. The latter seemed keen to reap higher profits from the New Deal, but they did not want to translate those profits into more investment. It seemed that the experiment in planning had not worked—indeed, that it had merely left the president politically vulnerable to a revival of populism. So, when the Supreme Court declared the NRA unconstitutional, few outside of organized labor mourned its passing. Whether that was fair is not clear: Roosevelt made a famously eloquent defense of the NRA at a White House press conference, almost nothing of which was quoted in the newspapers, while the Hearst press said that the end of the NRA restored "the rule of Christ."[22] And a poll a year later found public opinion almost evenly balanced.

In 1935, with another election only a year away, Roosevelt began his search for a different set of policies. The industrial policies of the Second New Deal were diametrically opposed to those of 1933.[23] Roosevelt, moving with the mood of the time, now blamed big business for the economy's problems. Old antitrust politics reasserted themselves, and the New Deal began to take on a distinctly Progressivist guise.

In 1935 Roosevelt sacked the planners and hired new free-market advisers. Tugwell, Moley, and Berle were out: in came a onetime Utah banker, Marriner Eccles, a Treasury economist named Lauchlin Currie, and the lawyer Felix Frankfurter; they dismantled the NRA and made no attempt to replace it. Roosevelt openly denounced big business: in 1936 he launched a campaign against wealthy tax evaders, many of whom were synonymous in people's minds with the captains of industry. Such cynicism had foundation: Jack Morgan responded to the campaign by saying that tax evasion by the wealthy was a very good thing. "The real enemy of capitalism is not Communism but capitalists," Felix Frankfurter told Roosevelt in disgust.[24] Trust-busting again became a goal of government economic policy.

The policies for which the Second New Deal was to become famous were concerned not with promoting recovery but with the provision of welfare; four or five measures stood out. The 1935 Social Security Act introduced an old age pension, unemployment benefits, and help to the needy. The Works Projects Administration (WPA), oversaw a vast program of public works, some of it wasteful though much of it valuable. The WPA not only built bridges and cleared slums but it also financed the creation of local history archives, provided free music classes for children, and commissioned murals for public buildings from struggling artists. The National Youth Administration gave part-time work to eight and one half million school children, allowing them to continue their education. The National Labor Relations Act, championed by New York Senator Robert Wagner, both expanded the government's role in industrial relations and strengthened the power of the unions. The Wealth Tax Act promised to reduce inequality by raising income tax rates for those on high incomes and by taxing excessive profits.

Although these policies stole the thunder from Roosevelt's rivals, exemplified by Robert La Follette Jr. and Huey Long (the latter was assassinated in September 1935), their effects on the American people were less clear. The unemployment pay lasted only twenty weeks at most, and recipients had to work for their payments. Worse still, no retirement pensions would be paid until 1942, and they were linked to previous incomes, so that those who had been poor would remain so in their old age. Although the Works Projects Administration built roads, bridges, hospitals, and many other pieces of infrastructure, Roosevelt insisted that the cost of the program, and of welfare support generally, should be met from taxation and not from extra borrowing. Keynes, in an article entitled "Can America Spend Its Way Out of Recession?" wrote, "Why obviously! No one of common sense could doubt it, unless his mind had been muddled by a 'sound' financier or an 'orthodox' economist," but Roosevelt remained fundamentally opposed to deficit spending.[25] Thanks to higher taxes, the 1935 federal deficit expressed as a share of gross domestic product was the lowest it had been in four years.

Once again, however, the government was unable to reconcile the president's fiscal conservatism with his activist programs, and over the next couple of years borrowing increased, in defiance of the president's intentions. As a result, total demand in the economy increased, and output and employment both rose. The effect was particularly marked in the South and Northwest; representatives of "new money," such as the Texan Jesse Jones, felt that the WPA provided their parts of the country with funds long denied to them by New York bankers.[26] Even Joseph Kennedy invested in new regions and industries helped by the WPA.

In 1937, however, just as American output seemed to have climbed back to the level last seen in 1929, the president pushed the economy back into recession. In an attempt to reduce the size of the federal deficit, Roosevelt cut government spending and raised taxes. Car production halved almost overnight—it looked like 1929 all over again. This time, however, there was no stock market crash to blame for the recession; instead, Roosevelt blamed monopoly price fixing by big corporations. He set up a Temporary National Economic Committee (TNEC) and told the committee to prove that big business was to blame for the new downturn. The story did not wash, though, and on April 14, 1938, Roosevelt admitted his mistake: He submitted to Congress his "Recommendations Designed to Stimulate Further Recovery," the Third New Deal.

Gone was the focus on competition policy. Instead, Roosevelt's new proposals reversed the fiscal conservatism to which he had long adhered. At last, an economic stimulus was to come through higher government spending, financed by borrowing rather than by taxes. Roosevelt had finally, and explicitly, embraced Keynes.

Even that was not enough. Roosevelt's 1938 package was still too modest to lift the American economy off the rocks, even with the help of the largest naval rearmament package in the nation's history, which Roosevelt announced that year. In November 1939 he secured the repeal of the Neutrality Acts, which had forbidden the sale of arms to belligerent nations, and within a year British orders for American armaments totaled a colossal $2.4 billion. In 1940 in a repeat of the World War I pattern, British—and, though briefly, French—spending on American armaments lifted the American economy clear of recession. Indeed, the British gave so much work to American factories that when the United States began to rearm, in mid-1940, there was barely enough capacity to meet demand.

## The Pecora Committee

Behind the New Deal another change occurred in the management of the American economy. Congress decided to scapegoat the great Wall Street banks, which had once masterminded the rise of American managerial capitalism, for the Great Crash and the Great Depression.

Wall Street was no stranger to congressional criticism. In 1912 the Pujo committee scrutinized the banks, especially J. P. Morgan, for signs of corrupt trading. However, Pierpont Morgan had insisted to the committee that his banking business was built on trust and honesty, and that self-interest kept him on the straight and narrow. Although they probably did not believe him, the committee failed to find any evidence of law breaking, and Wall Street survived the investigation intact.

Since then, however, Wall Street practices had clearly become sharper. During the twenties the stock market always seemed to be booming. As a result, the reputations of J. P. Morgan and other blue-chip banks such as Kuhn Loeb, which always stood behind any stock they launched, had become less valuable to potential savers. Critics in Congress were already beginning to suspect that the banks were cheating their customers when the Great Crash and the Great Depression completely undermined confidence in the financial system. So in 1932, with the Depression providing a dismal backdrop, Congress decided to have another look at Wall Street.

At first the Senate Banking Committee's investigation was a low-key affair: few senators really wanted an investigation of financial wrongdoing in which they or their colleagues might be implicated. Then, in January 1933 Congress appointed Ferdinand Pecora, a onetime New York assistant district attorney, to run the investigation. Pecora raked the muck and quickly found evidence that bank directors borrowed funds from their banks unwisely, often for financial gain, and that bank salesmen regularly persuaded vulnerable small savers to buy risky bonds. Worst of all, he found that the president of Chase had set up a Canadian securities firm in order to avoid American taxes, and had borrowed from his own bank to speculate in the bank's own shares.

As Pecora's discoveries mounted, the public began to pay attention. It seemed that there were two sorts of advice that the banks gave: bad advice to small savers, and good advice to bank cronies. The banks had made huge profits, even during the Great Crash and the Depression, and this suggested something more: that they acted as a cartel, excluding competition and so exploiting their customers in that way too.[27]

On March 22, 1933, Pecora asked J. P. Morgan, the bank that had built much of the United States and had helped to finance World War I, to open its books for inspection; as a private institution with no public shareholders, the bank refused. Pecora got the Senate to pass a resolution stripping Morgan's right to silence.

Reluctantly the bank complied, and two months later Jack Morgan testified in person to the committee, just as his father had testified to the Pujo committee.

Pecora listed Morgan's corporate clients, the ninety-odd corporations on whose boards Morgan partners sat, and he challenged Morgan to admit that there was something unsound about a bank ruled by one man and accountable to no one but able to decide the fate of such firms as General Electric, ITT, and Standard Oil. However, Jack Morgan, like his father Pierpont, would not be intimidated: he insisted that his standards of conduct were above reproach.

So Pecora tried another tack: Why, he wanted to know, had neither Jack Morgan nor any other Morgan partner paid income tax for the past two years? Jack had no answer. Worse followed: Pecora produced a secret Morgan list of people to whom the bank sold stock that, thanks to insider information, it knew would soar in value. The list included the present treasury secretary and one of his predecessors, the head of the New York Stock Exchange, the chairmen of the Democratic National Committee and of the Republican National Committee, Charles Lindbergh, General Pershing, the heads of General Electric and U.S. Steel, and a Guggenheim or two. The list even contained the name Calvin Coolidge.[28]

The bank denied Pecora's implicit accusation, but everybody agreed: J. P. Morgan bought both business and political patronage using inside information. The *New York Times* denounced the bank, and the Pecora committee made its recommendations for sweeping reforms of Wall Street.

The 1933 Glass-Steagall or Banking Act forbade bank directors from taking seats on the boards of companies to which they lent funds. It also prevented insurance companies and fund management companies from taking controlling stakes in industrial or commercial firms. Finally, at the suggestion of J. P. Morgan's great rival, the recently disgraced Chase bank, the Glass-Steagall Act ordered that banks could either take deposits or trade securities, but not both. The next year, the Securities and Exchange Act outlawed insider trading by requiring that any information supplied to one buyer of a stock had to be available to all other buyers, and it established the Securities and Exchange Commission to police the stock and bond markets.

These changes struck at the heart of the financial system that had supported the growth of American big business. J. P. Morgan reluctantly split itself in two, with the deposit-taking side keeping the old name and the securities business emerging as Morgan Stanley.

By ordering the restructuring, Congress sought to safeguard the interests of small savers. When it wrote the Securities Exchange Act, the Senate Committee on Banking and Currency said its purpose was to "protect the investing public and honest business."[29] In order to achieve this, the act required that savers be informed "of the facts concerning securities to be offered for sale" and protected savers against "fraud and misrepresentation." But did it? There was more truth than Congress realized in the claims of Pierpont and Jack Morgan that their bank valued its reputation for honesty.

Morgan won business because clients trusted the bank not to abuse its privileged position. The bank provided a stamp of approval on those companies that borrowed from it, and made sure that such companies were well managed.[30] J. P. Morgan and its better rivals showed great commitment to the firms to which they lent, yet Congress in its reforms showed no concern for the need to help corporate borrowers finance their investments. Corporate borrowers and those companies that issued securities, Congress assumed, could look after themselves. In 1933 and 1934 this attitude of neglect hardly mattered much; two decades later, however, it would become one of the factors hampering American companies in their competition against German and especially Japanese rivals.

## The World in Crisis

Global competition among big business was hardly an issue of immediate concern in the thirties. Much more apparent was the deleterious effect on American farmers of increasing competition in world food markets.[31] In 1933, most world food and raw material prices were between one third and one half of their 1929 level.

In part, the lower food prices were a delayed response to the overproduction of the twenties. Agricultural output had risen rapidly in the twenties as European farms recovered from the ravages of World War I. The Soviet Union also tried in the twenties to export grain in huge amounts in order to finance imports of capital goods. Agricultural output in Latin America and Asia also grew rapidly, as countries such as Argentina struggled to hang on to the new markets that they had acquired during the war, when European producers were otherwise engaged. Meanwhile, American farms mechanized and raised their production. The scene was thus set for a global collapse in food prices, starting in the twenties and intensifying into the thirties.

What was true for food was also true for other raw materials. Encouraged by price control schemes, huge investment took place around the world: starting during the war and continuing through the twenties, the investments covered all aspects of raw material extraction and production—coal mines, copper mines, rubber plantations, quarries, oil wells, and the rest. When industrial demand fell away as the world moved into a cyclical recession, primary producers found themselves struggling with vast excess capacity. The United States, as the largest mining and quarrying nation in the world, was highly vulnerable, but it was the farmers whose distress attracted the most attention.

Farm problems were not new, of course, but never before had they been so bad. Since the nineteenth century, industrialization and mechanization had reduced the degree of self-sufficiency at local, regional, and national levels; the expansion of world trade meant faster economic growth, but any slowdown would quickly feed through to global commodity markets. Prices would fall, but farmers and suppliers of raw materials would respond to declines in prices by increasing supply in order to maintain income. The policy was inevitably self-defeating: a small decline in demand from industry could thus do a lot of damage to farmers and those who produced raw materials.

In the nineteenth century this became a potential global threat for the first time. Because the world economy grew through most of the century, problems of this type seldom became severe; in the twenties and thirties, however, the picture had changed drastically, and unstable linkages between primary producers and manufacturers helped to make the global Great Depression much worse than anything that had happened before.

In the United States, Roosevelt felt bound to support American farmers. During the Second New Deal he decided to stem the advance of the dustbowl by helping farms to electrify, and so created the Rural Electrification Administration for that purpose—but electrification increased productivity, allowing farms to produce more at less cost, which drove prices down even further. This rebounded in the form of more farm closures, more job losses, and the demise of many rural banks and businesses—clearly the reverse of what Roosevelt intended.

If electrification impacted badly on American farmers, this was nothing compared with the damage that the farmers did to themselves by demanding tariff protection. In 1927, following the widespread tariff increases of the postwar decade, the World Economic Conference agreed to introduce tariff cuts, according to some program that had yet to be worked out. In February 1930 came another conference, to sort out the details. Twenty-seven nations attended the conference, but the United States was not one of them; American politicians were too busy refining what would soon become the Hawley-Smoot Tariff Act. The rot had started in May 1929, several months before the Wall Street Crash but at just about the time that the American economy began to move into recession. In that month the House of Representatives passed Hawley-Smoot, which promised to set prohibitive tariffs on a range of items. Originally these were just agricultural, but soon Congress extended the list to include many raw materials and manufactured items. The latter reflected Hoover's desire to placate small businesses; most large American firms opposed the tariff. In March 1930 the act passed through the Senate, and on June 17, 1930, Hoover signed it into law.

Other countries had already introduced new tariffs, but the passage of Hawley-Smoot provoked notable tariff increases in Spain, Switzerland, Canada, and France, as well as in many other countries. The world now knew for sure that the mighty United States, the world's greatest creditor nation, with the world's most efficient factories and farms, was not going to follow free trade policies. The American shift into protectionism meant that weaker nations would see their exports and hence their incomes fall, and thus they would be obliged to reduce their purchases from the United States—and, perhaps, renege on their debts to the United States.

The astonishing scale of the Hawley-Smoot barrier—40 percent—and the weight of the United States in the global economy made the act uniquely damaging. It was no great surprise that Hoover, who had begun to blame the rest of the world for American economic troubles, signed the act into existence; to his credit, however, he also agreed that another World Economic Conference should be convened in an attempt to reverse the rise in trade conflict and reduce instability in the international financial system.

Hoover was already out of office in June 1933 when the World Economic Conference opened in London. The conference took place against a grim background. The slide into protectionism was the result not just of global parochialism but also of the collapse already underway in the world's financial system. However hard it was to finance investment in the United States in the thirties, finding finance for international trade was even harder.

In the twenties it had been very different: thanks to the success of American industry, American firms in that decade were more efficient than those of any other nation and as a result, the United States ran a large trading surplus with the rest of the world. Americans were also net exporters of services and received income from their overseas investments, so their nation's balance of payments was almost always in current account surplus. The world economy had adapted to that fact: in particular, other countries borrowed funds from the United States with which to cover their trade and balance of payments deficits.

Problems began in 1929, though, when American lending abroad began to decline as banks diverted funds to prop up the domestic financial system following the Wall Street Crash. The banks had been lending abroad on the assumption that borrowing countries would grow rapidly in the thirties. However, for many countries the American recession, and the associated collapse in world food and raw material prices, damaged export growth, which in turn reduced their ability to service their debts, let alone to take on new commitments.

American banks faced a tough problem: if they stopped lending, their debtors would lose any incentive to repay existing loans (this happened, for example, in Brazil in January 1931, when the evaporation of international lending precipitated a default on existing debts); if, on the other hand, they carried on lending, the banks might just be throwing good money after bad. Furthermore, any one bank, by forcing the repayment of its own loans, could make it harder for others to obtain repayment on their loans. Since most of the lending banks were American, and since none of them could individually prevent the system from collapsing, but each of them individually could make a collapse more likely, there was a clear case for the American government to act on their collective behalf.

Adding to the problems of the banks and the need for some initiative from the American government were the continuing squabbles over reparations. Germany had rebelled once already, and when in 1929 reparations payments again came under threat, that endangered war loan repayments that Britain and France were still making to the United States. Accordingly, Hoover established a committee of experts under Owen Young, chairman of General Electric and a J. P. Morgan associate, to devise a successor to the Dawes Plan. The Young Plan, as it came to be called, reduced the capital sums of, and increased the repayment periods on, German reparations, as well as providing for a $300 million loan to Germany. However, by the time that the plan was due for implementation, in April 1930, the worsening economic situation had made even its reduced demands look impossibly onerous; in May 1931, with half of Europe's financial system in danger of collapse, President Hoover announced a plan for an international moratorium on the repayment of war loans and reparations.

Hoover's plan resembled that which Keynes had recommended over a decade earlier at Versailles, but it came too late. That month the massive Credit Anstalt bank in Austria collapsed, to be followed by others in central Europe. Both Rothschilds and the Bank of England tried to provide support, but neither was strong enough. That same month Montague Norman, the magisterial governor of the Bank of England who for decades personified Britain's global financial might, suffered a nervous breakdown, brought on by the impossible task of maintaining a position that no longer had any foundation. The government sent him off to Canada to recuperate.

Unfortunately, Britain's real problems were just beginning. International traders, sensing that Britain's financial position was not as strong as had long been pretended, began to sell pounds in exchange for gold from the Bank of England. By mid-August the nation's reserves were all but depleted, so on Sunday, August 23, 1931, the British cabinet under Labour prime minister Ramsay MacDonald met to discuss a secret plan to borrow heavily from the New York banks.

Late that evening a cable arrived in Downing Street from the Federal Reserve in New York. It seemed that New York's banks had decided that MacDonald might have the loan he wanted, but only on condition that he raise taxes and cut unemployment benefits.[32] MacDonald had already spent the day trying to persuade his cabinet to agree such a plan, without success; the Fed's apparent demand outraged his colleagues. The meeting ended in uproar, and that night, MacDonald tendered his resignation to the king.

The next day he was back in charge as the leader of a new coalition government, dominated not by the Labour Party but by Conservatives. MacDonald thus remained as prime minister, thanks to the promise of an American loan. His party said that he had sold out to Wall Street bankers, while the right in Britain were equally appalled by the apparent end of Britain's leadership of the global financial system.[33] It seemed that world finance would now be run by the United States or not at all.

On September 21, 1931, despite the change in government and the promise of the American loan (as well as one from France), and just before Montague Norman returned home, Britain abandoned the gold standard. With hindsight it seems a major tragedy that Britain and other countries in chronic deficit did not abandon gold much earlier. To remain on the standard, such countries needed to attract loans, and to get the loans, they had to follow the policies that the banks liked. The obsessive determination of governments such as Britain's to adhere to the gold standard thus forced them to pursue policies that kept interest rates and taxes high but spending low, resulting in a global recession. Had they abandoned gold, such polices would have been unnecessary—and the devaluations in their currencies would have improved their trade balances with the United States, provided that the latter did not devalue its dollar, and that its domestic economy was allowed to grow fast enough to absorb additional imports.

Keynes, a longtime foe of the gold standard, cheered when sterling was unpegged from gold, but the Bank of England and the British treasury soon regathered their strength and decreed that without the discipline (whatever that might mean) of fixed exchange rates it was even more vital than before that British economic policy should revolve around a balanced budget and strict control of domestic credit expansion. They even decided that Britain should introduce a high tariff, to improve confidence in sterling by increasing government revenues and reducing the trade deficit.[34]

Keynes's belief was that the departure of Britain and its pound sterling from the gold standard, and the currency's consequent depreciation against the dollar, would make British industry more competitive. However, in order to get the best of both worlds the British government used threats of financial embargoes to persuade a range of commodity-producing countries, mainly those of the empire, to peg their currencies to sterling, thus avoiding an increase in domestic costs from higher raw material prices. To keep these countries tied to Britain, the British government at the Ottawa Conference in 1932 gave them better access to the British market than they offered to Britain. Soon the "Sterling area" became as important to British policymakers as the gold standard had once been: it had efficient payment mechanisms, via the Bank of England (where Montague Norman was now back in control) and relatively free trade. Within limits, then, the British kept international economic liberalism afloat during the thirties, and Britain and much of the Sterling area avoided the worst of the depression from which the United States suffered.

Then in the preparations for the World Economic Conference in 1933 the British government presented a plan for the international economy, calling for the American and French governments to use tax cuts or higher spending in order to expand demand in the domestic economy, and to reduce tariffs; in return, Britain would return to the gold standard at the pre-1931 rate. The conference, stimulated by the British proposals and by a plan from Roosevelt's secretary of state, Cordell Hull, for reciprocal tariff cuts, looked as if it might produce the hoped-for recovery in the world economy. Roosevelt, however, had other ideas: he dropped a bombshell on the conference by sending a message that repudiated Hull's plan for tariff reform and scorned attempts at international currency reform. Roosevelt refused to expand the domestic American economy, and instead he aggressively devalued the dollar.

Roosevelt's attempt to use a devaluation to improve American competitiveness made one point quite clear: the president had no intention of acting as a global leader so long as isolationism remained a dominant issue in domestic politics. Admittedly Roosevelt did decide in 1934 that the devaluation had accomplished its purpose, and so he persuaded Congress to pass the Trade Agreements Act, which cut tariffs on a reciprocal basis. He nevertheless also permitted Congress to pass a law forbidding American banks to lend to any nation that reneged on its war debts; the British government took immediate offense, and promptly defaulted. The world economic system was now fractured, with no promise of repair and no sign that the Roosevelt administration understood the risks it was running.

## The Return to War

As the world's economic system crumbled, Germany's government moved toward delinquency. In the early twenties the German government had used expansionary policies, financed by heavy borrowing from abroad, to offset the problems created by Versailles and reparations demands. Unfortunately, rapid inflation, a rising burden of debt repayments, and the failure to settle the reparations issue undermined the confidence of lenders, most of them Americans. The Weimar government wanted to court international favor by paying reparations and reducing the current account deficit, and in 1925 it agreed to the Dawes Plan stipulation that it should peg the currency to gold and introduce austerity policies in order to restore confidence and quell inflation. Coming on top of a slowdown in world trade, this was highly damaging, and the economy crashed into recession. As a result, Germany needed to borrow all the more heavily; but by 1928 high American interest rates made such borrowing ruinously expensive.[35]

Furthermore, Germany's policy became increasingly unworkable after the American economy went into recession: getting the balance of payments into current account surplus when the major export market was in recession was a daunting task. There was effectively no interest rate that Germany could offer which would attract capital inflows on the scale needed to avoid domestic deflation.[36] The government refused to consider devaluation, reasoning that since world demand was so weak, export volumes would hardly rise, and that there was little scope for reducing imports below their present levels. Perhaps more important, devaluation would raise the value of Germany's foreign debts, which would make debt servicing and debt repayment even more burdensome and new capital inflows far more difficult to attract. Thus even if the balance of payments deficit fell, the deficit might become harder to finance.

It seemed that there was no policy that Germany could pursue which would satisfy the demands of global financial markets without plunging the economy even more deeply into recession. After 1933 the National Socialists took a radical approach to the problem:[37] they repudiated Germany's reparations debts and began immediately to spend heavily on reconstructing the German economy in pursuit of full employment. To sustain that, the German government needed trade barriers as well as price, wage, and exchange controls to prevent massive problems with the trade balance and inflation. In September 1934 the government rendered it virtually impossible to exchange marks for foreign currency without specific permission. Once started down that route, however, the economy needed quickly to become more self-sufficient, and so Germany began to produce materials such as aluminum and synthetic rubber, although at prices much higher than those prevailing in world markets.

Hitler saw that not as a problem but as part of a wider insulation of Germany from foreign, liberal influences. He did, however, recognize that Germany could not be *completely* self-sufficient; part of his strategy was to make trade deals with various central European and South American countries that, like Germany, faced difficulties trading with the rest of the world. Nobody else wanted the currencies of countries such as Hungary, for example, and the British and American banks would not lend to them. The German government thus made deals that, while they implied trade on terms favorable to Germany, were nevertheless better for the countries concerned than no trade at all.

After 1936 there was no room for backtracking and returning to the international liberal community: Hitler had embarked upon policies of rearmament, military threats, and domestic oppression. He had concluded that he had to seize control of another country, ideally the Ukraine—a country rich in both farmland and minerals. Germany thus moved toward war.

Another nation opted out of the liberal international order in the thirties—Japan. Its economy had grown rapidly in the nineteenth century, and, like the United States, it had benefited significantly from World War I.

Since the revolution of 1868, usually called the Meiji Restoration, the Japanese government had been happy to foster private enterprise. It created state-owned firms and then, once they were viable, privatized them at discount prices. The objective was clear: to make Japan strong. The slogan of the time was *fukoku kyōhei,* "enrich the country, strengthen the army." The government subsidized young industries and, once the so-called Unequal Treaties with the West expired in 1911, it protected them with penal tariffs on imports of many manufactured items, especially consumer goods. By the twenties, although many Japanese people still worked in agriculture, growing food for Japan's own consumption, manufacturing production was rising rapidly. The rate of Japanese industrial expansion closely rivaled that of Germany and easily exceeded those of recession-hit Britain and the United States.

As part of their industrialization strategy the Japanese offered open access to imports of the raw materials needed by their industries as well as insisting on the widespread reorganization and modernization of industry. The goal was for Japan to export manufactured goods as well as semimanufactured products.[38] The policy was much the same as that which Hamilton had once urged the United States to adopt, and not surprisingly its critics had a Jeffersonian cast. The promotion of rapid industrialization necessarily threatened Japan's still feudal social system, and the drive to modernize had to deliver results or suffer political reversal.

In the twenties the results came. Japan had a substantial trading sector, importing raw materials and reexporting them as semimanufactured goods. This trade supplemented and increasingly dominated Japan's traditional export business—selling raw silk, mostly to the United States and France. The major item that Japan imported, processed, and reexported was cotton, a market that Japan had taken from the British during the First World War.[39]

However, the rate of growth in imports tended to outstrip that of exports. As a result the balance of payments surpluses of the World War I period quickly disappeared, and to finance its net imports Japan was forced to sell off much of the gold and other assets gained during the war. As a result, Japan's economy became highly sensitive to fluctuations in the world economy: the collapse of foreign demand as the world went into recession in the early thirties hit Japan badly, and it too entered a severe recession. Especially hard hit were silk exports, but textiles and other industries also suffered badly. As its trading performance deteriorated and as foreign banks became increasingly conservative, Japan, like Germany, found it increasingly difficult to borrow. The country had either to cut back imports or boost exports despite the slump in world demand—but how?

Most of the raw materials that Japan needed were available locally. Manchuria and Korea were rich in coal and iron ore. The Dutch, French, and British East Indian empires were rich in rubber, oil, and many essential minerals such as manganese, tin, bauxite, and nickel. Japanese companies already exported to these countries, especially to Korea, Formosa, and Manchuria, but not enough to cover the cost of all the imports that Japan needed. However, with little hard currency to spare and almost no access to credit, Japan lacked the cash with which to buy raw materials on world markets. That threatened its ability merely to manufacture goods, let alone sell them.

Not for the first time, imperialism began to seem the way ahead.[40] The first target for Japan was Manchuria, a territory to which Japan had long laid claim, despite America's Open Door policy. In September 1931 the Japanese army, acting independently of the government in Tokyo, overran Manchuria, using an explosion (secretly set by Japanese officers) on the South Manchuria Railway as a pretext. Despite the affront to American sensibilities, there was little that Washington was able to do: an admonitory note from the State Department merely annoyed the Japanese, who formally annexed Manchuria and sent troops to attack Shanghai.

The invasion of Manchuria improved Japan's access to raw materials and obliged Manchurians to import from Japan rather than from other nations. Meanwhile, domestic rearmament brought back into use many resources made idle by the recession. As production increased, so Japanese living standards improved; within a couple of years, the Japanese economy was working at full capacity. Before long, however, the occupation of Manchuria began to drain the Japanese economy, for the rearmament drive sucked in even more raw materials than Manchuria could provide, diverting production away from export goods. Far from improving, Japan's balance of payments began to deteriorate once more.

The government tried to improve the situation by means of currency devaluations and export subsidies, but the problems remained, and so it took recourse to repeated attempts to cut its spending. The cuts fell heavily on the large military budget, though, which turned not only the army but also *the people* against the government: the armed forces were staffed largely by peasants, and much of the military budget went, via pensions and other payments, into a social security system benefiting farmers. As the peasantry became more alienated, it looked increasingly to the army for leadership.

In 1935 Finance Minister Korekiyo Takahashi warned that excessive rearmament was damaging the trade gap, was responsible for the flight of gold and of foreign exchange, and was producing rapid rises in inflation; rearmament, he insisted, needed to be checked. In February 1936 a faction within the military assassinated Takahashi; in 1937 a clash between Japanese and Chinese soldiers on the Marco Polo Bridge near Beijing threatened to precipitate a full-scale war. Alarmed, Roosevelt made a speech widely interpreted to mean that the United States might need to "quarantine" Japan. The Japanese were not much impressed, however, and in December Japanese warplanes sunk an American gunboat, the U.S.S. *Panay*, on the Yangtze River.

Since Japan no longer stood much chance of borrowing from abroad to finance trade deficits, the government resolved to increase exports. Further imperialism was one option, but not necessarily the best, since the annexation of Manchuria by Japan had become bogged down in fights against nationalists and communists, and so the Japanese government now looked to a voluntary, but no less autarchic, yen bloc with its Asian neighbors. The aim was to allow Japan to raise exports and secure imports, without having to find scarce dollars or pounds with which to do the deals.

In a limited sense, the bloc worked: its members sharply reduced their trade with third parties, especially the United States, and sought self-sufficiency. However, the bloc was not completely self-sufficient: for example, Manchuria could not produce coal and iron in the quantities that Japan needed, and Japan still had to buy oil and scrap metal from the United States and other commodities from other rivals (for example rubber from the British, who controlled Malaya).

President Roosevelt responded to events by increasing the naval ship-building program and discussing naval cooperation with the British. In November 1938 he signed an Anglo-American trade treaty, improving American access to markets in the British Empire. The U.S. Navy prepared its plans for war against Japan, and American public opinion moved toward support for an arms and trade embargo.

In July 1940 Japan declared its aspirations for a "Greater East Asia Co-prosperity Sphere" to include Korea, China, French Indochina, Siam, Burma, the Philippines, the Dutch East Indies, and a large part of the British Empire—Malaya, Borneo, India, and, later, Australia and New Zealand. Although Japan wanted these nations to join the yen bloc voluntarily, if they would not, it was willing to contemplate the use of force.

Already, President Roosevelt had abandoned all but the last vestiges of American neutrality. It had become clear that Britain could not afford to buy all the armaments that it needed to fight Germany. Roosevelt had briefly considered abandoning weapons sales to Britain in favor of a massive American naval and military buildup, but had abandoned the plan as unworkable; instead, he had decided to introduce lend-lease, and thereby to undermine the appearance of American neutrality. Accordingly, in July 1940 the president felt free to embargo the sale of aviation fuel to Japan; the Japanese government promptly sent troops into northern French Indochina, partly to strengthen Japan's position against Chiang Kai-shek. Later that year, Roosevelt also embargoed iron and steel exports. Relations between Japan and the United States quickly deteriorated, and in July 1941 Japanese troops occupied the remainder of French Indochina. Roosevelt then froze Japanese assets in the United States, but resisted a complete ban on oil exports, fearing that, without access to oil, Japan would invade the oil-rich Dutch East Indies. However, Vice President Henry Wallace and Secretary of State Dean Acheson had fewer scruples: they sidestepped the president and announced a total and indefinite ban on American oil exports to Japan.

Japan's government was now trapped. Without access to oil, its economy would collapse, but if it curried favor with the United States and withdrew troops from French Indochina in return for oil, it risked both military defeat and civil war.[41] Under these circumstances, Japan's military leaders felt that the only possible strategy was an immediate strike against the American fleet with a simultaneous invasion of the Philippines and the Dutch East Indies. On December 7, Japan bombed Pearl Harbor.

World War II produced a startling transformation of the American economy. American industry invested $2.6 billion in new capacity, half of it government funded, allowing the replacement of inefficient equipment dating from the twenties. Output doubled between 1939 and 1945, and the government recruited an army of eight million people; half that number again served at sea and in the air. American companies built three hundred thousand aircraft during the war, the equivalent of 150 years' output at prewar rates.

One factor that made the American war effort possible was the interventionist experience that the American government had acquired during the New Deal. Departments such as the Office of Price Administration and the Office of Science and Technology were reorganized and told to help coordinate the war effort. The Reconstruction Finance Corporation began to prove its use, while the War Production Board became central to the successful prosecution of the war. Because of the war, these institutions became fundamentally probusiness, rather than antibusiness as they had been during the Second and Third New Deals.

However, a more obvious factor behind the massive American mobilization was its huge popularity. Once it became clear that the nation was going to fight wholeheartedly, there was little fear of defeat. The American people may not have wanted war, but they certainly wanted work. British rearmament had lifted the American economy out of recession, and American rearmament would carry it toward prosperity. Far from requiring sacrifices from most of the American population, the war created jobs and raised incomes. Unemployment largely disappeared.

The war also provided people with new responsibilities and skills, offered them adventure, self-respect, travel, and new ways of living. Americans became less parochial. In the thirties, only those who were desperate moved away from home; in the forties, however, one in every five Americans did so. Many went to live in the new industrial cities and army camps of California. Los Angeles was just the biggest of many cities that grew rapidly thanks to the war. The divorce rate soared, as did the birth rate and life expectancy. At last, the United States really did seem to have the confidence to be a superpower. Few wondered how long it might last.

## Chapter Five

# RECONSTRUCTION

## Bretton Woods

In September 1944 the allied governments held a conference in Quebec. High on the agenda was a plan, drawn up by the American Treasury under secretary, Harry Dexter White, under which the Allies would extract reparations from Germany, once the war was won. The intention of the plan, which became known as the Morgenthau Plan after it was adopted by White's boss, Treasury Secretary Henry Morgenthau, was to reduce Germany from an industrial power to an agricultural land with a low standard of living.

Such a project alarmed many allies of the Americans, who remembered how their own insistence on reparations after World War I, and the American insistence on war debt repayment, had contributed to the global depression of the thirties and hence to the instigation of World War II. Nevertheless, Morgenthau persuaded Roosevelt of his views, and there was very little that the other Allies could do to prevent the plan so long as the Americans were determined to impose it. "I had to listen politely to long lectures from White on what I regarded as a crazy plan" complained one British official at Quebec, wearied by the garrulous and dogmatic American.[1] Edward Bernstein, one of White's own colleagues, lamented that the latter seemed determined to destroy all German steel production, whatever the consequences for a postwar reconstruction.[2] In fact, the Quebec Conference would impose a tight limit on postwar German steel production and would limit German industrial output to less than half its pre-1936 level.[3] In addition, the Allies agreed that Germany should pay widespread financial reparations, with the amounts to be settled at a later conference.

Fortunately, American attitudes changed. Admittedly, negotiations on reparations opened and played a large role in the Potsdam Conference of August 1945; the Soviet Union alone was promised $10 billion in reparations, and Poland was promised large territories of what was then Germany—but Truman had replaced Roosevelt, and the new administration was much less willing to contemplate crippling Germany. It realized that seventy million Germans represented a major potential market for American goods; more importantly perhaps, the Truman administration feared that German deindustrialization would provide a justification, if any were needed, for the Soviet Union to dismantle German capital goods and ship them east, thereby strengthening the Soviet economy. At Potsdam, therefore, the Americans relaxed their position: the conference decided to forbid Germany from building armaments, ships, or aircraft but to permit it however much industry it needed to match living standards in the rest of Europe.

---

The abandonment of the Morgenthau Plan left the way clear for another scheme, also devised by White, but much less reactionary in its purpose. That plan was the Bretton Woods Charter, which created a set of international financial institutions and a revised set of exchange rate rules. Ever since, Americans have been credited with the creation of a new liberal international economic order, the Bretton Woods System, which for a quarter of a century apparently supported faster growth in the world economy than had ever before been thought possible.

The charter was not written overnight. American deliberations on the future of the global economy had begun even before Pearl Harbor. In 1940 Roosevelt asked his staff to prepare an analysis of what the American economy would be like once war ended. The report, succinctly titled "After Defense—What?" and released in 1941, implied that if Americans wanted peacetime prosperity they would have to export much more to Europe than they had during the tariff-ridden thirties. Accordingly, the United States ought to care about the health both of Europe's economies and of the financial and trading links with Europe. In the same year, Roosevelt and Churchill signed the Atlantic Charter at Placentia Bay, Newfoundland, under which Britain agreed to help the Americans to create a liberal international trading system once hostilities ended.

Roosevelt was keen to gain open access to the markets of the British Empire, and was determined to force Britain to abandon the system of tariffs and quotas known as imperial preference, under which the empire discriminated against goods from outside, including those of the United States.[4] At Placentia Bay Churchill resisted and Roosevelt backed down, but his officials did not give up. Britain, financially almost destitute, needed to renegotiate the wartime Mutual Aid Agreement under which the United States had provided it with goods on credit. So the Americans made it a condition of renewing the so-called lend-lease deal that Britain agreed to abandon imperial preference. Still the British might have held out, believing that the Americans would never let them starve, but Whitehall officials knew of several Commonwealth countries that were negotiating bilateral deals with the United States. The British government acquiesced, its global leadership role unambiguously come to an end.

However, the American government realized that further progress toward free trade could not occur without a workable system of international finance. For three years, from 1941 to 1944, American officials struggled with the question of how to organize postwar international finances. In July 1944, at a conference at Bretton Woods in New Hampshire, the Americans won international agreement to their plans for a new world financial order. The conference took place under United Nations auspices, with representatives of forty-four governments attending, but the event was essentially a mechanism to ensure British acceptance of the American proposals.

Harry Dexter White, who led the American team at Bretton Woods, believed that Europe's war-torn nations would only need a year or two in which to recover their economic health. White was certain that the United States should provide Europe with emergency relief, but only as a temporary measure; he decreed that no further finance should flow from the American government to Europe after 1947 or so. From then on, if Europe needed any further finance, it would have to look for help from American banks.[5]

Fundamentally, White intended to restore much the same international financial system that had prevailed before the war. Like many others, he believed that the key to achieving this would be the restoration of faith in currency values. White reckoned that if people had confidence in just one or two currencies, then commercial banks would willingly hold these and traders would use them as media of exchange. Naturally, he decided that the dollar would be one such currency; he assumed that from 1947 onward, the pound sterling would be another.

A large part of the world's potential spending power was still denominated in sterling, and wartime restrictions prevented the sale of currencies. White and others feared that the end of such restrictions would precipitate a stampede to sell the pound, so the British government had to agree that, from 1947 onward, it would buy sterling from any foreign government wishing to sell pounds in return for American dollars. White reasoned that since there would always be a buyer for pounds, the markets would not expect sterling to fall, and so would not feel forced to sell the pound—indeed, he thought, people would be happy to take pounds in exchange for goods and services sold on world markets. Thus the restoration of official sterling convertibility would help world trade to revive.

Meanwhile, the American government would do much the same with respect to the dollar. Beginning in 1945, the American government would stand ready to convert into gold any dollars held by foreign governments. This, supposedly, would increase confidence in the dollar—a confidence that would rub off on sterling when that currency became officially convertible into dollars. These conversions were to occur at rates that would be fixed and stable, which, White reasoned, would boost confidence still further. Every other country would fix its own currency against either sterling or the dollar. When possible, all the relevant governments would agree to convert their currencies into one or other of those two currencies.

Besides this new regime of fixed exchange rates, White's Bretton Woods plan also allowed for controls on international capital flows as a temporary safeguard for the international financial system. He expected that, after a few years, such controls would cease to be necessary, and that governments would quietly dismantle them. However, White also accepted that some countries would have periodic short-term financing problems, which would make it difficult for them to honor the terms of the Bretton Woods agreement. As a result, White proposed the creation of a modest International Monetary Fund (IMF) to make small, short-term loans to governments willing to take steps to correct temporary imbalances.

The IMF was one of the two great international institutions to come out of the Bretton Woods Conference. The other was the International Bank for Reconstruction and Development (IBRD), better known as the World Bank, which was to finance longer-term investment in any of the world's poorer countries that, because of the fiscal problems in the thirties, were still unable to borrow from the commercial banks. Like the IMF, however, the resources of the World Bank were to be very modest and its loans consequently small, perhaps to persuade countries to adopt conservative policies of the sort that would endear them to commercial banks.

Behind the thinking of the Americans at Bretton Woods was their belief that they could shift the world away from protectionism and toward free trade, and that as a result, very few large, persistent trade imbalances would need to be financed. The Bretton Woods system thus required only a minimal role for government action in the sphere of international finance. Far from being a break with the past, the agreement actually perpetuated the laissez-faire thinking that had dominated prewar American policymaking, albeit with some attenuations. However, White's belief that postwar international trade and payments imbalances would be sufficiently small and brief to require little or no government intervention was at odds with experience. In 1944 the war was pummeling most of the world's economies, many of which were still smarting from the events of the thirties. It seemed likely that peace would bring with it *more* protectionism, not less, and that the need for reconstruction would place far greater strains on the world's financial system than any ever before witnessed. These were points that were indeed put to White at Bretton Woods, mainly by the British contingent, who favored a much larger transformation of the global system than he had envisaged.

Leading Britain's delegation, and fueling its radicalism, was Maynard Keynes, now ennobled as Lord Keynes and back in the employ of the British government, his calumnies at Versailles long since vindicated and forgiven. Indeed, it is often wishfully suggested that Keynes had drawn up the Bretton Woods system.[6] Unfortunately, however, Keynes's role at Bretton Woods was similar to that at Versailles: although he succeeded in modifying White's policies slightly, he did not persuade the Americans to adopt his own more radical thinking. "We made some changes. But we certainly didn't change the substance of our plan," said White's first lieutenant, Edward Bernstein.[7] A year earlier, in 1943, Keynes had published a proposal for what he called an international clearing union just as White revealed his own plan. In many respects Keynes and White thought along the same lines, but Keynes went much further: his international clearing union would recycle funds from surplus countries such as the United States to deficit countries, and would also require the surplus nations to take steps to increase their imports. In negotiations before the conference, and at Bretton Woods itself, Keynes told the Americans that they were severely underestimating just how much disruption the war was inflicting on the world economy, particularly in Europe. He said that the balance of payments problems that would follow peace would be much more severe than the Americans expected, especially in Britain, which had suffered severe disruption to its pattern of trade. He said that Britain would not be able to restore sterling convertibility by 1947, and certainly not at the pre-1918 rate demanded by the United States, which Britain had abandoned once already, in 1931.

At a deeper level, Keynes argued that even without the disruption of the war, trade imbalances between nations would in future be large, long lasting, and commonplace—requiring both the IMF and the World Bank to be much bigger and better than the institutions that White proposed. Finally, Keynes doubted whether confidence in sterling would ever fully recover after the war, and he thought that even the dollar would lose its appeal one day. He wanted to see a new international currency issued by the IMF, the "bancor": although initially it would be much the same as the dollar, since the Americans would be bankrolling the IMF, the bancor would gradually acquire a life and status of its own, ready for the day when international sentiment turned away from the dollar.

White did not accept Keynes's arguments. He denied that the dollar would one day fall from grace, and so he disagreed with Keynes's view that the world needed a new international currency. On the contrary, "we need limited liability, and we need discipline," said the parsimonious American.[8] White rejected Keynes's pessimism about the stability of the international economy, and he did not share his worries over severe balance of payments problems. Keynes had also tried to get White to agree to a massive loan to Britain to replace lend-lease; White assumed that Keynes was simply exaggerating problems in order to get a better deal on the loan. Apart from some minor increases in the finances available to the IMF and the World Bank, White held firm, insisting that Britain restore sterling convertibility in 1947. The resultant minimalist Bretton Woods system thus fell far short of Keynes's hopes. Time would tell whether Keynes's skepticism was justified.

## The Marshall Plan

White did not believe that he was treating Britain badly. In 1945 the American and British governments signed a financial agreement under which Britain agreed to pay in full for those lend-lease goods which were on order when the Americans canceled lend-lease, while the Americans would provide a loan on favorable terms to cover the cost. The Americans also waived payments for all the goods that had previously been obtained under lend-lease, which thereby became in retrospect free gifts. The Americans sold cheaply to the British government some surplus property in Britain, and, more important, they committed themselves to lend Britain up to $3.75 billion in July 1947, if at that time Britain made sterling convertible into dollars and abolished all forms of trade discrimination.

No similar deal was offered to the European nation that had probably been most hurt by the war, Germany. Fortunately, most of Germany's immediate postwar problems were smaller than they were at the end of World War I. Admittedly, German output in 1946 was probably only one quarter of its prewar level: shortages of coal, steel, electricity transport, and finance all created severe bottlenecks that affected all other parts of the economy.[9] Despite the wartime bombings Germany's manufacturing capacity had never been higher, however, and by the end of the year output from Germany's factories was beginning to increase. Food was often scarce, not least because ten million Germans had fled westward before the advancing Soviet army, but supplies from the United States reduced the problems. Two thirds of families had no homes, but with the factories intact, that was not an absolute barrier to economic recovery.

What was true for Germany was true for other parts of Western Europe as well. By late 1946, output in the rest of Europe was almost back to prewar levels.[10] On the surface, then, White had been right and Keynes wrong—yet by 1947 most of Europe's national governments were very worried. Many European countries experienced bad winter weather at the start of the year and worker unrest later; supply shortages increased, and some factories had to stop producing because they could not get the inputs they needed. The boom did not collapse, but it did teeter. Furthermore, there was a deeper problem: thanks to the rapid pace of reconstruction, European imports were rising rapidly, especially from the United States. Before the war the main manufacturer of investment goods in Europe had been Germany.[11] However, Germany's capital sector had been badly damaged by bombing, by the wartime government's preoccupation with munitions, and then by looting: the country was in no position to supply the capital equipment that Europe needed. As a result, the investment boom occurred only on the back of imports from the United States—but Europe could not pay for those imports with the limited number of goods that it was exporting.

Before the war, European nations had financed their imports from the United States with the proceeds of exports to the colonies or to Eastern Europe, but the colonies and the East Europeans were no longer buying. There was little chance of using tourist earnings since, not surprisingly, most people stayed at home. Nor could Europe earn much income from services such as shipping: those European ships which had not been sunk in the war had mostly been laid up, often because American freighters were underpricing European vessels for what little trade there was. Nor could European nations raise the cash to pay for American imports by selling off overseas assets: they had already done so or had pledged them to the United States to pay for the war. Indeed, debt repayment to the United States was a serious problem, as it had been after World War I. This meant in turn that American banks had little appetite for extending new loans to Western Europe.

The Bretton Woods plan had been that in 1947 the restoration of sterling convertibility would instantly restore confidence in Europe's financial situation and attract plentiful bank loans; clearly, however, this was not about to happen. White had believed that he was laying out a system whose stability was ultimately, if sometimes indirectly, backed by the American government and the Fort Knox gold reserves. However, the ultimate basis of confidence in any financial system is not the cleverness of its design, nor even the capital of the financial intermediaries, but the borrower's ability to repay loans—and World War II had destroyed that ability, so the banks would not lend. The Bretton Woods regime, far from boosting confidence, simply drew attention to the difficult state of European finances.

In 1947 Britain was due to implement its part of the Bretton Woods agreement. At the United States' insistence the British government ordered the Bank of England to announce its willingness to sell dollars, at a fixed rate, to any foreign government wanting to sell sterling. As the British feared would happen, foreign governments immediately stampeded to dump sterling and buy American currency instead. Within weeks the British government had used up almost the entire American loan, spent on buying in pounds that other governments did not want. With such reserves as Britain possessed starting to disappear too, there was nothing left for the British to do but withdraw the offer of convertibility.

The 1947 run on the pound merely reflected the common awareness that Britain could no longer pay its bills. Before the war, Britain had always run deficits on trade in goods, financing them by selling services and with earnings on the nation's vast stock of overseas assets. After the war there was not much international trade in services; and Britain had sold many of its assets to the Americans in order to pay for the war, and American war loans required servicing. Meanwhile, British imports, especially of American oil, raw materials, and manufactured products, were soaring. Perhaps one day the situation might turn around, but in the short term nothing stood behind sterling, providing security. In these circumstances it was unlikely that foreign banks or governments would want to hold the British pound.

Moreover, what was true for Britain was similarly true for the rest of Europe. Where the financial cost of the war was less than in Britain, the real cost in lost capacity and people was usually greater—and if the British had failed to make sterling convertible into dollars, there was little hope for other European currencies. The system that was supposed to gel in 1947, thanks to sterling convertibility, fell apart. As a result, American banks' willingness to lend to Europe, already limited, evaporated, and the governments of both Europe and the United States looked around for new institutions, agreements, or mechanisms to finance the recovery of Europe.

At the time, many people said that the crisis of 1947 was just a temporary setback. It was not really surprising that postwar Europe was short of dollars: Europe wanted to invest, and it had to borrow from the United States to do so. In time Europe's economy would strengthen, and its exports would earn dollars, they said; once that happened, the Bretton Woods system could be resurrected.

However, there was a deeper problem. The Americans were confident that the highly efficient companies of the United States would benefit most from the opening up of world trade. Since they expected that the United States would run large payments surpluses, it seemed to them appropriate that the dollar should be the world's main reserve currency. However, if that were true, then other nations would collectively run an equally large balance of payments deficits. White's whole argument against Keynes had been that nations should not be allowed to run large deficits, and hence that the IMF should be given only minimal funds to lend to such borrowers. It thus looked as if the spindly IMF that the Americans had set up might be inadequate after all, just as Keynes had said.

This presented the Americans with a choice—either lend Europe a lot more finance and with fewer conditions than originally intended or accept a smaller global role for the dollar than they wanted. Until they decided, neither European governments nor European banks could borrow the necessary dollars to pay for vital imports. Partly as a result, European output fell in the first half of 1947; many people's living standards fell, too, especially those who were already poor. Although most people in Western Europe were much better off than they had been in the last years of the war, the situation looked politically dangerous.

In May 1947 Assistant Secretary of State for Economic Affairs William Clayton wrote in a famous memorandum that "millions of people in the cities are slowly starving," and that the American government had to act to avert a catastrophe.[12] Whether Clayton was right and a complete collapse really was imminent is unclear; some people in Europe in 1947 were indeed starving, but not millions, not even in Germany. However, European governments had strong incentives to exaggerate to visiting American officials such as Clayton the severity of their nations' problems, since by doing so they could get American relief, if only from debt repayment burdens.

State Department officials were more than willing to believe such accounts. The State Department believed that by providing aid directly to Europe's governments, the United States could win political leverage over Europe—something the laissez-faire Bretton Woods system had never offered. Marshall, Clayton, and their colleagues feared a possible threat to American interests from communism in Europe. The communist parties in France and Italy were strong, and in Germany the American military said that the Soviet Union was courting the allegiance of the German people. The State Department believed that the United States had a duty to retain Western Europe within its own sphere of influence, and it wanted to swing Congress toward that view and away from its incipient isolationism.[13] Accordingly, on June 5 Secretary of State George Marshall launched the Marshall Plan, providing massive American government aid to the governments of Europe.

The State Department also quite rightly justified the Marshall

Plan purely in terms of American economic self-interest.[14] Economic expansion in Europe was important if American factories and farms were to be kept busy exporting, and the provision of finance to Europe would allow that to happen. Indeed, since most Marshall aid had to be spent on American (or, at a pinch, Canadian) goods, it was effectively a massive subsidy to American industry.

What the State Department could also have said but did not, was that Marshall aid was made necessary by the collapse of moves to implement the Bretton Woods system. The problem was to get finance flowing from the United States at a time when American banks were manifestly unwilling to lend to Europe. At Bretton Woods, White had argued that a minimalist American international economic policy would suffice, and that free markets would then do their work; the Marshall Plan now recalled Keynes's skepticism that the world would need much more.

Paradoxically, the Marshall Plan may have weakened rather than strengthened American control over postwar Europe. To administer the plan the State Department set up one American agency, the Economic Cooperation Administration (ECA) and an international body, the Organization for European Economic Cooperation (OEEC). Based in Paris, the OEEC was intended to allocate Marshall aid funds between Europe's various nations. This centralized arrangement was intended to be the first step toward a "United States of Europe," with a European customs union as an intermediate stage. The supposed economic justification was that if European companies could be made more efficient, then Europe's balance of payments problems would disappear. The way to achieve greater efficiency was to have a single large European market, so that companies could exploit economies of scale. The resemblance to the First New Deal, with its cartels and producers' agreements, was far from coincidental.

However, European governments were far from keen. They had few federalist ambitions and did not want the United States to use the Marshall Plan to remold Europe in its own image. Each government had its own agenda. Britain's main interest was the world outside Europe; France, in contrast, sought mainly to replace Germany as Europe's industrial leaders. The French government was under no illusions: if there was to be free trade, as still seemed possible, then the inefficient French economy would suffer. First, France had to modernize: to that end, the French wanted favored access to German coal and coke resources, and proposed the creation of an autonomous international state covering the Ruhr and Saarland, where these resources were located. The new state would supply the French steel industry, which would then expand and take over world markets that the Germans had supplied before the war.

The French plan was, sensibly and not surprisingly, vetoed by the Americans. An autonomous international state, created explicitly to help the French gain an advantage over the Germans, never sounded very reasonable; yet by emphasizing its economic and political hostility toward the Germans, France prevented the Americans from treating Europe as a homogeneous whole.[15] The French demanded to negotiate directly with Washington, and other nations then followed suit. The Americans agreed, and Marshall aid flowed into Europe according to the dictates of bilateral negotiations, strengthening rivalries between European nations. In particular, the French were willing only to form a customs union with their smaller neighbors and refused to cooperate with either Germany or Britain; the British for their part emphasized their economic ties to the old empire, recently refashioned as the Commonwealth, rather than to the economies of the rest of Europe.

Since the American government was now disbursing Marshall aid by bilateral negotiations, there was not a lot for the OEEC to do. The Americans had always wanted the OEEC to be led by ministers from the various governments involved, but the European governments had resisted, insisting that the organization be run at a less senior level. (It later metamorphosed into the Organization for Economic Cooperation and Development, or OECD, a sort of international think tank). Furthermore, once the Marshall Plan was in place, neither the IMF nor the World Bank seemed quite so important: when countries such as Japan needed finance over the next couple of years it was neither the IMF nor the World Bank that provided the funds but, rather, the American government directly. In practice, then, the Marshall Plan acted both as an anti-federalist European institution and as a substitute for the Bretton Woods institutions, doubly undermining American aspirations.

Through their many bilateral discussions with the American government, European governments quickly realized that in negotiating terms there was a balance: their own need for American cash against American fears that Europe would go its own way. To avoid the possibility that Europe would become an almost autonomous trading and financial region, Washington felt obliged to compromise. European governments were particularly unwilling to dismantle the national economic controls and bureaucracies that had got them through the war. The need to plan the recovery seemed just as acute as had been the need to plan the war.

Some American officials, such as Assistant Deputy Administrator of the ECA Richard Bissell, remained committed to the view that Europe should ape the United States by adopting both federalism and laissez-faire policies. However, most realized that they had to accommodate themselves to European ideas, as well as vice versa. Even if Europe united, which seemed pretty unlikely, it might not follow the laissez-faire model of the United States. Europe would probably find its own internal institutional arrangements, and would probably be much more interventionist than the American government.

## Toward the Common Market

Although the Americans still thought of Bretton Woods as "a sleeping beauty, in suspended animation and awaiting the kiss of completed European reconstruction to awake to a happy future," to the Europeans, Bretton Woods was "either moribund or a corpse."[16] The Americans hoped that Bretton Woods could be reconstituted if European governments devalued their currencies against the dollar: because lower exchange rates would be easier to defend, the British government would be willing to commit itself to convert sterling into dollars on demand, and Europe's other governments would make similar commitments.

The British government, however, refused to countenance such a move. The Labour Party was in power, and was desperately keen to avoid offending Britain's patrician financial establishment. The City's of London's earning power had always been predicated on a high exchange rate, and although that made Britain industrially uncompetitive, the City managed to dress up its self-interest as financial prudence and moral rectitude—and the Labour government kowtowed to City thinking.

The British hoped that at a pinch they could get by without the help of either the United States or Europe. The nations of the Commonwealth, plus one or two others in Scandinavia and elsewhere, still pegged their currencies to sterling; the British authorities half believed that they could revive the use of sterling for international settlements and simultaneously eliminate trade barriers within the sterling area. Most of the nations concerned were traditional trading partners of Britain, and the British romantically perceived strong cultural and natural ties with the nations of the sterling area. On that basis, the exchange rate between sterling and the dollar did not seem so important, nor did the lofty ambitions of the Bretton Woods Conference. Forget any new world economic order: Britain would look after itself.

Such views were at odds with the facts. In 1947 sterling area governments had been among the first to dump sterling in favor of dollars during the brief period of convertibility. Just as important, Britain was borrowing heavily from the United States, making the sterling-dollar rate a crucial problem for the British government. However, it takes a long time for the decline of a great power to be truly acknowledged, even by that power's successor. The Americans feared that the British would deny them easy trading access to large chunks of the world, and were reluctant to offend the British government by insisting on a devaluation, let alone on the abolition of Commonwealth trade preferences.

By 1949, however, Britain's borrowing had become unmanageable and a devaluation was almost inevitable.[17] Still the British denied the fact, managing even to negotiate several financial and trade concessions from the United States in return for "agreeing" on September 18 to devalue sterling against the dollar by just over 30 percent. Yet the British refused to promise to turn sterling into dollars on request, and they showed no willingness to discuss their policies with either the IMF or the OEEC—the two institutions that the Americans had created for precisely that purpose.

Although none of Europe's other nations had been warned let alone consulted about the devaluation (apart from the French, and this only at the last moment), they could not afford to be left behind: all of Europe grumpily and severally followed Britain's example, and devalued. They did not, however, show any desire to meet American aspirations by committing themselves to sell their currencies on demand for sterling or dollars. None wanted to repeat Britain's experience of 1947; to agree to defend a fixed exchange rate against the dollar and then watch their whole foreign exchange reserves hemorrhage in a matter of days seemed rather foolish. If the Americans wanted Europe's currencies fixed against gold and the dollar, then they would need to provide the necessary firepower, in the form of money for currency market intervention.

The fact remained that Europe could not ignore the need for international payments arrangements to replace the collapsed Bretton Woods system. Britain's abandonment of sterling convertibility, the arrival of Marshall aid, and the 1949 devaluations had resolved Europe's immediate balance of payments crisis, but problems still existed beneath the surface. Sterling still looked overvalued against the dollar, as did other European currencies, making it hard for Europe to earn dollars through increasing net exports. Furthermore, Marshall aid would not last forever: the scheme was scheduled to end in 1952, and it seemed unlikely that Congress would agree to an extension. Sooner or later, therefore, shortages of finance would reappear as a constraint on European growth.

Since January 1948 the French had been flirting with floating exchange rates in defiance of the Bretton Woods ambition of fixed exchange rates; as punishment France had been denied access to

IMF funds. Despite this, the French government had been secretly pressing for a scheme, known as "Finebel," in which France, Italy, and the Benelux countries would remove all capital controls with one another and allow their currencies to float. When in September 1949 the French minister of finance, Maurice Petsche, revealed his government's plans to the Americans, the latter objected: they did not like floating exchange rates, and they believed that if the French really would not allow the British into Finebel, then they ought at least to include Germany. The Americans threatened to stop Marshall aid unless Europe came to heel. Partly for that reason, the French backed down, and instead advocated a different scheme—this one including Germany—that would allow fixed exchange rates while involving pan-European policies of industrial intervention and industrial support. There would be a new European investment bank, partly funded by the Americans but under less American control than the IMF, and there would be little commitment to moving toward trade liberalization.

Again the Americans objected, and the new scheme came to nothing. However, the State Department now accepted that Europe could not be forced to revive the moribund Bretton Woods system, especially if Europe was to move closer to integration. So, much to the annoyance of the IMF and the Federal Reserve (among others), the State Department began to discuss with the Europeans the possibility of a European Payments Union (EPU), which would be broader than Finebel but much less ambitious than Bretton Woods. European countries would log all bilateral surpluses or deficits with the Bank for International Settlements. Countries would settle the resultant total surpluses or deficits in dollars, and credit agreements would even cover those in part. The American government itself would pour dollars into the pool to ensure that there was no liquidity shortage.

In August 1950 the Europeans and Americans agreed to the terms of the EPU. The agreement was "an assertion of European economic and political will as a reaction against American policy."[18] Although the arrangement promised to stimulate intra-European trade, it would do nothing directly for the rest of the world, nor for the role of the United States within the world economy. The EPU would not promote the role of the dollar at the center of world finance, and would use institutions that followed the existing contours of European ambitions rather than the American-inspired IMF.

In 1950, just as the EPU came into being, the French government proposed another scheme, addressing the single most important issue in European industrial policy—the future of the coal and steel industries. To the alarm of many in the American steel industry, the end of World War II had provoked massive investment in European steel making, especially in France. The exception was Germany, where occupying French soldiers set to work dismantling the steel mills and transporting them back to France. Although, as already noted, the Americans refused to allow the French to take the Ruhr and Saarland away from Germany, the French remained determined to prevent German domination of the European steel industry; at the same time, though, they wanted cheap access to German coke.

In March 1948 the Americans and Europeans agreed to the creation of an International Control Authority for the Ruhr. Much weaker than the original French proposal for an autonomous state, this arrangement nevertheless annoyed the West Germans, who by now felt themselves to be sufficiently successful economically not to warrant such external interference. Taking note of this, French Foreign Minister Robert Schuman, who believed in the central importance of an amicable accommodation between France and West Germany, began to search for a better arrangement: in 1950 he launched his Schuman Plan for the creation of a European Coal and Steel Community (ECSC).[19] On April 18, 1951, the governments of France, West Germany, Italy, and the three Benelux countries signed the Treaty of Paris, agreeing to remove all coal- and steel-related national subsidies and trade barriers against one another. The treaty created what was known as the High Authority, empowered to promote the maximum output of coal and steel within the community at minimum cost and common prices. This authority would coordinate the rationalization of mines, foundries, and steel mills throughout the community and provide support from a fund to which all the community's members contributed. The High Authority would be accountable to a council of ministers and to a legislative assembly.

For the Schuman Plan to work, though, it was essential that the community members should discriminate against imports from outside their area. The main source of such imports was the United States; and because the American government still had the right to veto any decisions of the West German government, it could have halted the Schuman Plan. At first it looked as if it might do so: the discriminatory principles governing the work of the new organization were the antithesis of free trade, and the ECSC was precisely the sort of interventionist body that the Americans disliked. Since coal and steel were such important sectors, the ECSC would compromise the whole liberalization ambition.

However, American objections were short lived. Shortly after the announcement of the plan came the Korean War. The French told the Americans that if they wanted European steel, they would have to allow the Europeans to run their coal and steel industries in their own way. The Americans withdrew their objections, and the ECSC formally came into being.

The ECSC provided Europe with its first step toward the creation of the Common Market. In May 1952, flushed with the success of the ECSC, the six governments signed a second treaty creating the European Defence Community, with the intention of forming a single European Army. That attempt soon floundered, confirming the common European view that economic integration was much easier to achieve than political union. Accordingly, Paul-Henri Spaak, a Belgian politician who had chaired the OEEC, led a committee to examine closer economic ties among the six ECSC nations; in 1956 his committee produced a blueprint for what became known as the Common Market, covering the removal of all trade barriers within the community, the creation of common policies for agriculture and transport, and a shift toward free movement of people and finance throughout the six nations. On March 25, 1957, the six nations signed the Treaty of Rome, creating the European Economic Community: committed to trade discrimination against the rest of the world and intervention in industry and agriculture within Europe, it was thoroughly different from the plans devised by the Americans long before at Bretton Woods.

## A New Trade System

Beyond Europe, American attempts to create a new laissez-faire world economic order that would run itself without the need for leadership were no less compromised. The point has already been made, in chapter 3, that World War I helped some of the world's poorer nations to develop and industrialize. As supplies of manufactured goods from Europe dried up, countries abroad began to produce their own local substitutes. The Great Depression, however, left the poorer nations severely weakened, so that by the time of World War II they had lost their ability to compete against the capital intensive industries of Europe, Japan, and especially the United States. By the mid-forties American production technology had become highly sophisticated, huge economies of scale were now available, and the cottage industries of the Third World (as we call it now) could not hope to sell against American products that were both better and cheaper.

As a result, when hostilities ended, the short-term gains to the poorer nations from World War II did not translate into long-term security. The war widened economic gaps between nations rather than narrowing them. Although in semi-industrialized countries such as India the production of munitions, ships, and other equipment rose during the war, there were offsetting falls in the output of other commodities such as coal, pig iron, steel, and even cotton.[20] In other even poorer nations, the war was positively damaging: occupying armies, especially those of Japan, ruined the agriculture of many countries, destroying farmland, grabbing all the food and crops they could, and disregarding the need to plant for the future. Colonial nations saw their industries turned over to war work, often with disastrous consequences.

Other, less direct problems, were if anything more severe. In

Bengal in 1943 massive war expenditure by the colonial Indian government resulted in a sharp rise in inflation. Those Bengalis who worked for the army, in the munitions factories or in other industries involved in the war effort, prospered from the economic boom. However, the price of rice moved far beyond what millions of Bengalis could afford to pay; wartime controls prevented the importation of food from other regions or countries, and so speculation, panic buying, and administrative chaos resulted. Three million people died in Bengal that year, thanks to the inflation that the war brought.[21]

Roosevelt was determined that peace should bring with it an end to European colonialism.[22] American soldiers did not fight to preserve the British Empire, nor that of any other elderly European power. Just as Europe had to be freed from Nazi dominion, so too countries such as India should be freed from British dominion. Not surprisingly, the Europeans felt differently: during the war Churchill repeatedly blustered that he did not become prime minister to preside over the breakup of the British Empire. In reality, however, it was practically impossible for the British to rule the empire from London while the war was in progress, and many countries such as India were already on the verge of independence by the time that the war ended.

In many cases, however, the British moved only slowly toward granting independence, while other imperial powers such as France were even more determined to hang on to their colonies—much to their own ultimate disgrace. Although such resistance to American anticolonialism was largely reactionary, it also contained a strong commercial streak. The Europeans knew that American moral high-mindedness masked a determination to break Europe's preferential trading arrangements with the old empires. Indeed as already noted, Cordell Hull made the abolition of imperial preference a condition for granting Britain lend-lease. Then in June 1945 the American government suddenly canceled lend-lease, leaving Britain desperate for funds; the condition set for a new loan was, again, the end of imperial preference. Reluctantly, the British agreed.

However, British officials insisted that the abolition of imperial preference had to be part of global tariff reductions. At meetings in 1943 and 1944 they and their American counterparts had planned an international convention to settle a system of rules under which countries would use trade barriers only to defend their trade balances by approval of an International Trade Organization (ITO). The British were in no hurry to introduce the new system, of course, and when the Republican Party won control of Congress in 1946, the Americans also began to drag their heels; as a result, it was not until spring 1947 that negotiations began on the rules to govern the new ITO.[23]

That autumn the conference moved to Havana (Cuba was then an American satellite). The British wanted to keep imperial preference, and the Americans had decided that they too wanted preferential tariffs to protect their trade with Cuba and with the Philippines. The British in turn said that as well as keeping imperial preference, they wanted to extend the conditions under which trade barriers would be permissible, to include the maintenance of full employment. Meanwhile, several of the world's poorer nations argued that they too needed trade barriers to protect their industries from the might of American competition.

Despite these problems, representatives of fifty-eight countries signed the Havana Charter in March 1948. The agreed-upon text fell far short of free trade, left imperial preference intact, made many concessions, and allowed many special cases, much to the annoyance of Congress, now once again heavily isolationist. Realizing that Congress would not ratify the charter, President Truman withdrew the legislation rather than face defeat. The charter and the ITO perished before they were born.

All was not lost, however, for in 1947 in Geneva a variety of nations signed over one hundred bilateral trading agreements with one another, some of them involving significant tariff cuts. The United Nations took the agreements, bundled them together into a single document and, with the much more ambitious ITO plans becalmed, persuaded first eight and then another fifteen nations to sign the resultant General Agreement on Tariffs and Trade (GATT).

Crucially, the agreement included a most favored nation clause, although participants agreed to let the British government reinvent the system of imperial preference in a diluted form as the British Commonwealth. They also waived the most favored nation clause for regional customs unions and free trade areas, and agreed to meet periodically at similar conferences to negotiate successive rounds of tariff cuts.

To many American government officials, GATT was a bitter disappointment and an ignoble deviation from free trade principles. Having championed the independence of former European colonies, the Americans found that those very countries refused to embrace free trade policies. More than that: in 1947 the Truman administration had made a remarkable decision to unilaterally reduce all American tariffs to their lowest levels since 1913, irrespective of the response of other nations.

The United States went out on a limb in favoring the rapid elimination of trade barriers, but other nations showed little inclination to follow. Thanks to the tariff cut, every nation in the world suddenly found itself able to export cheaply to the United States. Since countries could nevertheless protect their home markets from cheap American imports, it seemed that the whole world benefited twice over—at American expense.

From the American point of view the unilateral tariff cut of 1947 was far from foolish, however. Even with foreign tariffs to overcome, American companies could still export heavily; other nations were growing fast enough to want American products, which were pretty cheap in any case, thanks to economies of scale. Meanwhile, the absence of American tariffs meant that American imports were cheap, holding down domestic costs. Both the American economy and world trade boomed, rather as happened in the late nineteenth century when Britain pursued much the same policy.

It is likely that the Truman government's obsession with communism hijacked its policies toward both colonialism and tariffs.[24] State Department officials feared that as the British, French, and Belgian governments dismantled their empires, China and the Soviet Union would occupy the resultant political vacuums. The American government reasoned that if communism spread to the world's more vulnerable nations (and everybody seemed vulnerable to the State Department), and if such nations absented themselves completely from participation in the international trading system, then the United States stood to suffer both economically and politically. Thus the Truman government adapted trade policy to fit the views of nations vastly less powerful than the United States itself: better a global trading system crisscrossed with tariff walls than no system at all.[25]

## The Occupation of Japan

In some respects the question of what to do about postwar Japan was easier than the problem of settling a policy for Europe. The bombing of Hiroshima and Nagasaki meant that American troops under General Douglas MacArthur could take uncontested control of Japan, without having to share the victory with other allies such as Britain or, critically, the Soviet Union. So, following the occupation of Japan, MacArthur immediately became an American viceroy in a way that could not be said of Eisenhower in Europe.

Until July 1945 the State Department was planning a very different resolution to the Pacific War, which might have meant an equally different pattern to the postwar administration of Japan. In that month, Henry Stimson, secretary of war, submitted a memorandum to President Harry Truman.[26] Stimson paid tribute to Japan's fifty-year transformation from an isolated, feudal nation into a great industrial power. He recalled how, until a coup in 1931, Japan had been a responsible and cooperative participant in the world trading system, noting that the Japanese leadership included many people who considered the Pacific war to be crazily ill-conceived and unwinnable, and who shared American anxieties over Soviet-led communism in Asia. But he also said that the Japanese would fiercely resist any invasion—fiercely enough, perhaps, to take half a million American lives.[27] These considerations led him to urge Truman to offer the Japanese an honorable peace: the

United States should oblige Japan to demilitarize and to become democratic in practice. In return, Japan should keep its industry and its independence, and enjoy the benefits of the liberal trading regime that the United States was planning for the world.

Two weeks later, at the Potsdam Conference, Stimson again approached Truman, though this time his message was very different: he informed the president that the first atomic bomb had been successfully tested at Alamogordo in the desert of New Mexico. Stimson had little desire to see the bomb used; he still favored a diplomatic solution to the war, especially since the military was unsure whether it could repeat the Alamogordo success in action. However, Truman was determined to settle the war against Japan quickly, before the Soviet Union could intervene. The atomic bomb offered a means to do that, and Truman seized his opportunity.[28] The end of the war was thus vastly more traumatic for Japan than it might have been (although perhaps no more so than if the Soviet Union had invaded), and the transfer of power to the American government as embodied by MacArthur was, accordingly, far more absolute.

Japan had suffered even more during the war than had Europe. Two million Japanese had died, even before the dropping of the atom bombs, and American air raids had flattened about two fifths of Japan's towns and destroyed about one fifth of Japanese factories; much of the rest had either been turned over to military use or cannibalized for spare parts. For MacArthur, food shortages, rapid inflation, and falling output all meant trouble. Even (perhaps especially) with the American Eighth Army garrisoned in their country, the Japanese were liable to become politically restless.

In such circumstances, MacArthur looked like a dangerous man to put in charge of Japan. Truman, like most of the American establishment, thought that MacArthur was erratic, egotistical, and of dubious competence. In 1932 MacArthur had led the brutal eviction from premises near the White House of the Bonus Marchers, unemployed World War I veterans seeking early payment of a promised bonus; in 1944, with the war still being waged, he nearly stood against Roosevelt for the presidency. Truman was probably happy to exile MacArthur to Japan.

However, MacArthur displayed little hostility toward the ordinary Japanese people, blaming instead Japan's military dictatorship for the war against the United States. He was keen to achieve rapid reform, and reasoned that enlightened change, administrative efficiency, and popular support from the Japanese people would give him the perfect credentials for the American presidency. MacArthur thus initially committed himself to a wide range of liberal economic and political reforms, including the release of political prisoners, votes for women, free trade unions, a more equal distribution of income and wealth, and an end to the exploitation of tenant farmers by their landlords. Of special importance was MacArthur's intention to abolish the business conglomerates, *zaibatsu*, that dominated Japanese industry, and his hope that a move toward free trade would allow Japan to prosper via trade with its Asian neighbors.

Initially it looked as if MacArthur might be impeded by a separate American plan devised by Edwin Pauley, a Californian oil tycoon, to extract reparations from Japan's big industrial combines. With Truman's blessing, Pauley and a commission of advisers visited Japan in 1945 and determined that the United States should transfer resources away from the *zaibatsu* to nations elsewhere in Asia, thereby impeding the economic advance of the former while promoting the latter. Pauley's aim was to prevent Japan from becoming once again the economic and political center of the region by preventing the recreation in Japan of such strategic industries as munitions, iron and steel, and shipbuilding, and by handing Japanese industrial assets to host countries elsewhere in Asia. Japan, according to the plan, would concentrate instead on light industry and consumer goods.[29]

Although Pauley claimed that his policies would not lead to Japan's impoverishment, the already parlous state of the economy made such protestations look distinctly disingenuous. MacArthur opposed Pauley, partly because he resented interference in his fiefdom, but also because he thought such policies would be very bad for Japan. He stalled Pauley's plans for a year, by which time officials in Washington had also come to see reparations demands as quite unrealistic. The idea was quietly dropped.

Reparations was one of the few subjects on which MacArthur and Washington agreed. Two issues separated him from the American government: *zaibatsu* abolition and the case for American financial aid. The latter was closely tied to the issue of trade. Before the war, Japan had sold manufactured goods to China and other parts of Asia, and had imported fuel and raw materials from those same countries. The Japanese also imported some high-technology products from the United States and Europe, paying for them mainly through sales of silk and, to a lesser extent, through shipping fees and selling freight and shipping insurance. Now, however, Japan had to buy these commodities from the United States or do without. The war-damaged countries of Southeast Asia were unable to supply the raw materials that Japan needed, and were either too poor to buy Japanese exports or, in the crucial case of China, too preoccupied with civil war.

MacArthur clearly realized that recreating a circular flow of trade would help to revitalize the domestic Japanese economy, and he hoped that the introduction of free trade would allow Japan to deal with most of its economic difficulties. However, trade problems also meant financial problems. Before the war Japanese exports exceeded imports, but after the war the reverse was true: most Japanese exports went to Asia, whereas imports came mostly from the United States—but Americans were hardly likely to want payment in the currencies of China, Korea, or Taiwan. In consequence, Japan faced a dollar shortage that was even more acute than its overall trade imbalance suggested: without American loans or gifts, the Japanese economy simply could not function at all.

Nor did financial problems end there. In the early years of occupation American forces shifted $350 million per year of food and other necessities to Japan simply to prevent starvation. Japan needed such resources for survival, but it needed much more to finance vital industrial investment. MacArthur saw the problem, and accepted the humanitarian aid, as well as some money from the Reconstruction Finance Corporation, but he feared that additional American funds would mean more supervision from Washington and less power for himself. So the supreme commander for the allied powers repeatedly protested that there was no need for large financial transfers from the United States to Japan.

MacArthur was not alone in resisting American finance. Partly because of their unfamiliarity with Japan's language and complex customs, his staff governed Japan through the established Japanese civil service, who were as keen as MacArthur to avoid interference from Washington—even to the extent of not wanting American finance. MacArthur's staff and the Japanese government established a working method that, although sometimes testy, served both their needs: he would propose radical liberal reforms to satisfy his audience in the United States, and the bureaucrats would water down those proposals to satisfy vested interests in Japan before putting them before Parliament, known as the Diet. Neither paid much attention to such problems as food shortages, unemployment, or inflation, nor to the stagnation of production or the fractious mood of the ordinary Japanese people.

Their complacency was partly encouraged by the weakness of the parliamentary left. The socialist and communist parties, which had been persecuted before and during the war, remained disorganized and ineffective; in April 1947 they were just strong enough to win control of the Diet in that month's elections, but only through a fragile and quarrelsome coalition. In October 1948 the right regained power, in the form of the newly created Liberal Democratic Party—and remained in office almost to this day. Outside of Parliament, however, the left had much greater strength, not least because of MacArthur's decrees enabling trade unions to organize in factories and offices. With the economy apparently collapsing, organized unions and individual workers grew increasingly militant: there were frequent strikes and occupations, and in April and May 1946 there were mass demonstrations in Tokyo demanding more food, more pay, and the resignation of the government.

MacArthur fumed against the protests and issued a warning against "Mob disorder or Violence,"[30] delighting the conservatives and merely antagonizing the militants. Soon MacArthur was threatening to imprison strikers, with predictable consequences—the unions began to organize a general strike, scheduled for February 1, 1947. MacArthur banned the strike and soon launched a purge of suspected radicals working in industry, while Parliament outlawed collective bargaining and strikes in the public sector. The policies proved effective at dampening trade union militancy, but they did nothing to tackle Japan's underlying economic problems.

In Washington the State Department was watching events in Japan with increasing unease. One of Marshall's first acts on his appointment as secretary of state had been to create the Policy Planning Staff under George Kennan, who in 1946 had helped to push American policy away from collaboration with the Soviet Union and toward "containment." Together with Under Secretary of State Dean Ascheson and others, Kennan argued that Japan had to be rebuilt as a bulwark against the Soviet Union, and to a lesser extent China. In March 1948 Kennan visited Japan; his report for Marshall ran to forty-two pages, in which he blamed the collapse of the economy on MacArthur's purges, first of the right and then of the left, on his threats to dissolve the *zaibatsu* and extract reparations, and on his refusal to recognize Japan's desperate need for American investment finance. Soon Kennan was joined in Japan by a business delegation led by Percy Johnston, chairman of Chemical Bank, but organized by William Draper, himself a former banker but now serving as army under secretary. Johnston's group came rapidly to much the same conclusions as Kennan's.

The previous year some of MacArthur's staff had produced a report, known as the "Green Book," which set forth a plan in which the United States would provide Japan with $1.2 billion of aid and raw materials, to kick-start the Japanese economy back into life. MacArthur turned his back on the report, but Draper argued in its favor, persuading the State Department to make a start by asking Congress for a $180 million finance package for Japan, Korea, and the Ryukyu Islands—which supposedly made up a defensive perimeter against communism on the Asian mainland. The funds were to be spent on industrial raw materials, would be made available between April 1948 and June 1949, and would be known as the Economic Recovery in Occupied Areas (EROA) plan. The raw materials were for use in the manufacture of goods for export, mainly to the rest of Asia. Congress agreed, partly persuaded by the Johnston report and partly by a growing recognition that since there was little chance of containing communism in mainland China, Japan had to be the first line of defense. Although it reduced EROA funds to $125 million, Congress approved the legislation in June, 1948.[31] Congress also provided American textile mills with credit to spend on Japanese cotton. Finally in December 1948 President Truman appointed Joseph Dodge, a Detroit banker and close associate of Draper's, to be MacArthur's deputy and to implement Washington's plans for Japan's economy. The appointment infuriated MacArthur, who realized that Dodge would not assist but supplant him.

Japan now had its equivalent of the Marshall Plan. However, although the Americans offered reconstruction, they framed the policy very conservatively. Already Draper had ordered MacArthur that, henceforth, the budget of the Japanese government should balance and policy should promote price stability as well as production for export. Dodge arrived early in 1949, and for a year and a half he balanced spending on Japanese industry with cuts in government spending and reductions in the public payroll. Although Dodge created the Ministry of International Trade and Industry (MITI), he cut much government credit to small firms and canceled some of the finance that had hitherto flowed to Japan from the Reconstruction Finance Bank. These so-called stabilization measures were perhaps justified by the need to reduce inflation and curb government inefficiency and corruption, but they tended to dampen economic activity and undermine most of the boost coming from the reconstruction funds. Taken together with a new purge of suspected communists and measures to replace militant trade unions with more conservative unions, these policies—known as the "Dodge line"—represented a severe austerity program for Japan at a time when its economy was severely depressed. Unemployment doubled in the eighteen months following Dodge's arrival, and although inflation fell, it was not obvious that the new policies were much better than those of MacArthur.

The salvation for the Japanese economy, and the start of the so-called Japanese economic miracle, was not the Dodge line but the American military expenditure associated with the Korean War.

On June 25, 1950, after many cross-border skirmishes from both sides, North Korean forces crossed the thirty-eighth parallel into South Korea. The American government responded not just by sending troops to the south but also by greatly increasing its military and financial presence in the region. The major recipient of American personnel, equipment, and spending power was Japan.[32] Just as in the late thirties and early forties British rearmament orders had given the depressed American economy a much needed fillip, so American rearmament did the same for Western Europe and especially Japan in the fifties. In the period from 1945 to 1955, American military spending in Japan was twice the amount of direct American aid to the nation. Nor was the spending limited to food and small scale supplies: the American military demanded more hardware than could be shipped across the Pacific, so it signed contracts with Japanese firms to build items ranging from electronic equipment to whole ships. Toyota, a small and struggling motor company on the verge of closure, suddenly found itself in receipt of massive contracts to assemble jeeps for the American army. Japan's economic activity soared.

At first the Americans were wary of allowing the Japanese to manufacture weapons, so the Japanese initially developed an industrial structure oriented toward everyday items, for which there was also a consumer market, and toward basic heavy industry.[33] One of the legacies of the Korean War was an American embargo on Japanese trade with communist China, which threatened to damage the Japanese economy; it was partly in recompense that the American authorities agreed to use Japan as a major source for military hardware. The effect of that was to skew Japanese industry toward high-technology products, and to perpetuate the benefits to Japanese industry that the Korean War created.[34] Gradually the high-technology component of American military spending in Japan increased, and with the contracts came technological knowledge. The American orders were still for components, not complete weapons, but in consequence the Japanese found that with a little modification they could sell to civilian markets the products that they were making for the American military.

## The Emergence of Japan, Inc.

When MacArthur arrived in Japan he came armed with instructions from Washington to abolish the "large industrial and banking combinations"—*zaibatsu*—that dominated Japanese industry more completely than even J. P. Morgan had dominated American commerce. The State Department claimed that in the thirties the *zaibatsu* had depressed domestic Japanese consumption by paying unfairly low wages and had promoted Japanese military adventures abroad for the sake of markets to conquer and cheap fuel and raw materials. Thomas Bisson, soon to become one of MacArthur's officials, wrote that "if the zaibatsu are permitted to survive . . . they will be able to prepare even more thoroughly for the next attempt to conquer East Asia by force . . ."[35]

Strictly speaking, there were four real *zaibatsu*, created in the nineteenth century when the Meiji government gave control over great swaths of Japanese industry and finance to four families— Yasuda, Mitsui, Mitsubishi, and Sumitomo. These families were vastly wealthy, and American proposals to break up their business empires threatened them with disaster; rather than waiting passively for that to happen, they took steps to dissuade the Americans. In October 1945 representatives of the four families offered a deal to Raymond Kramer, the colonel responsible for deciding on a reorganization of Japan's economy. They promised to dissolve the holding companies at the center of each *zaibatsu*, to deliver to the occupation authorities the resignations of all *zaibatsu* family members from the boards of subsidiary companies, to sell family shares in the holding companies to an American liquidation commission, and then to invest the proceeds in Japanese government bonds.

With MacArthur's approval, Kramer agreed to the plan, and on November 6 occupation authorities issued a directive to that effect. The *zaibatsu* could hardly believe their victory: although the family members had to sell their shareholdings in their holding companies, they did not have to sell their shares in their subsidiaries. The sales were not required to be open to the general public, and stocks could instead be offered to *zaibatsu* sympathizers, who would allow the family leaders, *honsha*, to remain in power—thus the *zaibatsu* seemed destined to remain almost entirely intact.

Although the State Department was not yet much interested in Japanese economic affairs, MacArthur's apparent capitulation appalled men such as William Clayton, who persuaded the Justice Department to dispatch a special mission to Tokyo to check on the arrangements for the *zaibatsu*. The Edwards mission, as it was known, arrived early in 1946 and very swiftly denounced the occupation directive for failing to break up the *zaibatsu*, proposing instead that all affected stock should be sold to smallholders, that the *zaibatsu* families should receive only partial compensation, and that new antitrust laws should prevent the resultant companies from gaining any new monopoly powers. The report also recommended similar treatment for other business groupings.

Having asserted its authority, though, the State Department soon lost interest in the matter; although in May 1947 it formally sought the approval of the Far Eastern Commission for the Edwards plan, it did so without much enthusiasm. The manifest failure of the Japanese economy to recover was placing great strains on American government finances. Washington decided that the only way to get Japan's economy moving again was to rehabilitate the *zaibatsu* and effectively pass control back to them.

Ever resentful of outside interference, MacArthur's response was to insist that the Japanese government introduce accelerated legislation in the Diet to disband the *zaibatsu*. In October George Kennan denounced MacArthur's attack on the *zaibatsu*, saying that it would end in "economic disaster" and "near anarchy."[36] In October, William Draper cabled MacArthur, instructing him to delay Diet consideration of what was called "the *zaibatsu* deconcentration bill." MacArthur refused, and in November and December respectively the lower and upper houses of the Diet passed the legislation. In February 1948 the new Holding Company Liquidation Commission ordered the dissolution of over three hundred Japanese companies.

Since the dissolutions did not occur immediately, the battle was not yet over. In March, MacArthur overreached himself: he declared his candidacy for the presidency. Although he claimed to do so with humility, MacArthur's hubris was soon evident, and he found almost no one willing to join his campaign. By May, faced with near-certain humiliation in the next month's Republican convention, MacArthur was already a spent force; that month Draper dispatched a Deconstruction Review Board to Tokyo to examine the companies listed for dissolution and to recommend to MacArthur whether the proposals should go ahead. When the board told the supreme commander that almost all the firms on the list should not be dissolved after all, MacArthur acquiesced: the *zaibatsu* were safe, at last.

Formally the four *zaibatsu* all ceased to exist in 1948, but informally they all survived, slimmed down, without their former close financial structures but still with a bank at the core of each group and a complex set of informal ties linking member firms. These arrangements outwitted the lawyers who framed the antimonopoly law, and soon the former *zaibatsu*—now known as *keiretsu*—were joined by others. Some of the newcomers were centered around banks such as the great Daiwa Bank, which included the securities giant Nomura within its orbit, while others centered around industrial firms such as Nippon Steel, Toyota, or Matsushita.[37]

Each *keiretsu* operated in a range of markets, with its member firms eschewing competition with one another and instead competing fiercely with companies from other *keiretsu* while assisting other corporate family members in their own struggles against outsiders. With most Japanese markets regularly growing at 10 percent per year, there was almost no market in which a *keiretsu* did not want to participate, so each *keiretsu* operated in as many markets as possible—and in each it sought to be a major player. The result was fierce battles between small numbers of powerful firms trying to dominate each other.

As soon as the Korean War kicked life back into the Japanese economy, the *keiretsu* got to work. Economic expansion followed a steeply rising curve, driven by heavy investment at the expense of short-term consumption. Japanese firms invested during the fifties and sixties because they believed that their markets would grow; the investments themselves raised output and demand in the economy, thus becoming self-justifying.[38] The Japanese had easy access to state-of-the-art American and European technology, and each company made sure that it never lagged behind in the race to assimilate Western technology. Thanks to the *keiretsu*, Japanese banks were usually among the largest shareholders in the nation's biggest companies, but they were seldom able to divest themselves of large stakes in a given company; one result of this was an unusual, and almost permanent, bond between owners and managers. Because the Japanese economy was growing rapidly, incomes usually ran ahead of spending plans, and thus the private sector saving rate was generally high. The banks had plenty of deposits to lend, and their close links to the big corporations meant that they were happy to take long-term views; industry invested accordingly.

Important though the Korean War and the *keiretsu* were in generating Japanese recovery, the investment boom of the fifties and sixties would have failed had the investment not embodied a new age of Japanese technical and managerial innovation. For while some older sectors such as coal and steel faced long-term decline, others expanded more than fast enough to take their places.

The most important form of innovation that Japan pioneered was not a particular product but a method of production. In 1950, quite soon before the outbreak of the Korean War, Eiji Toyoda of the Toyota company journeyed to Detroit to examine Ford's mass production methods. Shortly before, Toyota had suffered a collapse in sales, a damaging strike, and heavy redundancies. Eiji's uncle, Kiichiro Toyoda, had been forced to resign as head of the firm: it seemed that a new direction was needed, and copying Ford might be an option. Eiji reported that the Ford company built more cars in a day than Toyota had made in its entire history. "You might as well compare a pebble with a boulder," he said.[39] As a result, Toyota simply could not replicate Ford's mass production methods.

The Japanese government said that the solution was for Toyota and other motor manufacturers to merge. However, even the combined companies would have been tiny by comparison with the big American firms. Until the Japanese market grew to be vastly larger than it was, Japanese firms could not begin to enjoy the benefits of American-style mass production—yet the market would not grow unless employment first increased on the back of higher production. The Korean War offered a partial escape from this vicious circle, but even massive American military orders were insufficient to lift Japanese production to levels comparable with American industry.

So Eiji Toyoda turned his back on copying Detroit and looked instead for inspiration from Taiichi Ohno, his chief production engineer. Ohno had spent several years trying to find a way of making small batches of a component as cheaply as enormous companies made large batches. American manufacturers used presses to shape metal; because changing the presses was very time consuming, firms would make tens of thousands of a single part, then alter the press to make tens of thousands of another part. However, there is a high cost associated with carrying inventories, so the method only makes sense for firms that make hundreds or even thousands of cars every day. The much smaller Japanese firms, then, could not use existing presses efficiently; instead, they had to make cars virtually by hand. This was much less reliable, of course, and even with low Japanese wage levels much more expensive.

Ohno's goal was to find a way of reducing the time it took to change a press. If he succeeded, it would mean that production runs would not need to be so long. Throughout the fifties, Ohno focused on this task, and by the end of the decade he succeeded: Toyota could change a typical press in three minutes, whereas in Detroit it took all day. Toyota could now make cars in small numbers as cheaply as Ford made them in large numbers.[40]

Toyota's new manufacturing method employed small numbers of adaptable presses to produce large ranges of car components, keeping inventory levels to a minimum, which held down costs. Whereas American firms operated with weeks of idle inventories, Japanese firms had only a few hours of inventories. The consequence of this "just in time" method was that Japanese lean production, as it became known, could compete in cost terms with American mass production.

There were several by-products from lean production. Japanese companies such as Toyota could not afford to have as many defective components as could American companies like Ford, since total stock levels were so much lower, so the production methods developed in Japan in the fifties and sixties depended on a much higher commitment to quality from the start of the production process. Lean production was essentially a continuation of the journey away from European-style craft techniques—a journey that had taken in the American system of manufacturing and mass production before moving toward lean production via an intermediary stage, known as the *kanban* system.[41] In the nineteenth century the American emphasis on interchangeable parts had removed the need for fitters to file down clumsily made components until they fitted together; even so, mass production factories in the first half of the twentieth century still delayed quality checking until the products came off the end of the assembly line. In contrast, lean production shifted responsibility for quality control back to production line workers, making it easier to discover why quality problems arose, and reducing the need for remedial changes to products coming off mass production lines.

One implication of the Japanese approach was that this higher quality and reliability of products created important marketing opportunities that American firms, duped by market research analysis, had overlooked. As a result, Japanese manufacturing competitiveness was able to approach that of American firms. On the surface the Japanese had a low commitment to pushing forward the boundaries of product innovation; beneath the surface, though, they were innovating just as fast as the Americans once had. This allowed Japanese companies to achieve growth rates that would have been impossible, had they simply decided to follow in the footsteps of their American rivals.

However, in order for lean production to generate higher quality, workers had to be more skilled and more committed than were those of Detroit—they had to be able to identify and rectify problems that American production workers would simply let slip through. Japanese firms could not afford to pay desperately high wages, so they made great efforts to build loyalty. Pay based on length of service already made it very difficult for workers to move from one firm to another, so firms were able to obtain loyalty while also paying low wages. Although potentially highly exploitative, the system worked for very large companies so long as sustained and rapid economic growth prevailed and the firms continued to enjoy the larger share of the growth. Under these circumstances, workers could be confident that their wages would rise through time, and that their jobs would be secure. To buttress that confidence many workers in such firms were offered lifetime employment pledges, sweetened with wages based on length of service, subsidized housing and health, and profit-related bonuses. It was the antithesis of Detroit's approach to employment policies; however, since Japan's economy was growing rapidly, the approach worked very well— and posed a challenge that Americans themselves would recognize only when it was almost too late.

*Chapter Six*

# THE GOLDEN AGE REASSESSED

*The New Industrial State*

In the fifties American companies had an impressive capacity for delivering the goods—jobs, security, profits, opportunity, and, for those at or near the top, excitement. American corporations still had their critics, of course, but few said they were economic or commercial failures. When in 1956 William Whyte published *The Organization Man* he argued instead that American corporations manipulated the minds of their workers and managers by fostering attitudes of conformism. Similarly, Vance Packard argued in *The Hidden Persuaders* that advertising manipulated consumers, and a year after that, in 1958, John Kenneth Galbraith wrote in *The Af-*

*fluent Society* that Americans could only produce consumer goods so cheaply by neglecting social welfare considerations and at the cost of gratuitous pollution. Galbraith saw public squalor hidden behind private affluence, but he did not doubt that the latter existed.[1]

The sector that still represented American industry at its most awesome was motor manufacturing. By the fifties there were only three mass manufacturers of automobiles in the United States, and they virtually monopolized the domestic market. By 1955 this meant an output of seven million automobiles, double the production of the rest of the world put together. Such a massive industry reflected and reinforced other developments: the sprawling nature of American society and the low price of gasoline notable among them. The United States was still self-sufficient in oil; although crude prices had risen sharply in the late forties, prices were back down again in the fifties. The vast Saudi Arabian oil fields were coming on stream and beginning to depress global price levels. For the oil-addicted American economy, anything that held down prices was desirable, especially since it was American companies, Texaco and Standard Oil of California (Socal), that won the Saudi contract to pump the oil from the ground.

Economic success and market concentration were apparent in other industries too. Three banks dominated American retail banking, just as Ford, General Motors, and Chrysler monopolized the market for automobiles. The Glass-Steagall Act had turned out to be no deterrent to concentration and size in banking: the three were the Chase Bank, which merged in the fifties with the Manhattan Bank to form Chase Manhattan; Citibank, formed from a merger of First National City Bank and the First National Bank of the City of New York; and Bank of America, which did not need to merge with anybody to become the largest bank in the world, so strong were the benefits that it reaped from servicing California's aerospace and other industries.[2]

Aerospace was another huge and highly concentrated industry, and one that benefited greatly from the support of the American government. During World War II, aircraft manufacturing had been the largest industry in the United States. It was centered in California, primarily, although strong in Seattle and St. Louis as well. As early as 1944, however, the orders for new aircraft started to dwindle as the American and British armed forces reached saturation levels. In 1945 the atomic bombs dropped on Japan seemed to seal the industry's fate: atomic weapons offered the politicians the promise of an awesome military capability from just a handful of aircraft and bombs. Boeing immediately closed the factory making the Super Fortress, the U.S. Air Force's big bomber. Over the next two years while most American industries boomed, production of aircraft dwindled.

As with Japanese industry, the Korean War was the savior of American aircraft manufacturing—indeed, of the armaments industry more generally. The war showed that there was little peace for the wicked, and that the old-fashioned killing methods were still the best. Then came the Cold War, and later the Sputnik, which guaranteed that Pentagon orders would keep flowing. These resulting contracts were then used to cross-subsidize civil manufacturing: Boeing and Douglas developed new jet airliners, the 707 and the DC8, on the back of contracts for military aircraft.[3] There were only four companies in the aircraft industry, competing with each other through intensive Washington lobbying for vast contracts covering many years of production; their close symbiotic relations with the Pentagon famously caused President Eisenhower in his farewell message to warn against "the acquisition of unwarranted influence, whether sought or unsought, by the military-industrial complex."[4] The fact remained that by maintaining a massive military presence—there were three million Americans on active service in 1955, a year of peace, compared with a quarter of a million before the Great Depression—the government kept the economy operating at a much higher level of demand and activity than would otherwise have been the case.[5]

## Policymaking

Partly thanks to the strength of American corporations, a new era of macroeconomic stability had entered American affairs after the war ended. During the Truman presidency the economy grew at an underlying rate of about 4 percent a year; under Eisenhower the figure was a little below 3 percent.[6] Consumers kept on spending, and American production lines kept on flowing. Admittedly, the two political parties did what they could to pick fights with one another: Republicans criticized their opponents for excessive government spending, and Democrats replied that the Republicans were neurotic about inflation and complacent about unemployment. These were, however, disagreements over margins, not over matters of principle; it seemed that growth was both easy to achieve and largely unproblematic.[7] There were recessions in 1949, 1953, 1957, and 1960, but they were all quite mild and did not threaten the economy fundamentally.

The strong performance of the economy also owed a lot to economic policies. The 1946 Employment Act had imposed on the federal government a responsibility to monitor the state of the nation's economy and to adjust policies quickly in order to prevent a repetition of the Great Depression. That meant that the administration was committed to stand ready to use taxing and spending decisions to stabilize the path of the economy and to prevent mild fluctuations from developing into acute crises. In 1945 the new Truman administration cut taxes and provided cheap loans to companies in order to tide them over the difficult period of adjustment as the nation demobilized and war contracts ended. The Serviceman's Readjustment Act of 1944, known as "the G.I. Bill," also provided funds to ex-servicemen who wanted to set themselves up in business or farming, or even to train or go to college. Thus spending held up, and fears of a postwar surge in unemployment did not occur.

Admittedly, Truman was deeply uncomfortable with the idea that governments should sometimes deliberately run budget deficits. The same was even more true of Eisenhower who, if he was ever forced to choose between conservatism and Keynes, opted for caution and a balanced budget. In 1959 and 1960 for example, Eisenhower sought to balance the budget following a sharp rise in government spending, despite the slightly sluggish state of the economy. On the whole, however, such problems were rare. The rapid growth of the economy meant that tax revenues rose strongly in the forties and fifties, and demand for welfare and health benefits fell, so that the federal government found it easy to balance its budget. The rapid growth was itself encouraged, though, by the confidence that business felt that the federal government would not allow the Great Depression to revisit the United States.

The economic policies of the Kennedy administration were initially just as conservative as those of his predecessors, although that did not allay the doubts of the financial markets, which instinctively distrusted the young leader and, according to Paul Volcker, saw Kennedy as "a young man of unknown financial credentials—and he was a Democrat." The markets sold dollars, requiring the Fed to support the currency—as Volcker says: "Against this background, we began losing more gold."[8] However, his treasury secretary, Douglas Dillon, said of Kennedy that "he was also financially conservative . . . I think it was the influence of his father."[9] Kennedy lacked strength in Congress, lacked experience, and was overshadowed by his Republican predecessor as well as by his father, all of which probably pushed him toward conservatism; his advisers, too, were cautious, counseling him not to try to undo in a year the "inadequacies of several years."[10] Accordingly, the new president espoused economic orthodoxy, just as his predecessors had: there was no tax cut in 1961, and there were no big spending plans. After an unplanned budget deficit in 1961 to accommodate extra military expenditure following the Berlin crisis, Kennedy had to be dissuaded by his advisers from raising taxes.[11] Nevertheless, he presented a balanced budget proposal to Congress in January 1962.

The president's hope was that, despite his restrictive budget, the economy would grow by 4.5 percent, and that unemployment would fall to 4 percent.[12] By June 1962, though, that optimism looked quite untenable: Kennedy's advisers told him that the economic expansion of 1961 was about to falter unless he took definite action. With an election approaching, Kennedy was forced to choose between growth and fiscal orthodoxy.

After great deliberation, the president announced in a speech at Yale that he had set his back against conservatism and opted for growth. In January 1963 he asked Congress for large cuts in both personal and corporate income taxes. Americans had seen nothing like it for thirty years. Kennedy had decided to turn away from respectability: "I am not talking about a quickie or a temporary tax cut" he said, which only made his decision more striking.[13] The greatest challenge that Kennedy's policy posed to prevailing ideas was his assertion that, since the tax cuts would stimulate economic activity, they would raise revenues and reduce the need for welfare payments, and so would be largely self-financing. Whether this theory was entirely correct is rather doubtful, and in any event Kennedy (not for the first time) failed to impress a hostile Congress: the legislature was still resisting the proposed tax cuts on November 22, 1963, when Kennedy died in Dallas.

Lyndon Johnson took over the Kennedy tax proposals, added to them, remodeled them as the Revenue Act of 1964, and then rammed them through Congress. He also won congressional approval for extra spending on health, education, and welfare, as well as for sweeping civil rights reforms. Indeed, the spending measures were much closer to the president's heart than were the tax cuts: a pork barrel career had taught Johnson that the way to keep people happy was to spend money on them. Thus the president defended the 1964 tax cut as a means to avoid recession and support growth, whereas he depicted the Great Society spending program as an heroic "unconditional war on human poverty." To a degree he was right, but many of his proposals did more to help the middle classes than people at the bottom of the income scale.[14]

Johnson's Great Society program had a less personable sibling —the Vietnam War. The conflict was directly, if morbidly, beneficial to many Americans, since it boosted output, profits, and employment in the United States, just as previous wars had. Companies in the armaments, aerospace, vehicle, and electronics sectors prospered in particular and the war provided considerable employment throughout the Sunbelt. It was hardly surprising, then, that many of the politicians who advised first Johnson and then Nixon to deepen the conflict represented, or were associated with, states whose industries benefited from the war.[15]

Thanks to the economic growth induced by the war, tax revenues rose and government health and welfare spending declined, in comparison with what they would otherwise have been. Admittedly, war spending spiraled way beyond the predictions of the Defense Department, and the president found himself sacrificing some of the Great Society program as a result; but, with the exception of 1968, when the federal budget deficit exceeded $25 billion, government borrowing generally remained low; in 1969 there was even a surplus.[16] Nevertheless, the Great Society and the Vietnam War left the American economy with very few idle resources. In the mid-sixties, with little or no slack in the economy, prices began to move sharply upward, imports increased, and companies diverted their selling efforts away from exports and toward the buoyant domestic market, with the result that the current account of the balance of payments deteriorated and inflation increased. By 1966 unemployment was well down—and inflation was a dizzying 3 percent. Eight years of almost continuous strong economic growth had closed the gap between the output actually occurring in the economy and the productive potential of which the nation was capable.

In such circumstances there seemed to be a strong case for increasing taxes. However, Johnson refused to act, reasoning that tax rises would be unpopular: the president did not want it to be said that the middle classes were having to pay, either for the Great Society or for the Vietnam War.[17] In December 1965, faced with presidential inaction, the Federal Reserve acted to raise interest rates. Investment, especially housebuilding which had grown rapidly during the upswing, immediately fell away. Public outrage was considerable, and the president severely criticized the central bank.

The Fed nevertheless stuck to its guns and kept interest rates high through 1966; only in 1967 was there some relaxation. By then, the Fed had helped to prod the government to take some action of its own: in January 1967 the Johnson administration asked Congress to approve a temporary tax surcharge. The legislature was reluctant, and it was not until June 1968 that it finally agreed to the surcharge, including some retrospective provisions. Washington was now openly admitting that there was a deep-rooted inflation problem in the United States.

## Underlying Issues

In the fifties, few people paid much attention to any competitive threat posed to American industry by companies in Japan and Western Europe—even though economic growth in those countries was already much higher than in the United States. Between 1950 and 1955 the American economy grew at an average rate of 2.4 percent per year, compared with 2.8 percent for Britain, 3.3 percent for France, 5.0 percent for Italy, 7.3 percent for Japan, and 8.1 percent for West Germany. In the 1955–60 period American growth fell sharply to just 0.6 percent a year; growth also fell in Germany, but the latter still grew nearly ten times as fast as the United States.[18] Few Americans considered the possibility that European and even Japanese firms might be catching up with, let alone overtaking, American companies. In terms of the crude volume of total output, there was clearly no contest; in terms of efficiency gains, productivity growth and even technological innovation, though, American leadership was already vulnerable.

Part of the reason why the problems were not apparent was that whereas in the fifties the United States was a net importer of goods and services from Europe, during the sixties it became a net exporter for the first time ever. That must have felt good to quite a lot of American companies. Yet the loss of their share of a market that was growing much faster than that of the United States was less easy to face. Furthermore, although the United States exported more capital equipment and chemicals than it imported, the reverse was true for consumer goods, semimanufactured items, and components for assembly. For such items, the American trade balance with the world was going badly into deficit.[19] Furthermore, during the sixties the United States became a net importer of steel on a very large scale, and in 1968, for the first time in its history, the United States imported more motor vehicles than it exported. Meanwhile, the United States was also shifting from being a net exporter of energy—mainly oil, but also coal and gas—into a net importer.

Although American industry was easily the most productive in the world, other nations had already gained in the long struggle to catch up with the Americans. In the first half of the fifties, output per head in German and Japanese manufacturing industry rose three times faster than it did in the United States. During the second half of the decade, manufacturing productivity increased ten times as fast in Germany as in the United States; in Japan it was stronger still. It seemed that no sooner had the United States established itself as overwhelmingly the largest economy in the world than other nations started to catch up.

While such statistics should not be taken at face value, the basic point remains that the fifties were a decade in which the United States faced new difficulties. For the next thirty years, successive administrations continued to ignore these problems, masked as they were by the apparent might and success of giant American companies. As a result, by the sixties the United States had a serious competitiveness problem. American productivity growth was faster than it had ever been, as was the rate of innovation—but both were lower than elsewhere, threatening American competitiveness in both price and quality terms. The large current account surpluses were destined to disappear. A dollar devaluation might provide an escape, but even that was not certain.

By the mid-sixties, furthermore, American productivity growth was starting to slow. The rapid economic growth in the decade's second half became increasingly dependent on rising government expenditure to fill the place formerly occupied by genuine industrial and commercial advance. It has become fashionable to say that the higher government spending of the sixties squeezed out the enterprise sector. On the contrary, it is more plausible that slower American productivity growth caused a vacuum that the government, rightly or wrongly, chose to fill; by doing so, it prevented the productivity problem from fully showing up at the level of overall economic growth.

Slow growth in American productivity had another effect: American companies could only prevent massive reductions in their market shares by increasing pay much more slowly than did European and Japanese firms. As a result, American costs per unit of output did not actually rise relative to costs abroad; in that sense American industry suffered no erosion in its competitiveness during the period.[20] Nevertheless, the damage was there: it was simply the workers who carried the cost, since their wages grew more slowly than did those of workers abroad. Perhaps they reckoned that the alternative was unemployment; more likely, they did not know just how much faster things were changing abroad. Either way, most Americans accepted the arrangement.

So why did it happen? To say that during the sixties low growth in real incomes masked an underlying decline in American competitiveness is to raise the question of what was going wrong. One answer—a powerful one—is that nothing was going wrong: it was just that other countries had special advantages. Americans provided other nations with help, starting with the Marshall Plan, which allowed those nations to challenge the United States for global market share. When reconstruction ended, American finance kept flowing, often accompanied by American technical and managerial knowledge. So companies in Europe and Japan grew rapidly by copying American methods. If American productivity growth in the sixties reflected genuine innovations in technology and organization, other nations achieved larger productivity gains simply by exploiting earlier American achievements.[21]

Furthermore, Japan and the nations of Europe were busily shifting resources away from low-productivity sectors, such as agriculture, into industry. The United States had done that long before and clearly could not repeat the process.[22] Finally, the reductions that Europe made in its internal trade barriers stimulated growth within the region; the United States, not part of that process, could hardly expect to benefit from lower European trade barriers.

The question remains: Why did the United States not find new ways to improve its economic performance and prevent other nation's from eroding American leadership? At first, perhaps, it did. In the fifties the American government spent $100 billion on forty-one thousand miles of interstate highways, an improvement to the nation's transport system that had an effect on the economy almost comparable to Europe's reductions of internal trade barriers. Of greater excitement was heavy American military and space spending, which gave the United States an early advantage in many industries, and also boosted the skills level of the workforce, thanks to the training provided by the army, navy, and the airforce. The government also invested heavily in the fifties in scientific and engineering research, spending much of its money on the space program and on military projects, and channeling it through academic institutions such as Stanford and MIT. According to the National Science Foundation, Americans in the fifties produced four out of every five major technological innovations in the world.[23] In that decade the employment of scientists and engineers grew at nearly four times the average rate of increase in employment. From the mid-fifties to the mid-sixties American expenditure on research and development almost doubled as a share of the gross national product.

Of particular importance was investment in new communications technology. Initially funded by the armed forces, the investment boosted the growth of the telecommunications industry and of television, so that by the late sixties Bell Labs, for example, which had started with wartime government contracts, had fifteen thousand people on its payroll. A similar story applied to RCA, which dominated the production of radios and later televisions, and which cleverly based its huge research facility at Princeton. RCA pioneered the development of computers, although it was IBM which did the most to promote their adoption by combining in true American-style innovation with a sharp focus on marketing. Thanks to IBM, computers spread through American industry long before they became important in other countries, conferring advantages across a range of activities from basic inventory control to the design of advanced technological products.

Unfortunately, during the sixties the pace of American innovation began to slow as both companies and government reduced the share of their resources that they devoted to research and development.[24] By the middle of the decade, the National Science Foundation has reported, Americans generated only one out of every two of the world's major technological innovation. No single country was as large a source of innovation as the United States, but collectively the rest of the world was now on a par with the United States. A 1968 research published by the OECD painted a similar picture: the United States no longer had an overall technological lead, and the OECD questioned whether in such important industries as pharmaceuticals, steel manufacturing, bulk plastics, and machine tools, American leadership had ever existed.[25] In computers and electronics the United States was still well ahead, but mainly thanks to government support.

In the second half of the sixties American research and development expenditure declined in real terms.[26] The bulk of the cuts fell on long-term and high-risk research; the number of patents granted to American individuals or firms peaked at the end of the sixties and declined through the seventies. Exceptions were in pharmaceuticals and agricultural chemicals, both industries in which activity was accelerating in other countries too; this followed a trend already established of fewer inventions making it to market. In the early seventies the growth in employment of scientists and engineers fell to just one third of the average rate of employment growth, and the average age of American scientists and engineers increased sharply—a sure indication of an ossification of the research function within companies.

By the seventies the impact of slow growth in research and development expenditure was becoming increasingly apparent in world trade shares. During the previous decade the American share of world trade in technology-intensive products had barely changed; in the seventies it fell by about a fifth. Japanese companies were the victors.[27] When asked to explain these trends, American companies lamely said that breakthroughs seemed harder to achieve than in the past, or that government regulations were becoming too onerous.[28] More to the point, however, government subsidies were dwindling due to the end of the Vietnam War and the running-down of the space program. Companies were also attempting to "improve" the management of their research and development effort by placing greater emphasis on short-term profit gains and on meeting performance targets.[29]

In the sixties, for perhaps the first time, foreign markets began to rival the domestic market, in terms both of growth and size, and as a result firms such as Ford and International Telephone and Telegraph (ITT) began to pay increasing attention to overseas sales prospects. Many American firms decided to set about establishing production facilities in Europe and the Third World, where production costs were low and productivity growth was high.[30] Others that had been operating overseas since the start of the century raised their commitments. For obvious reasons the oil industry had been shifting abroad since the forties, when it accounted for a third of all American postwar overseas direct investment, but other industries now followed. The automobile industry, too, greatly increased its existing foreign investment—Ford had been making automobiles in Britain since 1910—as did chemicals companies and those in the electrical sector. By the end of the sixties the output of American companies located abroad outnumbered American exports four to one—and many of the exports were simply transfers from one part of an American multinational corporation to another. By 1970 thirty-five hundred American firms had overseas subsidiaries, while ITT, the quintessential multinational, had two hundred thousand employees in Europe alone.[31] The largest economy in the world was the United States; the second largest was American companies operating abroad.

The fact that American companies could set themselves up in

foreign countries and win large market shares was testimony to the abilities of American firms, in particular to their organizational strengths.[32] Many American firms tended to produce only semi-manufactured items and components in the Third World, since American and European tariffs did not discriminate against those items and they could be sold cheaply in the United States as well as in the Third World itself. Such giant American firms often conducted certain activities in some parts of the world and other activities elsewhere, developing global structures that brought a large proportion of world trade within their bureaucratic structures—replicating on a global scale what men such as John Rockefeller had done in the United States almost a century earlier. Although there were costs involved in such bureaucracies, operating abroad was still more profitable than operating at home, and the largest American companies made one third of their profits abroad.[33] For the firms that was not a problem, but for the American economy it represented a possible source of danger.

The increasing tendency for American firms to look abroad for new markets for existing products rather than to invest at home in product innovation was reminiscent of the transformation that occurred in Britain in the late nineteenth century. It was argued in chapter 2 that the change that took place in Victorian Britain was partly a reflection of the economic and political strength of the nation's financial community, and the weak ties between industry and the banks. The same can perhaps be said of the United States in the sixties and seventies. Although in this period the United States ran a balance of payments surplus on its current account, a declining part of the surplus was generated by the nation's factories and an increasing proportion by its banks, service companies, and earnings on earlier overseas investments. The United States was becoming a rentier economy: the banks wanted and got a strong dollar, which was bad news for American industry that needed a weak currency to protect its competitiveness, so American companies built factories abroad rather than at home.

The division between banks and corporate borrowers deepened in the sixties, as the big American banks shifted at the margin away from conventional deposit taking and lending, and toward new methods of finance.[34] The effect was to push banks and their clients even further apart, exacerbating the mistakes made in the thirties following the Pecora committee. In 1961 Citibank pioneered the issue of certificates of deposit (CDs) in which the banks issued pieces of paper or CDs stating that they held funds on deposit from particular corporate clients, and the clients then sold the CDs on the open market to other savers. Soon an equivalent arrangement developed for the deposits of American companies operating abroad—the Eurodollar market. On the lending side, companies such as General Motors would issue so-called commercial papers or CPs in exchange for cash from pension funds and other big institutions, and the banks would merely manage the transactions, picking up fees for doing so.

The banks knew little about the firms for whom they arranged finance, which made it even more difficult for them to take long-term views on the relative strengths and weaknesses of different corporate borrowers. This put pressure on American companies to achieve high profits in the short term, rather than adopting a more relaxed approach, since otherwise they could not readily obtain finance. Partly as a result, the corporate sector was deflected from intensive technology-led growth and toward extensive market-led growth. Together, these developments discouraged heavy investment in research and innovation, since such activities implied risk; instead, it encouraged American companies to look abroad for markets and production opportunities, since high sales, rapid productivity gains, and low wages were all more immediately available abroad than in the United States.

The rise of market rather than bank financing had another effect. In such a system, the cheapest financing costs went to the largest companies—but only if they used their size to increase their security rather than to allow themselves to take risks by innovation. The merger boom in the sixties rivaled that of the last years of the nineteenth century, but this time as American companies grew they became less, not more, innovative. Whereas in the fifties large American companies grew faster than medium-size ones, during the sixties the largest firms only kept pace with the economy as a whole, and the real innovation was confined to smaller firms such as Hewlett Packard and Texas Instruments.

## The United States and Free Trade

In the fifties American industrial problems were yet to manifest themselves fully, and Americans were impatient about the slow progress toward the global free trade that they had been promised in the forties, and that was described in chapter 5. Part of the blame for that rested with Congress, which remained as protectionist as ever. In 1945 it insisted on an escape clause in all future tariff negotiations, allowing the United States to renege on tariff cuts, and in 1948 it established a tariff commission whose job it would be to set minimum levels below which the president could not reduce tariffs. In 1955 Congress decreed that no tariff cuts could be agreed relating to the arms industry, a provision that was extended in 1958 to cover many other industries supposedly vital to national defense.[35]

Against that background it is hardly surprising that the attempts made by successive American administrations to use the GATT mechanism to secure agreements to tariff cuts failed. This became serious in 1958, when the creation of the European Common Market promised a new era of rapid growth in intra-European trade, from which the United States naturally would not directly benefit. In American eyes, Europe's preoccupation with promoting intra-European trade was a distraction from efforts to improve transatlantic trade agreements. At worst, Europe was denying the United States full access to its markets, and thereby stunting the natural growth of the American economy. In 1960 the fifth round of GATT talks got underway, but the tariff commission impeded the administration's attempts to achieve worthwhile tariff cuts, and little was achieved.

In any case, the Eisenhower administration had itself become more protectionist by then, and neither the president nor his staff made much attempt to change congressional thinking. Kennedy, in contrast, came into office in 1961 a committed free-marketeer with the ambition of reasserting American global leadership in the trade sphere as in other areas of policy.[36] Accordingly, the new president proposed that the United States (and Canada) should gain entry to the Organization for European Economic Cooperation (OEEC), which would be suitably renamed the Organization for Economic Cooperation and Development (OECD). He spoke grandly of an "Atlantic partnership" between Europe and the United States—but since the OEEC had never quite taken off as the body charged with integrating Europe's economies, Kennedy's initiative achieved little.

More impressive was Kennedy's success at getting Congress to agree to a new trade bill, passed in 1962 as the Trade Expansion Act, which empowered him both to halve all tariffs and to negotiate with the European Economic Community (EEC) for the reduction of the especially high tariffs that the United States operated against the Common Market. Armed with that power, Kennedy asked for a further round of GATT negotiations on tariff reductions, with the primary purpose of persuading Europe to reduce its discrimination against American exports. Where previous GATT rounds had focused on negotiating tariff cuts, industry by industry, the intention this time was to seek agreement to a general overall tariff cut, covering almost all industries, to be implemented in stages. Although perhaps a riskier approach, it offered the possibility of a great success for Kennedy.

The initiative immediately faced problems, though. The Europeans refused to discuss tariff cuts for iron and steel, chemicals, textiles, and food—a fairly long list. Furthermore, Congress had only given the administration permission to reduce tariffs against the EEC on those products for which American-EEC trade accounted for 80 percent of the world total. In 1962 Britain was applying for EEC membership, and since Britain was still a major trader, the congressional stipulation promised to cover a wide range of products. In January 1963, however, France's President De Gaulle vetoed British entry to the Common Market: without Britain's inclusion, the number of products covered by the 80 percent rule was much reduced, and the potential significance of the Kennedy round reduced accordingly.

It took until 1967 for the United States to secure a GATT agreement with Europe and the rest of the world, and although the resultant deal is often described as a great triumph, it was modest in comparison with the original ambitions of the American government.[37] Participants agreed to tariff cuts averaging 35 percent on sixty thousand different goods: American tariffs on manufactured goods came down to about 10–20 percent, as did Japan's, and Europe's tariffs came down to an average 10 percent. However, world trade was already rising rapidly, and the GATT settlement merely gave that process a further boost.

One source of the growth in world trade was Japan, which by the late sixties was emerging as a major player. For the first time, Americans began to buy Japanese consumer goods in large quantities—something that quite literally brought home the strength of Japan's trading challenge. In Washington, politicians began to complain that the Japanese denied foreigners access to their own markets while having easy access to other countries' markets.

It was certainly true that as Japan had become increasingly independent in the late fifties and sixties it had used import restrictions, export subsidies, and other measures to bolster its economy. Despite that, from the early seventies the Japanese were importing just as much relative to their gross domestic product as the Americans; and although their export-to-GDP ratio was higher, it was less than half that of the European average. The peculiarity of world trade in the seventies, then, was the very low level of American exports, not the trading performance of Japan.[38] The real trade villains of the late sixties and early seventies were probably the Europeans, who explicitly discriminated against imports from Japan and much of the Third World, in blatant violation of GATT. Much of the discrimination took the form of nontariff measures, as did American trade discrimination. In 1970 Congress sensibly rejected a bill imposing automatic quotas in any industry in which imports reached a certain share of the domestic market, but in 1975 it approved the American Trade Act, giving companies the right to apply for tariffs against imports in industries in which companies abroad obtained government subsidies. By then, the United States already operated quotas—disguised as voluntary agreements— against Japanese, Korean, and Taiwanese products.

It was to deal with such behavior that the next round of GATT talks was convened in Tokyo in 1973. By then, trade barriers were effectively higher in real terms than they had been a decade earlier.[39] The Tokyo talks dragged on, just as the Kennedy discussions had, ending only in 1979. Although the talks resulted in general agreements to reduce nontariff barriers and to establish a set of codes of good behavior, the Europeans still insisted that they would, if necessary, exercise their right under GATT's Article 19 to discriminate against "disruptive" low-cost imports. Furthermore, the Tokyo Round led to the Multi Fiber Agreement, under which countries adopted bilateral quotas for trade in textiles. Thus adherence to the basic GATT principle of nondiscrimination would occur only on a case-by-case basis, rendering it not much of a principle at all.

Neither the Kennedy nor the Tokyo round was a great triumph for the United States. In its attitude toward trade and GATT, Congress had veered between skepticism and open protectionism; the same was true, if less markedly so, for various administrations (with Kennedy's short presidency being the main exception). Under these circumstances, there was a permanent temptation to abandon GATT, with its protracted and acrimonious negotiations, and instead to strike bilateral deals with foreign governments. The fact that the United States did not do so, and instead struggled on with GATT, is probably a testimony to the potential threat to American trading interests posed by the Common Market.

The Kennedy and Tokyo rounds did little for the Third World— a failure that would later come to haunt the United States. In 1947, at the Geneva Conference, almost all the world's developing nations had denounced GATT, saying that it was designed to prevent them industrializing. GATT's unequal tariffs allowed countries to impose higher tariffs on imports of finished manufactured goods than on raw material imports, thus tending to keep industry located in the nations that were already highly industrialized. Thus during the fifties, representatives of the Third World called for a more equal trading regime than GATT apparently offered.

However, in 1964 the secretary general of the newly created United Nations Conference on Trade and Development (UNCTAD), Raul Prebisch, published a now famous report, "Towards a New Trade Policy for Development," in which he argued that even if tariffs were equal, the Third World would still be disadvantaged by trade.[40] Prebisch argued that over the long term the world prices of fuel, food, and raw materials were bound to fall in comparison with the prices of manufactured goods and services. Thus if Third World nations exported only commodities and imported manufactured products and services, they would find it ever more difficult to make their trade numbers add up: they would need an increasing volume of commodities exports to finance existing imports of manufactured goods and services. Indeed, the amount of the latter that they could afford would probably decline inexorably.

Prebisch's advice, like that of many other experts, was for Third World nations to reduce their need to import. He advised developing nations to manufacture goods that they currently imported from the industrialized nations, just as Latin American nations such as Argentina had done in the thirties and forties, and to export not just the old cheap commodities but also advanced manufactured goods and services.

Prebisch, like Hamilton two centuries earlier, rejected the liberal principle of nondiscrimination, advocating instead what became known as "import substitution." He argued that GATT's emphasis on equality of tariffs should be dropped in favor of a so-called generalized system of preferences, under which industrialized nations would grant tariff reductions on particular imports from developed countries on a nonreciprocal basis. Prebisch even argued that tariff cuts between industrialized nations should not occur, since the world's immediate need was to allow the Third World to export more to the industrialized nations, and high tariffs between industrialized countries would encourage precisely that.

Some of the evidence seemed to support some of Prebisch's arguments. Japan in particular prospered in the fifties and sixties on the back of cheap oil and cheap raw materials. Furthermore, when oil and other commodity prices rose in the seventies, Japan's prosperity rose still further as companies economized on fuel and raw materials, and as they increased the value-added content of their output. These gains seemed to be made at the expense of much of the Third World.

To make matters worse, Japan and the other industrialized nations supported their own farmers and kept out cheaper food from abroad. In many cases, the West even extended that policy to embrace old and inefficient manufacturing sectors, thereby further limiting the opportunities available to developing countries. For many Third World governments, then, Prebisch's import substitution policies seemed the only viable approach to development.

However, most of the evidence showed that import substitution worked better in theory than in practice. Countries such as Brazil and, to a lesser extent, Mexico found that after a decade of pursuing Prebisch's policies, they were still exporting the same low-value commodities they had been exporting in the forties, yet were consuming domestically produced goods that they could have bought more cheaply from abroad. Nor did their imports fall: rather, as they focused on raising domestic production of certain goods, they found themselves importing *more* of other things, ranging from food to machinery and equipment. Even the basic premise that the prices of their exports would tend to fall relative to the prices of their imports proved to be incorrect.[41]

As a result of the failure of import substitution, increasing numbers of Third World governments turned to American and other foreign companies in order to establish manufacturing and other facilities in their countries. This met the needs of the firms themselves, and it accorded with the latter's growing belief that global free trade was becoming just a dream. As in the interwar period, the way to avoid the effects of tariffs was to spread production around the world.[42]

While governments in most Third World nations welcomed multinational corporations, many radicals feared that the multinationals were more powerful than the governments of the countries in which they operated. They saw the multinationals as agents of American imperialism. Although the multinationals were by no means all Americans, and there was no explicitly imperial system governing their workings, it was generally true that apart from those who worked directly in them, most multinational operations conferred few additional benefits on their host countries. Firms such as Exxon, General Motors, and IBM did not generally disseminate much technology, nor did they distribute much profit locally. In many cases, especially the old mining and quarrying firms, the multinationals also obliged their workers to accept appalling working conditions and deprivations in return for minimal wages.

Furthermore, when host governments sought to introduce policies that the multinationals did not like, the companies would often look to their own governments to bring political pressure to bear on their behalf. In the case of American firms, there was often much that Washington could and did do. In 1954, for example, the CIA sponsored right-wing Guatemalan guerrillas who, in league with the local military, overthrew the government of Jacobo Arbenz. The government had been about to confiscate unused land held by the region's largest company, the American-owned United Fruit Company. A former member of United Fruit's board of trustees, Allen Dulles, was head of the CIA when it backed the Guatemalan coup, while Secretary of State John Foster Dulles was a former member of the law firm that advised United Fruit.[43]

A decade and a half later, in 1970, Chile's newly elected Allende government attempted to revive its economy by restricting repatriation of profits and by nationalizing American firms and renegotiating interest payments. These policies rightly disturbed many American firms, and the American government embarked on a campaign to undermine Allende, orchestrated a financial blockade, and gave support to the military, which in 1973 launched a coup and murdered the president.

Such political machinations might have mattered less if the Third World had shared more equally in the expansion of the world economy. In developing countries in the sixties, however, many nations lost ground compared with the industrialized West; even the better-off nations such as Argentina failed to participate in the long boom of the West, so in relative terms they lost ground. The result was that as the twentieth century progressed global poverty, far from diminishing, became worse. Many Third World nations criticized the West, certainly for failing to give enough help, and perhaps for growing at the expense of the poorer nations.

Frustrated by the Kennedy round of GATT talks, developing countries instead placed their faith in UNCTAD, which had been meeting every four years since 1964. UNCTAD had continued to advocate its generalized system of preferences (GSP), under which industrialized nations would grant tariff reductions on particular imports from developed countries without expecting any reciprocal tariff cuts from their trading partners. For a decade the United States continuously opposed the GSP. However, in 1974 the United Nations adopted a Charter of Economic Rights and Duties of States, expressing the desire of Third World countries for a New International Economic Order (NIEO).[44] The world's poorer nations asserted the right of commodity-producing countries to form cartels as well as the right to nationalize foreign-owned companies. The NIEO also articulated the case for international regulation of multinational corporations.

Faced with this threat, the United States remained implacable. In contrast, in 1975 the countries of the European Common Market and forty-six nations from the Third World signed the Lome Convention, agreeing to nonreciprocal tariff cuts on particular items.[45] A second Lome Convention followed in 1979. Under the terms of these treaties, Europe offered free access to its markets for almost all items from most of the countries of Africa, the Caribbean, and the Pacific, while allowing those countries to discriminate against European exports. In addition, the European Development Fund would provide grants and interest-free loans to the poorest countries whenever world demand conditions caused their export earnings to fall below certain levels.

These deals offered potentially great benefits both to Europe and to the Third World participants. Along with smaller deals in the seventies, they occurred quite outside the GATT framework that the United States had championed, and thus further signified the importance to the world of the European Common Market.

## The Fall of the Dollar

However, the most visible sign of the limits of American economic influence occurred not in the trade sphere, but in the area of currency management. During the fifties the world operated with two international financial systems: on the one hand, the European Payments Union (EPU), which extended to most of the colonies and former colonies that used European currencies in their international settlements; and, on the other, the American-led dollar area.[46] Mechanisms existed for settlements between the two areas, which assuaged American anxieties about being frozen out, but the fact remained that much of the world conducted its trade not in dollars but in European currencies, especially in sterling. It was this European system, and not the ideas or institutions of Bretton Woods, that was central to much of the international economic expansion of the fifties.

As the decade progressed there was heavy selling of the dollar in the international currency markets. Since the Federal Reserve was committed to keeping the currency stable, it was forced to buy up the dollars that other central banks were offloading, and hence sell large amounts of gold. The American government was reluctant to devalue the dollar, since it felt that such a move would reduce the nation's financial leverage over Europe and the world generally—a view that was tenable only if one believed, against the evidence, that such nations would continue to be desperate for American finance.[47] Instead, in December 1958 the major European governments announced that they were finally willing to buy or sell dollars on the open market in exchange for their own currencies. This announcement, often referred to as the long-awaited instigation of the Bretton Woods system, signaled the Europeans' confidence in the strength of their own currencies relative to the dollar as a result of the remarkable economic performance of the European economies in the fifties. Europe's currencies were now just as solid as the dollar.

The announcement threatened to provoke a stampede out of the dollar; to avoid such a crisis, and to give the Americans time to get their house in order, the Europeans waited until February 1961 before they put their plan into action. Even so, the American authorities spent the remainder of the sixties worrying about the manifest overvaluation of the dollar and the likelihood that the currency would collapse. In the middle of the decade the escalation of the Vietnam War added to the reluctance of both American and foreign institutions to hold American assets. The Vietnam War used up all of the United States' spare resources, and so made the country more prone to inflation. The trade account deteriorated as American industry concentrated on meeting military demands rather than selling to consumers and industries at home and abroad. For these reasons alone, the dollar came under inevitable pressure, but that became much worse as it became increasingly clear that the United States had no easy way to win the conflict, and that the war was creating severe political and social tensions at home. In these circumstances any economic policies that the administration might devise were bound to lack credibility, destroying market confidence in the dollar and, indeed, in American prospects more generally.[48]

In the second half of the decade American and foreign bankers and economists made repeated attempts to devise a new composite currency, in order to take the pressure off the dollar. Although American officials hoped that such an initiative would make the American currency stronger, in truth the efforts recalled Keynes's view that a synthetic currency would eventually be needed, to replace the dollar as the center of a system of fixed exchange rates. In 1968, after protracted negotiations the IMF issued the new currency, confusingly called Special Drawing Rights or SDRs, to debtor countries. The scale of the issues was so small that the SDRs made only a tiny difference; the dollar remained under heavy selling pressure, and the Federal Reserve had to sell increasing amounts of gold to support the value of the American currency at the rate fixed in 1958.[49] Both to help the Americans out and to maintain the fixed exchange rate regime, Europe's central banks, especially Germany's Bundesbank, also bought dollars, although in their case they had to sell their own currencies in exchange. The Bundesbank had already secretly promised the Americans in 1967 not to sell dollars, apparently in exchange for a commitment that the Americans would not relieve their financial problems by withdrawing troops from Europe.

None of that was enough, though: in 1968 the American government finally announced that while it would abide by the existing system of fixed exchange rates in its dealings with central banks, it would no longer promise to buy dollars and sell gold at the hitherto fixed price of $35 per ounce when dealing with private individuals, companies, and institutions.

From then on, however, the situation only worsened. It soon became clear that President Johnson's 1968 tax rise had done nothing to slow the economy. Part of the problem was perhaps that the government undermined its own policy credibility by describing the tax increase as merely a temporary measure. Although he modestly tightened fiscal policy, President Nixon continued this approach and was careful to describe his policies as gentle and only temporary. He did not want to create the impression that defeating inflation was going to be a long hard haul. That failed to match the realism of American companies and consumers, who reckoned that inflation had been growing for several years, was putting down roots, and would be hard to dislodge.

By 1969 inflation was 5.5 percent, and the unemployment rate was only roughly 3.5 percent: inflation was higher, and unemployment lower, than generally expected. This suited Nixon, who had plenty of political problems arising from the Vietnam War, and preferred not to add to his difficulties by presiding over high unemployment. From an early stage in his presidency, he had refused to consider policies that might increase unemployment. However, the Federal Reserve had different priorities, and it again attempted to slow the economy and protect the dollar by raising interest rates—an act that provoked widespread criticism, not least from Milton Friedman. In an article for *Newsweek*, Friedman accused the Fed of overreacting to inflation and undermining American economic growth.

In fact, the tighter monetary policy did not affect inflation, although in 1969 economic growth did slow sharply; it seemed that inflation was not only rising higher but was becoming harder to fight. Nixon had little stomach for such a battle. When, in 1970, he was presented with the opportunity to appoint a new chairman to the Fed's board of governors, he gave the post to Arthur Burns, a longtime political ally and former adviser to President Eisenhower. Two weeks after starting work on January 31, 1971, Burns relaxed monetary policy; it remained that way until after Nixon's reelection.

In 1971 the American trade account went into deficit for the first time since World War II, and in August of that year Treasury Secretary John Connolly discovered that the Treasury had only $10 billion in gold and foreign currencies with which to defend the dollar. Connolly persuaded Nixon that something had to be done, so they removed to Camp David for a conference, accompanied by Arthur Burns and Paul Volcker, then number two at the Treasury. Connolly's view was that for a decade Europe had been dictating American policy, and that European governments had kept their currencies artificially low, forcing the Americans to accept an overvalued dollar.[50] Initially in the early sixties most European governments were indeed well aware that they benefited from the overvalued dollar; but by the end of the decade, with mounting problems in their domestic economies, the prospect of a dollar devaluation scared them.

For Connolly, this seemed a great advantage: he believed that a lower dollar would pull the American economy out of recession, and that this should be achieved in a way that would blast the Europeans out of their complacency. His assumption was that after a period of turmoil in the world's currency markets, governments would get together to reconstruct a new set of parities involving a more competitive dollar—and that *those* parities would then be sustainable and defensible.

Connolly and Volcker put together a New Economic Policy for the United States, consisting of three elements. First, prices and wages would be frozen: the government would suspend the price mechanism. Second, imports would be taxed: free trade was forgotten. And third, the dollar would be floated: the United States would abandon the symbolic centerpiece of its leadership of a stable world economic order.

Shortly after taking office in 1969, Nixon had promised the American public, "we will not take the nation down the road of wage and price controls."[51] He now reneged on his promise, and imposed a prices and wages freeze: with inflation at 4 percent and rising, the White House announced on August 15, 1971, that for ninety days there were to be almost no increases in either prices or wages. Three months later came phase two: prices could now be increased in line with costs, and wages could be increased by 5.5 percent per year, or more in special cases. The inflation rate dropped down below 4 percent, and the economy continued to grow; the policy, it seemed, was working and phase two remained in force throughout 1972.

Nixon's staff designed these rules and regulations as much to impress the nation as to have a serious impact on inflation.[52] Soon they replaced phase two with phase three, a less restrictive set of measures that utterly fell apart when inflation reached double figures in June 1973. Nixon then imposed a complete freeze for two months, under the strange name of "phase 3½"—surely a sign of an administration that had lost its grip. Then came phase four, which lasted until April 1974, when the government abandoned the whole frustrating apparatus and buried it without mourners.

Even so, there were some superficial successes. From the start, farm prices and the prices of imported fuel and raw materials were exempt from the controls. Investment piled into these sectors, all the more so because their prices were rising sharply. The inflation problem remained, but initially it had been squeezed into a very narrow range of commodities. (The same was to happen in the eighties when inflation shifted away from consumer prices and toward financial asset prices.) However, this move only made it hard to spot: look at what's happening to the money supply, warned Milton Friedman and other monetarists. But Washington was not yet ready to listen.

Beyond the United States the decisions to unpeg the dollar and impose a tax on imports provoked the most astonishment. For Japan's leaders, these came as a particularly severe shock. Only a few months earlier, John Connolly had promised the Japanese government that the dollar would not be devalued, so the Japanese could hardly believe it when it happened. They seemed to get no guidance from Washington, were given no advance warning of the measure, and were not advised afterward what the reasons for the policy were. Toyoo Gyohten, a senior official in the ministry of finance, writes that "we were not sure what the Americans were really aiming at . . ."[53] In the resulting climate of distrust, the Japanese government suspected that the Americans and Europeans were ganging up against the Japanese to devise a new international monetary order that would exclude the yen.

Japan's sense of betrayal was boosted by the fact that the dollar devaluation was the second "Nixon shock" to which they had been exposed within a month: in July, Washington had announced that Henry Kissinger had recently visited Beijing, and that President Nixon would visit China in 1972. The alliance between the United States and Japan against China had been a pillar of Japanese politics; now the American government had unilaterally undermined that arrangement, at a time when it was already embarking on a withdrawal from Vietnam. The humiliation of not being consulted probably cost Prime Minister Eisaku Sato his job. In future, the

Japanese would try to be much smarter about making sure that their interests were considered by other nations, however mighty.

Europe's response to the Nixon devaluation was more measured, since European governments and central bankers had been much better placed to see the policy reversal coming. Indeed, the Bundesbank had debated floating the deutschemark in May 1971.[54] After the dollar devaluation the European governments negotiated a new exchange rate regime, which came into force in April 1972; although the dollar was again fixed against the European currencies as a whole, the Europeans developed sophisticated arrangements for allowing modest currency fluctuations without letting them get out of hand, arrangements to which the dollar was not party. Meanwhile, rising inflation in the United States and a worsening American balance of payments were beginning to make even the new dollar parity look too high. As a result, in February 1973, the dollar was devalued once again. A month later, the American government finally abandoned the idea of a fixed exchange rate for the dollar. Despite the supposed preeminent role of the dollar, the fixed exchange rate system had always seemed like a European club; now this had become more or less official. In the management of the world economy the United States was, it seemed, being left behind.

*Chapter Seven*

# CRISES

# IN THE

# SEVENTIES

## *Power Shift in the Oil Market*

In April 1959 the governments of the main Arab oil-producing
nations met in Cairo: British Petroleum, one of the world's largest
oil companies, had decided unilaterally to reduce the price that it
paid for oil, and the Arab governments wanted to agree to a collective response.[1] However, the conference failed to produce a consensus, leaving BP and the other oil companies congratulating
themselves on their victory over the producing nations. What they
did not know was that in secret sessions held at a deserted sailing
club on the outskirts of town, the Cairo meeting continued: together with "observers" from other oil-producing countries, the

Arab ministers laid out plans for a producers' cartel that would grab power away from the Western oil companies.

By the end of the meeting the producers had concluded a gentleman's agreement but lacked the determination to make it stick: each country always wanted the Western companies to take more of its own oil, and with the Soviet Union exporting heavily, prices stayed depressed. Under such circumstances the putative Arab cartel posed no risk to the West; on the contrary, the oil companies were alarmed by just how much oil was coming onto the market from various sources, and Standard Oil of New Jersey (later Exxon) decided to teach all the producers a lesson. In August 1960 it repeated the BP move and cut the price that it paid for oil; other oil companies followed suit.

In September the oil-producing nations held another conference, in Baghdad. The mood was more militant, and the participants agreed to create a cartel in order to give them bargaining power over the oil companies. Thus OPEC, the Organization of Petroleum Exporting Countries, was born. Initially, the oil companies showed no concern: although OPEC's members produced four fifths of the world's oil, the Soviet Union was supplying the world with as much oil as it could, and explorations in Africa promised a new source of crude that would marginalize the position of the Middle East. Furthermore, the Arabs were ill at ease with one another. Indeed, the most important nation in the region, Iran, was not even Arabic, and was often at loggerheads with Saudi Arabia. As long as there were no more clumsy attempts from the oil companies to slash prices without consultation, OPEC would, they believed, remain divided and unimportant.

For most of the sixties, this held true. However, demand for oil was rising sharply. The United States was massively inefficient in its use of oil; pressure from the domestic oil companies prevented successive governments from doing anything that might reduce that inefficiency, such as increasing taxes on gasoline. The growth of the United States was also heavily skewed by investment in consumer goods, cars, trucks, and capital equipment—all intensive users of gasoline or of oil-based products such as plastics. As new highways crisscrossed the nation, the more fuel efficient railway system fell into disrepair.

The world economy also grew rapidly, led by Japan, which, with few energy resources of its own, had an increasing impact on the global oil market.[2] Even in Europe reliance on oil products increased as coal fell out of favor. War in Vietnam, too, added to the rising demand, and for a while civil war in Nigeria, now an important producing country, added a further upward influence on prices.

And still the crunch did not come. In 1967 the Arab nations announced a boycott of oil shipments to the United States, the United Kingdom, and West Germany as punishment for supporting Israel in the Six-Day War. The boycott was a failure, though: prices barely responded, and the three nations found plenty of other sources of oil. It was, rather, the producers who suffered—Egypt in particular almost bankrupted itself, thanks to the combination of defeat by Israel and a failed boycott. Soon world production was higher than ever, and rising faster than demand.

Eventually, however, the balance was bound to tip. The 1969–70 winter was the coldest for thirty years. Demand for oil in the United States began to outstrip supply. Oil import quotas, introduced in the fifties by President Eisenhower to protect American oil companies from foreign competition, prevented the nation from importing all that it needed; although Richard Nixon had entered office wanting to scrap the quotas, he had backed down in the face of oil industry lobbying. After years of government protection and underinvestment, American oil firms were now finding it difficult to get enough oil out of the ground to satisfy the domestic market, let alone exports. This state of affairs prevailed until 1970, when for environmental reasons, a court injunction halted work on a pipeline to Prince William Sound: the Alaskan oil field was to have been the new Texas, but instead it stood idle, some feared perhaps permanently. For the first year on record American wells were pumping at full capacity.

In May 1970 a tractor accidentally ruptured the Trans Arabian Pipeline in Syria; the resulting increase in the world oil price was ominously sharp. Seizing the moment, Muammar al-Qaddafi, the new leader of Libya, demanded that prices paid to his country should rise; if not, he would close down the oil industry that supplied one third of Europe's oil. When Qaddafi won agreement, the other oil-producing nations gained confidence from the Libyan example and began to raise prices, one after another.

The oil companies became impatient. In view of the price leapfrogging that was taking place, they thought it better if they negotiated only with OPEC as a whole. Both the Iranians and the Saudi Arabians warned that doing so would give a boost to the radicals, who would win over the moderates, with the result that the price eventually agreed upon would be very high: indeed, a complete OPEC boycott of all the importing nations was now a serious possibility. In February 1971 the oil companies heeded the advice and agreed on a price with Iran and the Gulf states. Two months later they agreed to pay Libya, Saudi Arabia, and Iraq a higher price.

In 1971, as part of the wider anti-inflationary policy introduced with the dollar devaluation, the American government finally froze gasoline prices. Demand really did outstrip supply: in 1972 the utility companies warned of possible power cuts. Still the president did nothing about oil quotas: he had an election to win. Then in April 1973, with the election under his belt, Nixon finally abolished quotas, transferring the problem of the oil shortage from the domestic to the international arena. The United States soon became a net oil importer, for the first time in history.

From 1971 to 1973 the world experienced a sharp boom in industrial output as governments abroad expanded their economies; they hoped that by doing so they would offset the effect of the Nixon devaluation. With demand stoking up in the industrialized world, bottlenecks developed as economies found themselves operating close to full capacity. Crop failures in the Soviet Union and elsewhere helped to drive up food prices, while underinvestment, after a decade of low prices, helped to push up industrial material prices.

Although many journalists and officials busied themselves writing articles and memoranda predicting an oil shortage and a sudden sharp increase in prices, the American government ignored them: the same story had been heard before and had been wrong. Furthermore, so long as global excess demand was contributing to the rise in commodity prices in the early seventies, no individual country could expect its domestic prices to stabilize. The traditional remedy for inflation—squeeze the economy—was unlikely to work unless other countries applied it too; policymakers recognized the fact, and used it as an excuse to do nothing about inflation.[3] By the first half of 1973 the *average* growth rate of the industrialized economies was an annualized 8 percent. Non-oil commodity prices increased by more than half compared with their 1972 level; by the end of the year, prices had doubled.

Meanwhile the Egyptian government was preparing to break the diplomatic deadlock that had persisted since the Six-Day War with Israel. There had been a number of armed skirmishes, but now the Saudi Arabians had agreed to finance a full war, and would use an oil embargo to make the United States abandon its support for Israel. Although several Arab governments warned the American government about the plans, Washington made no attempt to alleviate diplomatic tensions in the region, and placed no pressure on the oil companies to strike an early and amicable agreement with OPEC. As a result, OPEC and the oil companies were still negotiating in Vienna in October 1973 when the Middle East went to war; two weeks later came the oil embargo.

The embargo itself did not work very well—it lasted only until December. However, the OPEC price that replaced the embargo was four times higher than the oil companies were accustomed to paying. Although governments in the United States, Japan, and Europe busied themselves encouraging their citizens to reduce energy demand, they knew it would not work: higher oil prices were a fact of life. Policymakers in the United States and in other industrialized countries were appalled at the problems that the OPEC price hike seemed to have visited upon them: the worst inflation, the worst recession, and the worst balance of payments problems since the thirties.

The industrialized nations, especially the United States, responded quickly to the OPEC embargo. The fundamental dilemma was that the higher prices were likely to exert forces both inflationary and deflationary at the same time—inflationary because they directly added to the costs of consumers and manufacturers, threatening a spiral of higher wages and prices, and deflationary because the increased revenue would go directly to the OPEC nations, few of which had much need to spend their windfalls. In 1974 the increase in oil prices took about $65 billion out of the world economy; only $15 billion was put back in the form of higher expenditure by the OPEC nations.[4] Partly because of that, and partly because governments in the industrialized world decided to deflate their economies in order to reduce the inflationary threat, the world went into recession.

The United States in particular dealt with higher oil prices not by economizing its use of oil but by moving into recession. In 1974, with commodity and oil prices going through the roof, the Fed raised interest rates in an attempt to slow the growth of credit expansion. The action had an impact, and in 1974 output fell sharply: the American gross national product fell by almost 8 percent from its 1973 peak to a low point in 1975. It was the largest fall since the Great Depression. Industrial production fell at double that rate.

Unfortunately the impact on inflation was much less and, for the first time, inflation coexisted with high unemployment. The recession that followed the first oil crisis was unusually long and unusually deep both at home and abroad, reinforcing the sense that the world economy had become much more badly behaved than it had been through most of the postwar period. There had been lots of recessions in the fifties and sixties, but they had been mostly small and short lived, whereas in the present episode economies seemed unable to bounce back. Governments lamented that they could no longer deliver the full employment and reliable growth that a decade earlier had seemed so easy.

In October 1974 President Ford had decided to raise taxes in order to reduce inflation, as part of a policy launched under the risible title of "Whip Inflation Now."[5] In 1975, however, with Americans in the grips of the worst recession since the thirties, he was forced to reverse his decision. In an agreement with Congress, and in response to a need to raise spirits damaged by the trauma of Nixon's disgrace and long-prevaricated resignation, Ford decided to cut taxes and stimulate recovery. The recession ended: growth was restored, and for a while inflation faded as a problem.

Unfortunately for Ford, the policy confusion did little for the hapless president's image. Over the next couple of years Congress, not the White House, ran tax and spending policy, and during his election campaign in 1976 Jimmy Carter made much of Ford's lack of strategy. Carter proposed a long-term policy that would involve both tax cuts and, supposedly, a progressive reduction in budget deficits. This extended various initiatives instigated under the Ford regime but never followed through on, notably the new creed of "supply-side" economics. In 1977 Carter, now president, announced to the slightly mystified nation a long-term plan: he would abolish outmoded regulations, reduce total federal spending, increase spending on measures to deal with unemployment, encourage new sources of domestic energy, cut personal taxes, and reform corporate taxes. The results of these allegedly supply-side measures would be higher growth rates for American output, investment, and productivity: there would be lower inflation, less poverty, a balanced federal budget, and a trade surplus. There would even be reduced vulnerability to oil shocks and an improved climate of international opinion.

A year later it was all forgotten: according to the *Economic Report of the President*, the government needed to switch from "efforts to strengthen growth in economic activity to measures to restrain inflation."[6] Inflation was again climbing sharply, and the Carter White House produced a whole range of policies—voluntary wage control, deregulation, monetary restraint, and so on—allegedly geared to keeping inflation down. Within a year OPEC had again sent inflation skyrocketing and plunged the nation into another energy crisis. President Carter appeared on television in front of an unlit fire, wearing a woolly sweater, talking about energy conservation. It was altogether too homespun even for the American electorate. In 1980 Carter was voted out of office.

## Japan Adapts

No nation was more shattered by the first oil price shock than Japan. Oil accounted for a huge proportion of Japan's energy needs, and all of it was imported. The cost of fuel and raw materials rose faster than the prices that Japan could charge for its traditional manufactured exports, and in 1974 there was a very large swing into current account deficit. Meanwhile, Japan's inflation rate soared to 24 percent, the highest rate in the industrialized world. The gross national product fell for the first time since World War II, and business confidence was in threads.

Initially the government seemed uncertain what to do, other than to suggest that men should wear suits with short sleeves during summer in order to reduce the need for air-conditioning. A new two-pronged strategy did, however, emerge—economize on energy and raw materials, and move manufacturing industry toward higher value-added and more profitable activities. During the seventies Japanese industry shifted its industrial structure away from industries such as steel, synthetic fibers, and bulk chemicals, all of which used a lot of energy and raw materials;[7] once the backbone of the Japanese economy, these industries shifted abroad, making way for new technology-intensive industries such as the production of sophisticated machine tools and electronic equipment. As a result, for the first time since the twenties, Japan began to import large volumes of low-technology manufactured goods. Since Japanese firms had built factories in many other Asian countries, and Japanese banks had provided loans to such nations, it was from them that Japan tended to import. Meanwhile, Japan's new high-technology industries had to export enough to pay for those imports, as well as for oil and raw materials. Thus the assaults on American and European markets had to be doubly powerful.

New technology brought with it higher productivity, new products, and new production methods. Japanese firms began to encroach on markets formerly the preserve of the more advanced Americans and Europeans—all of which meant more output, more employment, and more optimism at a time when Japan's rivals were still unable to think of a world without "stagflation."

Whereas in the seventies American companies showed no interest in energy efficiency, Japanese companies invested heavily in energy-saving technology; for them, the seventies were not a lost decade but a period of intense activity.[8] By the end of the seventies Japan was again growing faster than any other major industrialized economy, and it boasted low inflation and a healthy current account surplus. Japan was on course to become a new superpower. Other nations could only gasp at the efficiency with which Japan had dealt with the oil price shock.

The Ministry of International Trade and Industry coordinated the process of choosing which new sectors to develop and which to abandon. MITI had once operated by force, requiring companies to do as it wished by allocating vital foreign exchange to those firms which cooperated with its plans. Without foreign exchange, firms could not buy fuel or raw materials. However, in the sixties Japan had become a consistent surplus nation, and suddenly foreign exchange was in plentiful supply, so MITI switched tactics: now it dispensed "administrative guidance" about which sectors were likely to produce the highest long-term growth rates. MITI advised companies to invest in those sectors, even if short-term profit considerations suggested investing elsewhere.

Superficially less didactic than the old method, the new approach retained a powerful element of force. During the recession MITI excluded from the temporary industrial cartels that it organized any firm that did not cooperate with its strategy. As a result, outsiders had to bear the brunt of economic downturns. The most important of the cartels were the rationalization cartels set up by MITI in the seventies in response to higher oil prices. The cartels created the new industrial structure for the Japan of the eighties.

Cartels worked because the *keiretsu*, the industrial groupings that had replaced the *zaibatsu*, backed them; MITI dealt with co-ordination between companies from different *keiretsu* operating in the same industry. The groupings provided for cooperation between companies in different industries. Since their creation with American backing after World War II, the groupings had become immensely powerful; by the seventies they had built elaborate webs of cross-holdings, partly to thwart hostile takeovers and partly to strengthen collusive relationships between companies, allowing firms in different sectors to share employees, finance, research ideas, and market intelligence. These developments helped MITI to achieve its plans for industrial reorganization.

Apart from investing in order to improve products, Japanese companies invested to improve production processes. In the seventies and eighties lean technology, whose origins were described in chapter 5, became more widespread in Japan as the nation's manufacturers pioneered the use of computer-aided manufacturing. Such a transformation from low-technology to high-technology industry might have faced heavy opposition from workers: in the fifties and sixties, under similar circumstances, there had been frequent strikes and fierce industrial disputes as workers in declining industries such as coal and steel attempted to prevent their jobs from disappearing. In the seventies, however, the story was very different; firms such as Sony and Honda worked hard to maintain the loyalty of their employees by, for example, preserving lifetime employment systems.[9]

In a nation where firms still paid most workers according to their length of service, a lifetime employment promise from an employer was a welcome offer, since only the young could change jobs without suffering sharp losses in wages. However, even those Japanese workers who were displaced in the seventies could often find work elsewhere: a demographic slowdown meant that Japan was moving toward labor shortage, so that workers who left the manufacturing sector found jobs in companies less exposed to international trends. Employers often arranged the moves on their employees' behalf. Others took jobs with the multitude of very small firms providing low-technology support on subcontract to the nation's large capital-intensive firms.

Admittedly the story was not all sweetness and light. Even in those firms offering lifetime employment some layoffs occurred, and many firms evaded their commitments by retiring people early or by cutting their subcontractors loose. Many workers suffered pay cuts, and companies cut bonus payments and reduced the working week; those who took jobs with small firms frequently experienced little security and few fringe benefits. Many workers, especially women and older people, did not find work and returned to their homes, unable or unwilling to claim state benefits. Nevertheless, the fact remained that, despite the tough global climate of the seventies, Japanese manufacturers entered the eighties much more streamlined and efficient than were their American or European competitors, and able to offer better long-term job prospects. Although manufacturing employment fell by 2 percent in Japan between 1973 and 1979, while in the United States it increased slightly, the fact that Japan's manufacturing productivity rose at double the American rate meant that Japanese firms were both able and willing to invest for the long term. For the United States, the implications of this would soon be severe.

## Global Economic Problems

Rather than squeeze their economies in response to higher oil prices as the United States and most other industrialized nations did, or modernize as Japan decided to do, most Third World countries took upon themselves the full increase in trade deficits resulting from the higher oil prices. Thus, the Third World acted as the major stabilizing influence on the world economy after the first oil price rise. On the one hand, it maintained its imports of American and European goods, despite reduced export markets and higher oil bills; on the other, industrialized nations cut down their purchases from, and increased their exports to, the Third World.

Financially, then, the Third World came to the aid of the industrialized economies.

Furthermore, it was Third World countries, as well as some of the centrally planned economies of Eastern Europe, that bore the brunt of the squeeze on inflation. With employment still high in the industrialized West and trade unions strong, anti-inflationary policy had only slightly more impact on wages than on oil prices.[10] Thus it was commodity prices that took much of the strain; as these fell, Third World countries suffered from higher import bills and falling export receipts. By 1975 they were in danger of being crippled by their current account deficits, whereas the industrialized nations were in modest surplus on current account; it was a remarkable achievement, given that the price of their largest import had quadrupled, but one that had its counterpart in a big swing into deficit on the part of the Third World.

The money to fund the deficits did exist—it always does. The OPEC nations had surplus funds to match the Third World deficits. Initially, central bankers, economists, and assorted pundits insisted that it would be impossible to recycle OPEC surpluses without first revamping the world's international monetary institutions. Thus the IMF acquired a special "oil facility," and the Bank for International Settlements was asked to manage a "safety net," both of which were designed to facilitate recycling. The first had little impact, the second had none: as political devices, they came with policy strings, and because this was a controversial area the strings were tangled. Once again, the facilities never became very substantial.

While the politicians and the bureaucrats squabbled, though, New York and London bankers acted. As much as $60 billion had suddenly shifted to the Middle East, so the bankers climbed into their Boeings and chased after it.[11] With little to spend their money on apart from armaments, the OPEC nations were happy enough to place their new wealth on deposit with the commercial banks; and if the Third World nations needed money to finance their expensive oil imports, then the bankers were happy to oblige. The OPEC money flowed into New York and London, then on to South America and the rest of the Third World. Thus the commercial banking system did the work while the government officials did the talking. It was a policy the bankers were later to regret: as the developing nations began to pay interest on huge loans from American banks, so the Third World debt problem was born.

When the world began to recover in the second half of 1975, it was the American economy that set much of the pace; as a result, trade balances deteriorated. In Germany and Japan output also initially increased, but in both cases the governments were nervous about inflation, especially since commodity prices were again getting frisky. The rapid inflation of recent years had caused monetary growth to accelerate, and the German and Japanese governments tried to dampen this; meanwhile the recession caused government budget deficits to rise, and as soon as recovery got underway, the Japanese and German governments tried to cut these deficits back. As a result, growth slowed in both countries.

Such German and Japanese caution meant that the world recovery was both slow and fragile. This affected householders as well as corporations, and many began to think that the days of sustained, rapid growth might finally be over. Both groups planned accordingly, and companies in particular decided not to invest heavily, which made the global recovery all the more fragile.

On the positive side, however, governments were well aware that the recent inflation, recession, and slow recovery were international phenomena. Most politicians had either become more conservative or been replaced by those who were, but they were still uneasy about neglecting their longstanding commitments to full employment. An international solution to the problems of slow growth and high unemployment seemed appropriate.

According to the principles espoused long before by Keynes, in a period of very low world growth those countries with relatively healthy balance of payments positions and relatively low inflation ought to expand their economies. By doing so, they can create vibrant export markets for everybody else; in this way, strong countries can pull weaker countries along. The leader who most espoused such a view was President Carter, who was frustrated by the caution of his German and Japanese counterparts. A pattern of annual economic summits between the leaders of the major industrialized nations had been established in 1975, and now Carter invested these with new significance.[12] In London in May 1977 he lobbied Germany's Helmut Schmidt and Takeo Fukuda of Japan to raise their economic growth rates, and thereby help to strengthen the growth of the global economy.

By the standards of his immediate predecessors Carter was an idealist, but his attempt to introduce new cooperative international economic policies was backed by threats: if the Germans and the Japanese did not expand demand in their economies, he would massively devalue the dollar. In a world economy that was struggling to grow, such a threat was far more alarming than anything that Richard Nixon had done in the easier climate of 1971. Even so, both Japan and West Germany initially resisted American pressure, and both countries opted for slow, cautious growth in 1977 and early 1978, with the Germans especially reluctant to acquiesce to American pressure. Perhaps the Germans liked being both "geopolitical client and geoeconomic freerider," leaving it to the Americans to take the inflationary risks involved in expanding demand in the economy.[13] When the markets realized that neither the Japanese nor the Germans were prepared to help reduce the large American current account deficit, the dollar began to fall— with Carter's treasury secretary, Michael Blumenthal, standing by watching.

After the dollar had lost one fifth of its value, the Japanese and German central banks finally felt obliged to intervene, spending $35 billion to support the American currency, or rather more than Carter had wanted their governments to spend on domestic economic expansion via tax cuts or more spending. Still, however, the dollar looked weak. By June 1978 the dollar had fallen further; the American trade balance was improving, but it looked as if the global recovery might fade altogether. At a summit meeting in Bonn the Americans finally persuaded the West German government to expand demand in their economy, on condition that other countries, both weak and strong, would do the same. In the rather contrived terminology of the time, the Germans said that they would not be a "locomotive" but that they would lead a "convoy."[14] The Japanese increased their efforts to expand demand, and all the countries of the EEC agreed to do their bit too.

Still, however, the dollar was in distress. In October 1978 the Carter administration reluctantly tightened its budgetary policies and asked the Federal Reserve to tighten monetary policy. With inflation at 9 percent and the dollar worth only three quarters of its January value, the Fed needed little persuading, although it was reluctant to do anything that might imply panic. The foreign exchange markets were less amenable: still the dollar fell. So Anthony Solomon, then in charge of exchange rate policy at the Treasury, asked for help. From the German, Swiss, and Japanese central banks he borrowed $15 billion, and he borrowed more on the open market; he even went to the IMF for $3 billion. In total, Solomon secured a rescue package worth $30 billion.[15] The dollar recovered—it could hardly do otherwise—at the cost of the United States' financial humiliation.

Nor was that the end. In late 1978 the German-led convoy of industrialized nations fell victim to Iran's Islamic revolution, which sent oil prices rocketing once again as Iran suspended oil sales. Western stocks were low, the winter was cold, and the rise in price caused hoarding and a spiral of further price rises during 1979. The same shock had occurred twice in a decade; planners started to question whether a fundamental determinant of half a century of world economic growth—abundant cheap energy supplies—was now over.

The Iranian Revolution reflected the problems of the Iranian economy:[16] for three decades a combination of vast oil wealth and a powerful secret police had allowed the Shah's government to govern Iran unchallenged. By the late seventies, though, the consequences of maladministration were so serious that further suppression became impossible: Iran was no longer self-sufficient in food, its industry was in decline, and its infrastructure in tatters. In a nation with more oil than almost any on earth, electricity was frequently scarce: in Teheran householders ran their washing machines in the middle of the night to avoid the regular evening blackouts.

Opposition centered around the Shiite clergy, whose lands and power had been stripped by the Shah's government but whose propaganda skills far outstripped those of the government. There was sporadic violence, and by late 1978 strikes bedeviled the country. In November the oil industry was operating at only one fifth of its normal rate; on December 25 exports ceased altogether. The world's second-largest oil industry had all but closed down.

The potential damage to oil prices from all of this was, however, negated by the efforts of Saudi Arabia and the other producers, which immediately acted to maintain market stability by boosting output. There was no global shortage of oil, and hence no reason for oil prices to rise, but speculation and hoarding nevertheless gripped the market. Oil companies, governments, and wealthy individuals bought for speculative reasons, driving prices up further still. When the Shah fled and his successors declared an Islamic republic, no one doubted that Iranian oil was sure to flow again—but no one knew when or on what terms. It seemed possible that other nations in the region might suffer similar revolutions, and this prospect led speculators to buy even more. Market psychology was much like that of the 1929 Wall Street Crash, only operating in reverse.

So in 1979, it was the American and European oil companies —not OPEC, nor the Iranians—that tripled the price of crude oil. Oil companies and their big customers such as the chemical companies rushed to build up their inventories before the price went even higher—and thus drove it higher still. By March, Iran was exporting again, at a healthy two thirds of its previous rate. Inevitably, however, the OPEC nations, including though to a limited extent moderate Saudi Arabia, profited from the price rises; a few of the more militant states sought to drive prices up further—the value of their oil, after all, had been severely reduced by the earlier declines in the dollar. The episode's real significance for the world was that the oil market had been shown to be much tighter, much less flexible, and thus much more volatile than had been hoped. That implied that the inflationary risks associated with expansionary policies were much greater than previously thought.


## The Americans Rethink

The slowdown in American economic performance in the seventies occurred against a background of heightened aspirations. In the 1961 election campaign both Richard Nixon and John Kennedy had promised that economic growth would accelerate in the sixties. Americans, who had done so much better than expected in the fifties, wanted to do even better in the new decade. Demographics added to the pressure: the baby boom of the fifties manifested itself in a clamorous generation of teenagers. The products of a decade of affluence, they were more demanding and more assertive than their predecessors: more young people had their own cars, jobs were easy to get. Such changes meant that young people could be more independent of parental authority than were earlier genera-tions. Their independence was worth little unless they flaunted it, though, so spending increased.

Most important of all, in the sixties the poorer people of the United States began to clamor for a fairer distribution of the na-tion's wealth. As the economy grew, so it needed more and more labor, bringing people on the margins of society into the economic mainstream. Many blacks left the South for the inner-city ghettoes of the Midwest and the East Coast; there, the absence of proper health, education, and welfare provision hurt them much more than it had in their former homes. It was a trend that Kennedy did not initially notice: in his one year of campaigning and two years of office, he only began to address the deepening divides within American society. Although he did eventually commit himself to legislation on civil liberties, he kept his back turned firmly against rising government expenditure, despite the manifest inadequacies of the American minimalist welfare state. Kennedy, who committed the American nation to reach for the moon, favored tax cuts that mainly helped the middle class, rather than spending on education, welfare, and hospitals for the poor.

In contrast, President Johnson launched the Great Society program as a way to ameliorate the antagonisms and conflicts that would otherwise threaten his survival at the White House. The economy was operating at full capacity, and the rivalry for the nation's resources meant potentially dangerous conflicts between Americans of different class and ethnic backgrounds. Under the circumstances, higher government spending made it possible for the pressures to dissipate themselves in higher inflation. This was not such a bad outcome: the Johnson spending programs converted a rising tide of social conflict into a form that was not profoundly dangerous to the very structure of society.

In the seventies, however, the cumulative problems of the economy became too great to mask. By then, the relentless rise of American aspirations could only be satisfied by rising indebtedness —personal, federal, and eventually national debt, when the balance of payments moved into deficit and Americans began to borrow heavily from abroad. Many economists recognized this, but in a rather twisted way, gaining attention by arguing that the fundamental problem was too much public welfare provision. Supposedly, public support had grown far beyond the provision of a safety net for the most disadvantaged, and was reducing enterprise and the incentive to work. The same economists claimed that marginal tax rates were far too high and government regulations far too onerous: high taxes, they said, reduced the incentives to work and to invest. These supply-siders wanted lower tax rates (but a wider tax base), lower government spending (and a narrower welfare base), and fewer government regulations.

In 1987 Michael Boskin, a former Reagan official, wrote, "from the late 1960s to 1980, the nation's primary economic goal shifted from increasing to redistributing wealth."[17] The claim is at best an exaggeration: for example, although taxes did indeed rise in the seventies, the rise was modest—average marginal tax rates

increased from about 25 percent to about 35 percent in the decade—and it still left taxes low by most nations' standards.[18] It is also
true that welfare spending and transfer payments grew in the seventies from a little more than one third of federal government expenditure in 1970 to just over one half in 1980; but since the
American economy was at the top of an economic boom in 1970
and was in recession in 1980, this is hardly surprising. After com-
pensating for the cycle, the increase in the welfare bill was much
less than the crude figures suggest. Much of the increase in spending
and the need for higher taxes reflected demographics: more elderly
people in the seventies meant that more welfare needed to be paid
out, especially because the large numbers of retired electors meant
that politicians had to start boosting the living standards of the elderly, who had long been neglected.

Elsewhere, federal spending came under strong downward
pressure in the seventies, especially after the end of the Vietnam
War reduced the political pressure for domestic welfare programs.
The government made cuts in welfare programs, and it put on hold
many legislative and spending gains from the sixties. All in all the
decade was not in fact marked by profligate spending—at least on
the part of the federal government. Nevertheless, with the nation's
income now growing much more slowly than people's aspirations,
there was widespread agreement that a radical response was
needed.

In 1980, in the face of severe global and domestic economic and
political problems, Americans turned to a presidential candidate
who offered them simple solutions for complex problems. Pro-
claiming that government was the problem not the solution, Ronald Reagan proposed to give decisions back to market mechanisms,
and to make the United States a more laissez-faire economy than
at any time since before the Great Depression.

In the United States, many people blamed the rising trend in
American inflation on the weakness of the Federal Reserve, which

was supposed to be responsible for the nation's anti-inflationary policy, but which instead had a reputation for wobbling between inactivity and slavish support for the government of the day. Thus, for example, Kennedy's New Economics growth policy took it for granted that the Federal Reserve would do nothing to undermine the president's dash for growth. Instead, in 1962 the President's Council of Economic Advisors tried to control inflation by announcing "guideposts" to signal what rates of pay increases industry could afford; the council reasoned that in order to avoid inflation, wages in the United States should grow no faster than productivity. So the government hoped that if it pointed this out, then everybody would moderate their wage demands. There was no suggestion that the Federal Reserve should use interest rates or restrictions on monetary growth to deal with inflation.

A small band of economists, led by Milton Friedman, had long argued that the best explanation for the rise in inflation during the sixties and seventies was the accelerating pace of monetary growth. Accordingly, they blamed the Federal Reserve for inflation, arguing that the Fed failed to perform its basic job of controlling the expansion of the money stock. The monetarists believed that if the Fed had prevented an acceleration in monetary growth after the first oil price shock, then it could have prevented higher oil prices from generating a sustained rise in inflation.

Seemingly a dry, technical notion, the monetarist claim had strong political reverberations. They rejected all compromise as far as inflation was concerned, and hence they rejected the full employment commitment made (at least nominally) by all governments since 1946. Although the majority of economists and government officials remained skeptical whether monetary stringency would directly produce lower inflation, they did believe that it would produce recession, and that the latter would reduce inflation. So if the politicians had decided that reducing inflation had to be the top priority, then economists in government and on Wall Street were willing to let the monetarists pursue their misguided path toward that goal.

In 1979 William Miller, chairman of the Federal Reserve, was the latest in a series of chairmen who behaved more like White House staffers than independent central bankers. Formally, the Fed had already embraced monetarism, but at a time when the Carter government had little credibility with financial markets, Miller lacked the authority to convince traders that a policy once started would be followed through. "Not since the Great Depression has the Federal Reserve seemed so ineffective, so listless, so demoralized," one of its staff complained.[19] With the American economy close to recession, the markets doubted whether the Fed had the courage to act against what seemed to be a rising problem with inflation.

President Carter accepted, however, that psychology needed to change. In August 1979, following his famous retreat to Camp David, Carter replaced Miller with a senior Treasury official, Paul Volcker, who possessed all the financial experience and credibility that Miller, an ex-businessman, lacked. The president's intention was to restore confidence in the Fed's independence and in its commitment to curbing inflation. Volcker was already known to be committed to using monetary control to defeat inflation, and once in office he wasted no time in putting that into practice. On October 6, 1979, exactly two months after taking office, the new chairman announced an "improvement" in operating procedure designed to allow much tighter monetary control. Officially, the purpose of the change was to *enable* the Fed to do its existing job better;[20] in truth the so-called Saturday night special marked a new *determination* to do the job, irrespective of the political consequences. (A few years later a Reagan White House official would complain of Volcker's independence that "trying to question [him] is like shooting a slingshot at an elephant."[21]) American interest rates immediately soared as the Fed applied an unprecedented squeeze to the American banking system; the banks in turn squeezed their customers, and the American economy plunged into recession.

For the official commitment to monetary control to be really convincing, however, another step had to be taken: the government and the Fed had to eschew any other policies that might, by their nature, compromise the determination to tighten monetary control. In particular, the Fed could not guarantee that it would exercise tight control over monetary growth if it was also operating under government instructions to stabilize or support the dollar in the world's currency markets. For monetary control to mean anything, therefore, the Fed needed a promise from the Treasury that the latter would refrain from policies geared to fixing, stabilizing, or otherwise intervening in exchange rates. Under President Carter, however, the Treasury would make no such commitment. When he gave control of the Fed to Volcker, President Carter hedged his bets by giving William Miller the post of treasury secretary, thereby limiting the Fed's new extremism. Carter remained committed to the ideal of international coordination of economic policies, and hence to the ambition of stable exchange rates.

The arrival of the Reagan administration changed this situation. The new administration distrusted government intervention in the domestic economy, and it also opposed the international coordination of economic policies. Accordingly, in April 1981 Beryl Sprinkel, the Treasury's under secretary for monetary affairs and a onetime student of Milton Friedman, made an announcement: the American authorities would no longer make any significant interventions in currency markets. Except in rare circumstances— Sprinkel cited the previous month's assassination attempt on the president—the authorities would not even try to smooth temporary ups and downs in the dollar; still less would they attempt permanently to alter or preserve currency rates. The dollar would have to fend for itself.

The Reagan administration claimed that by letting the dollar float it was reordering its priorities away from the international economy and toward domestic matters.[22] Since the nation's high unemployment reflected its high interest rates, and since these were caused by high inflation, which itself reflected the oil price hike, the attempt to distinguish between international and domestic policy issues was clearly disingenuous. It was probably more accurate to say that, following the diminution of American influence around the world, the new American administration felt *unable* to influence foreign governments, and so it concentrated on domestic policy measures, because those were the only tools it had available. The irony was that, far from improving the domestic economy, the government placed the economy in a new and even greater peril.

## Chapter Eight

# A DECADE
# OF NEGLECT

## *Without Keynes*

After the Sprinkel announcement the dollar strengthened sharply in the currency markets. From 1980 to 1985 it rose by 70 percent against the deutschemark and 30 percent against the average of all major currencies, while the American trade balance deteriorated rapidly. This clearly disturbed the old-fashioned Keynesian economic establishment, which believed that problems with the American trade balance made such an appreciation quite irrational. It was, as one British economist later remarked, like the Indian rope trick, but with the added refinement that this new trick took place in full view of the whole world—the original version was only ever seen by a friend of a friend.[1]

Furthermore, Keynesians also argued that the rise in the dollar would damage the American economy. Instead, though, once the economy recovered from the 1981–82 recession, it experienced a period of historically high growth and declining inflation. That too seemed to confound the pessimism of the old establishment.

However, as the years went by, the trade balance went further and further into deficit. In 1984 it exceeded $100 billion for the first time in American history. The volume of American exports had not changed much since President Reagan entered office; in contrast, though, the volume of imports *had* increased rapidly— Americans were spending much of their increased incomes on imports. Furthermore, domestic firms were even losing existing business to foreign competitors. Factory utilization remained obstinately low, and by 1985 it was falling. Manufacturing employment was two million lower than it had been when Ronald Reagan first took office. It looked as if the Keynesians were right after all—and that sooner or later the currency markets would have to acknowledge the fact and dump the dollar.

Even Paul Volcker had severe reservations.[2] The practical problems that faced him at the Fed led Volcker to temper his early monetarism with increasing amounts of pragmatism. When the Fed embarked upon its monetarist experiment in October 1979, it had been convinced that its attempts to apply strict monetary control would neither affect nor be affected by its desire to maintain a stable banking system. Although the fight to achieve and maintain monetary control might create temporary liquidity and capital problems, the Fed believed that these would be neither endemic nor permanent. In perfect circumstances this might have been true; in the circumstances prevailing in the early eighties, however, it was far from true. Meanwhile the American banks believed, quite reasonably, that they enjoyed implicit guarantees against failure. In extreme circumstances the Federal Reserve would act to protect depositors—so the banks behaved accordingly, leaving the Fed with little option but to honor the supposed guarantees.

So in 1982 the Fed reversed its 1979 policy priorities. It opted for banking stability in preference to monetary orthodoxy and cut interest rates in response to anxieties over the health of American banks.

The cut in interest rates got the economy moving again, but with the dollar defiantly high, it also fueled still more imports. In his public statements Volcker blamed rising American trade deficits squarely on the large budget deficits, but privately he knew that the currency played a part too. He worried that the rise in the dollar was helping to generate the large trade deficits, and that the deficits would eventually trigger a dollar collapse. By the mid-eighties, Volcker had come to believe in managed currencies and had all but abandoned his earlier monetarist thinking.

In contrast, both Beryl Sprinkel and Treasury Secretary Donald Regan remained highly doctrinal: they could not understand why Volcker was not more successful at bringing down monetary growth, a goal they believed would lead to lower interest rates and faster economic growth.[3] The Fed and the Treasury repeatedly clashed in private. Although Volcker remains diplomatic, another ex-colleague says of Regan that he was "a man of little guile and no subtlety," and another referred to him as "officious" and subject to "trademark Irish temper tantrums"; a third colleague said, more bluntly, "I despised him. He was so arrogant."[4] Fortunately, however, Volcker's prestige was the greater, and in July 1983 Regan failed in an attempt to block Volcker's reappointment as chairman of the Fed.

Volcker's unpopularity at the Treasury partly reflected the belief on the part of Sprinkel and Regan that the Fed was largely to blame for the increased budget deficits that had come to dominate the economic policy debate. In the early eighties high interest rates and the sharp rise in the dollar brought down American inflation, both by making imports cheaper and by pushing the economy into recession. Volcker thus reduced inflation, but by causing recession he also pushed up government spending and reduced tax revenues. For those at the Treasury who believed that the budget ought to balance, Volcker thus had much to answer for.

Attempts to scapegoat Volcker were predictably unsuccessful. The Reagan administration came into office determined to cut taxes, reasoning that lower taxes on incomes would stimulate people to work harder (and, of course, make the president more popular). Accordingly, in 1981 Reagan presented Congress with his Economic Recovery and Tax Act. In this legislation he proposed to make annual across-the-board cuts in income taxes for the next three years; Congress passed the legislation, largely intact.

Between them Congress and the administration boosted demand in the American economy in order to court popularity at home and to raise American prestige abroad. Tax cuts increased both personal and corporate spending, while the federal government flooded military and naval contractors with new orders. Consumer confidence grew, and householders as well as companies felt able to borrow more and save less. Spending continued to increase, even when the government reduced its own contribution to the process.

However, the new administration, like many before it, dreamed of balancing the budget.[5] Accordingly, the president also presented plans to Congress to cut back Social Security spending: he wanted to eliminate minimum benefits, abolish many students' benefits, and cut the pensions of people who retired before the age of sixty-five. It is not clear whether the spending reductions would have been sufficient to cover the cost of the tax cuts; it is clear, though, that unless the economy grew very rapidly the Federal budget would not balance. Thus Reagan's dream of achieving a balanced budget was indeed just a dream. The budget would not have balanced even if Congress had approved the spending cuts *and* Volcker had not depressed demand in the economy. Furthermore, the president also committed himself to accelerate the increase in military and naval spending that had already got underway in the final year of the Carter presidency.

Such policies were potentially quite dangerous. Congress authorized the tax cuts and the extra military and naval spending before there was any extra revenue (or sufficient welfare spending cuts) to pay for them. This might not have mattered too much except that Reagan's attack on welfare spending brought him into bitter conflict with Congress, which in turn made it impossible to come to any agreement on ways to finance the extra military and naval spending and the cuts in taxes. Although the resulting rise in federal borrowing was not necessarily harmful, it directly contradicted Reagan's promise to balance the budget. Furthermore, Reagan's pledge that the tax cuts would last forever precluded future measures to reduce borrowing, should they be needed. The commitment amounted to an abdication of the government's future right to raise taxes—a right for which Americans had once fought. Meanwhile, those cuts in welfare spending that did take place exacerbated the alienation already felt by many disadvantaged Americans and contributed to the spiraling costs of policing (let alone living in) an increasingly divided society. The deregulation of business and the regressive nature of the tax cuts added to the risks by creating new opportunities for the rich to become richer and the poor to become resentful.

For a while, however, the threatened catastrophes did not occur. The Reagan government eschewed involvement in any major wars, and at home those who suffered from welfare cuts did not rebel, at least not collectively. Americans found that they could easily finance their increased spending by borrowing heavily from abroad. However, since they spent much of the extra borrowing on consumption rather than investment, and since the nation had to service and eventually repay its borrowing, the American growth rate increased only in the short term. Meanwhile, the budget deficit spiraled.

Over the next seven years the administration's attempts to return to the path of financial orthodoxy grew ever less convincing. By the second half of the decade the runaway federal deficit was a source of much embarrassment. Some blamed the administration for lack of sophistication, some blamed Congress for refusing to believe that somebody would have to pay for the tax cuts; some almost, but not quite, blamed themselves.[6] Few were willing to acknowledge just how much the deficit contributed to the American growth rate—nor would they admit how difficult it would be to reduce the deficit without pushing the economy toward recession. Fewer still ever questioned the general assumption that the deficit was unduly large. In fact, throughout the decade the deficit was no larger in relation to gross national product than the deficits of other leading nations. The idea that the federal deficit was a monster was simply untrue.[7]

## The Revenge of the Free Market

Ronald Reagan's policies were clearly driven by more than purely macroeconomic considerations. "In the four years that I served as Secretary of the Treasury I never saw President Reagan alone and never discussed economic philosophy or fiscal and monetary policy with him one on one," remarked Don Regan.[8] In his election campaign Ronald Reagan proposed to increase military and naval spending so that foreigners would again know their place; he proposed cutting welfare spending and taxes so that the government would no longer waste the income of successful Americans on the unsuccessful. Under his new regime, the obligation to take care would no longer fetter the instinct to succeed.

A particular element of what soon became known as "Reaganomics" was the president's promise to reduce or abolish many curbs on the behavior of business. Deregulation had been on the political agenda ever since the economic slowdown in the late sixties. As successive governmental attempts to restore fast growth by means of macroeconomic policies apparently failed, so business leaders got together to bemoan their plight. They agreed that a major problem was government regulation, which, they said, restricted market expansion and impeded the efficient allocation of resources. So various business-funded think tanks set to work, devising arguments in favor of deregulation, and various politicians took up the cause. Deregulation thus featured in the programs of all the seventies administrations, from Nixon right through to Carter. By the eighties the weight of political pressure for deregulation was immense, and Ronald Reagan determined that his government should accede to that pressure.

Companies wanted deregulation to increase their own freedom to maneuver. Rather than have the federal government or the courts decide on market structure, businesses wanted to make the decisions themselves, as Pierpont Morgan and the robber barons had once done: they wanted to compete where they wished and to reduce competition where they wished. Companies also wanted fewer controls on pollution, health and safety, land use, and their activities generally.

For a while in the eighties Americans gained the tantalizing impression that deregulation and the return to laissez-faire policies were working. The economy expanded rapidly, and many people became much better off as employment increased from 90 million people at the start of the decade to 106 million by the end. It seemed as if the removal of business fetters really had produced a significant improvement in business performance, particularly since the decade saw sharp increases not just in employment but also in investment in new machinery and equipment—especially with re-gard to the information and computer technologies that swept across the nation during the eighties. Now, with its new technol-ogy, American industry could exploit its unmatched engineering design and management skills.

Although, for example, American car manufacturers could no longer make profits from turning flat steel into car bodies (the Tai-wanese and Koreans could now do that more cheaply), it was nev-ertheless now possible for the Americans to compete with better design and quality, if they chose to do so. Each year these latter factors contributed more to the value-added of the car than ever before, and this fact gave American firms the opportunity to im-prove their nonprice competitiveness. In a similar way, American steel manufacturers no longer made profits from manufacturing an alloy from iron and carbon; rather, the new technologies gave them the opportunity in the eighties to make large profits from manufacturing the specific quality, weight, tolerance, and shape that their customers needed. Information technology applied in the manufacturing process allowed firms to fabricate products to customer requirements, which ought to have given American industry a huge competitive advantage over industry in other nations. Design could be more market led, so American firms would no longer need to persuade customers that existing products met their needs; instead they could persuade customers to define new needs for themselves, and then produce the goods to meet those needs.

Unfortunately, this is not what happened. For one thing, much of the deregulation that occurred failed to have its desired effects on competition, let alone on competitiveness. After the federal government deregulated the airline industry, for example, the number of carriers initially increased sharply; later it decreased until the industry became more concentrated than ever. Some airlines achieved almost total dominance over travel from specific airports (the "hub and spoke" system). Similarly, although the AT&T breakup introduced competition on long-distance calls, local calls became the monopolies of the regional firms into which the courts divided AT&T.

Nor did the wave of new investment that swept over the United States in the eighties produce the promised restoration of American competitiveness. The main reason was that the wave was just not large enough: American companies did not make sufficient profits from their investment in the new knowledge-based technology to offset the losses that stemmed from the mechanistic parts of production. Although their longstanding commitment to marketing should have given the Americans an advantage, they had deskilled marketing—like so many other activities—in response to the economy's growing failure to produce skilled workers. American firms were also slow to relate marketing back to research activity. Information technology promised to revolutionize the process of "learning by doing" in which firms reappraised their products in the light of customer requirements; however, American companies appeared reluctant to exploit such opportunities without a guaranteed quick return.

Furthermore, much of the investment in information technology in the eighties occurred not in the manufacturing sector but in the provision of services. Banks, shops, wholesalers, hotels, and restaurants installed new electronic equipment; by 1986 nearly one in three office workers had computer work stations. Those manufacturers who did invest heavily spent mainly on improvements to their distribution, communications, and financial systems, rather than on design and basic manufacturing, and the capital equipment that companies did buy tended to come from Europe, Southeast Asia, or especially Japan.[9] Also, the Reagan administration's declaration that it intended to abolish tax breaks on investment caused many firms to bring forward their spending, thereby creating an investment feast in the early eighties, but a famine later in the decade once the tax breaks were gone.

A similar story concerned the apparent recovery in American research and development effort, which grew faster in the eighties than it had in the seventies. The increased research spending was, however, largely the result of increased military and naval budgets: "Star Wars," the Strategic Defense Initiative, may have been scientific and technical nonsense, but for contractors in Texas and California it meant a brief period of lucrative business. In 1985, nearly 70 percent of government-funded research and development in the United States was spent on developing weapons. The government spent almost nothing on industrial development, though, and if one excludes military spending, American firms spent less on research and development than their Japanese competitors.

There were other problems. Whereas in other industrialized nations output growth in the eighties was associated with rising productivity, in the United States productivity improved only slowly: instead, companies used extra workers to generate the extra output. This was very good for the government's claim to be getting Americans back to work, but with wages rising much faster than productivity it meant a squeeze on margins. Americans were mortgaging their future. The poor productivity trend was a reminder that the American economy was not as innovative as it had once been; it was also a reminder that the Reagan administration's supply-side policies were leaving a troublesome legacy for George Bush.

There were other legacies too. A wave of mergers and takeover bids followed the new liberal approach to antitrust policy. These bids, which involved household names such as RCA, General Electric, Gulf Oil, and Nabisco, were not driven by any industrial logic, not even the raw desire of men like John Rockefeller to monopolize the markets in which they sold; they reflected, rather, the imperatives of Wall Street.

In the thirties Congress placed legal limits on the interest rates paid by banks on deposits. The idea was to prevent banks from weakening their capital by competing excessively with one another. The policy was very crude, and when nonbanking financial intermediaries began to offer competitive interest rates it became ineffective. By the late seventies the American financial system had twisted itself into a knot, as regulated investment banks tried to find ways to compete on equal terms with unregulated saving institutions. Thus banks set about devising new products to exploit loopholes and to overcome the constraints imposed by tight regulations.[10]

Prominent among the new products that the investment banks set up were money market mutual funds (MMMFs), devices by which savers invested in financial assets such as stocks and bonds without going directly to the markets. These promised to produce better returns for savers than conventional deposits—as at first they did. In the eighties, however, thanks to Volcker's high interest rates the funds underperformed. The banks controlling them worried about lucrative business slipping away, so they looked around for high-performance assets to put in the fund portfolios. What they found were "junk bonds," bonds without proper backing.

At the time the markets treated companies that issued these bonds with disdain. Although the bonds generally outperformed conventional bonds—so that the more junk bonds a fund held, the better it performed—respectable pension funds and insurance companies refused to buy such bonds in any quantity, believing them to be highly risky, and Wall Street's prestigious investment banks refused to involve themselves in trading them.

For Wall Street's less august investment banks, however, junk bonds offered a rare opportunity to be a big player in a market that firms such as Morgan Stanley and Goldman Sachs disdained. Most prominent among these banks was Drexel Burnham, formed in 1971 by the merger between the patrician but fading firm of Drexel Firestone and a small but streetwise firm known as Burnham and Co. The man responsible for trading low-quality corporate securities at Drexel Burnham was Michael Milken, an accountant's son who had studied business administration at Berkeley in the mid-sixties. When every other student seemed to be enjoying the counterculture of drugs and antiwar protest, the sober Milken studied research on the long-term portfolio performance of low-grade junk bonds. What Milken discovered (or thought he had) was that junk bonds were no riskier than high-grade assets. At Drexel Burnham he became the junk bond champion, always willing to spend the firm's money buying such assets; always able, due to his awesome selling skills, to pass the bonds on to others for a profit. By 1977 Drexel Burnham controlled three quarters of the junk bond market.[11]

Milken's only problem was to persuade companies to *issue* junk bonds. At first it was a tough task: no company would dare issue a junk bond unless its managers believed that it could run with the wind to pay them off. Few managers believed that, though, and few companies were investing so heavily that they needed an extra source of finance anyway. In the early eighties, however, the investment bankers hit on their solution, leveraged takeovers: companies that wanted to take over other companies would raise the cash by selling bonds to the public. Hitherto, the company selling the bonds would have real assets to back the bonds, in case something went wrong; now firms such as Drexel Burnham persuaded small companies to make takeover bids for large companies. The bonds they issued would be "backed" not by their own negligible assets but by the much greater assets of their victims.

For every pushy get-rich-quick company in the United States it was a dream come true: now the way to deal with your larger competitor was to buy it. The little guy *could* beat the big guy— that was what American business was supposed to be all about!

Thanks to junk bonds, there were four times as many corporate takeovers or mergers in the eighties as in the seventies. Even the likes of Goldman Sachs and Morgan Stanley joined in the business, and large, well-capitalized companies took to issuing the bonds too. Junk bonds were a cheap way of raising money, since there were few tiresome regulations to satisfy in the issuing process. More important, however, even the largest firms now needed the money: any day they might find themselves victims of a takeover bid from some small, aggressive firm, of whom previously nobody had ever heard. Many such predators existed, motivated not just by the greed of their own directors but by that of men such as Ivan Boesky, Wall Street's most awesome arbitrageur, who encouraged outrageous bids for major American corporations so that he could profit from the deals.[12]

There were obvious problems. One was law breaking. Wherever there is trading there are always a few cheats, but usually it does not matter too much: a bruised apple in the bottom of the bag, a secondhand car with a bald spare tire. With junk bonds, however, there was plenty of scope to cheat, and incredibly high rewards for those who did. Unfortunately, the cheating often only emerged later, when economic or financial downturns left companies unable to pay their debts; the subsequent scrutiny then revealed that corners had been cut, problems covered up, and rake-offs as the deals were put together.

The jail sentences later passed on Ivan Boesky and Michael Milken serve as the most obvious symbol of the American junk bond period. Perhaps more serious than the crimes themselves was what junk bonds did to the structure of American industry. Admittedly, some commentators tried to argue that junk-financed merger mania improved industrial efficiency: by reallocating the control of companies to those who were most entrepreneurial and ambitious, some said, the takeovers made the American economy more competitive.[13]

Perhaps American industry did need restructuring to help it focus on the markets and products that would offer the best prospects for the decades ahead. However, few could pretend that the restructuring taking place was of that sort. What really happened was that owners' loyalty to companies, already a rare quality in the United States compared with Japan, disappeared. The mutual funds became the new owners of the American corporate sector, and they cared only about how their assets performed from quarter to quarter, which meant that the managers of the companies they owned had to care too. Instead of making investment decisions intended to improve long-term competitiveness, companies spent their profits on projects designed to reap short-term rewards. Often that meant buying other companies; for some firms, this was their only reason for existing.

The most serious problem with junk bonds was that the changes made companies far more vulnerable than before to economic downturns. When interest rates rose, highly geared companies found themselves teetering toward bankruptcy and unable to service their heavy borrowing. As the decade progressed this worry increasingly preoccupied the Federal Reserve; unfortunately, it was initially not a problem about which the Reagan administration wanted to hear.

Nor did the government want to know about another related problem. In the late seventies the sleepy and provincial savings and loan institutions first came to the attention of Wall Street's mighty investment banks. On the whole, Wall Street did not much like the S&Ls: the New York bankers were jealous that these thrift institutions received federal insurance, enabling them to offer more security to depositors. They believed that the government mollycoddled the S&Ls, which had only themselves to blame for the fact that they found it very difficult to break even and meet their obligations to their clients. However, for the investment banks the

S&Ls had their uses—very lucrative ones. The thrifts could pay high interest rates, thanks to the general quality of their asset bases. So Wall Street banks started to put their own clients' funds on deposit with the S&Ls: the business was extremely profitable, and firms such as Merrill Lynch were always looking for a thrift that could accept a vast deposit of "brokered funds."

Nevertheless, the investment banks had a problem. Although President Carter had liberalized the thrifts, federal law still forbade S&Ls from accepting more than 5 percent of their total deposits through accounts that exceeded $100,000. This meant that, month by month, the number of S&Ls able to accept brokered funds dwindled, to the great frustration of the investment banks.

Then in 1980 came the Reagan presidency and the appointment of Donald Regan as secretary of the treasury. Regan had been the head of the brokerage firm of Merrill Lynch: the very company that invented MMMFs in the seventies and the first firm to lure thrift institutions into the giddy world of Wall Street finance. Regan's appointment was not a bright day for the S&L industry: in March 1982 he ended the 5 percent limit on brokerage funds. Wall Street firms could now split large deposits into amounts of $100,000, place them with thrifts, and benefit from federal insurance. The new legislation also allowed S&Ls to offer interest-bearing checking or "super NOW" accounts to a wider range of customers than Carter had permitted, and it allowed the thrifts to compete head-on with the MMMFs by offering money market deposit accounts (MMDAs) subject only to a minimum balance requirement of $2,500.

Thrifts could now draw in almost all the deposits they wanted, which was rather a lot—for Congress deregulated the loan side too. The thrifts could now buy state and local securities and could make commercial, consumer, and educational loans, even to high-risk borrowers involved in activities such as real estate and construction.[14]

Congress also abolished the restrictions on thrift ownership. Under the terms of the Garn–St. Germain Depository Institutions

Act, the Federal Savings and Loans Insurance Corporation was given authority to permit mergers between thrifts and nonthrift institutions, as well as between institutions in different states. Now anybody could own a thrift and invest its deposits almost as he or she saw fit.

Finally, the Reagan administration had celebrated its arrival in Washington by pushing out many incumbent officials from the Federal Home Loans Board (FHLB) and replacing them with less zealous regulators; the administration also cut FHLB jobs and vetoed pay rises. The quality of FHLB thrift supervision, never especially high, collapsed: the crooks moved in. The new owners of the thrifts extended loans that could only be repaid if oil prices, property, and other asset prices increased forever—and perhaps not even then. Indeed, in numerous cases the borrowers were the new owners.

The subsequent crisis needs little description. The existence of some problems was apparent from early on, but it was not until the mid-eighties that the scale of the thrifts' insolvency became clear. Oil, property, stock and bond markets all turned down, and thrift after thrift found itself unable to pay back depositors. Yet still it was difficult for the authorities to act, even if they had the courage: to shut one thrift would undermine confidence in all the others, and hence make their collapse inevitable.

Neither Don Regan nor Ronald Reagan was willing to act, creating a power vacuum in the Oval Office and making the situation ripe for a Washington coup. In January 1985 James Baker was the president's chief of staff. With Reagan much less active than in the early years of his presidency, the post conferred almost no power. Accordingly, the ambitious Baker accepted a proposal from Don Regan that they swap jobs. In his new post as Treasury Secretary, Baker could make things happen: he quickly obtained congressional agreement to a $10.8 billion lifeboat for the thrifts— an amount that was dwarfed by the $500 billion of unbacked thrift liabilities. Quietly, in the closing months of the old administration and the first year of the new one, the government took over thrift after thrift. Their assets were now backed by government guaranties, until the government sold each of them at knockdown prices to friendly purchasers.

The eventual response to the S&L crisis showed that the American government was willing to intervene in the economy when it suited its own interests. The objective of the S&L bailout was not to keep the S&Ls in business, since they were manifestly no longer viable, but to get George Bush elected.[15] Jim Baker was Bush's campaign manager, and it was he who delayed the real S&L reckoning until after 1988.[16] There were few prosecutions of those who had broken the law, and despite the high-profile trials of men such as Milken, many people later looked back on the Reagan period as one in which the government, through its laissez-faire policies, assisted a handful of unscrupulous individuals to rob their fellow citizens of countless millions, even billions, of dollars.

However, such an account misses a crucial point. The law breaking was an accompaniment to, not the rationale for, the policies of the Reagan administration. In the eighties the Reagan government rejigged the American financial system so that borrowers could continue running large deficits for longer than had ever before been possible. The desire to borrow reflected the poor state of the economy. Consumers borrowed so that their spending could grow faster than their wages; the government borrowed so that its spending could rise faster than its revenues. Companies borrowed not to buy capital equipment with which to compete more effectively in the world market but to buy one another. Takeovers meant that individual companies could grow very fast by swallowing others, but this did not make the economy as a whole grow faster, any more than the consumer borrowing or the government borrowing did. Debt increased out of all proportion to underlying assets or real growth in the economy. The ratio of financial assets to gross domestic product in the United States rose sharply.

Significantly, the increase in financial flows came mostly through the securities markets.[17] Junk bonds were just the most hair-raising manifestation of that; in contrast, old-fashioned bank loans and deposits grew only slowly. Americans convinced themselves that extraordinary high borrowing levels were not risky, so long as they bought assets—commercial paper, equities, junk bonds, and so on—that they could sell if need be. Liquidity thus meant security, or so the investment bankers said.

However, that was precisely the conceit that half a century earlier Keynes had dismissed as the "fetish of liquidity": the belief that everybody can avoid risks by buying tradable assets. As stockholders discovered in 1929, and again in 1987, there is no such thing as a safe tradable asset when everybody wants to sell together. When the junk bond market collapsed after the NJR-Nabisco debacle, the fallacy exposed by Keynes, and mentioned at the end of chapter 3, once again became clear for all to see.

## The Third World Debt Crisis

Meanwhile the Reagan administration had other problems that it preferred to disown. Between the first and second oil price shocks, several major Third World nations suffered continuous current account deficits on their international payments. American and European banks financed the deficits and prided themselves that they were taking long-term views. Supposedly, the growth prospects of such countries as Argentina, Brazil, and Chile were better than the prospects in domestic American and European markets. The banks also reassured themselves that they had diversified their loans across many countries. Furthermore, the banks mainly lent to national governments rather than to individual companies or people. That made the loans safer, didn't it? The loan amounts were vast, the administrative costs modest, and the banks could charge premium interest rates. By the end of the seventies the major American banks were making fully half their profits from lending to the Third World. In the case of Citicorp, Third World loans provided three quarters of the bank's profits.

In 1979 the second oil price hike disturbed the picture. When the industrialized nations including the United States began to ramp up interest rates, the complacency became even more striking. Governments in the industrialized nations decided to protect their balance of payments from the effects of higher oil prices. By deflating their economies and putting up with recession, they were almost bound to succeed at reducing their international payments deficits. Meanwhile, however, the oil-exporting countries were obviously experiencing large improvements in their payments positions. It is hardly surprising, then, that the burden of adjustment once again fell elsewhere, on the oil-importing countries of the Third World and the centrally planned economies of Eastern Europe. It was these nations that carried most of the burden of higher oil prices.

Admittedly, like the governments of the industrialized nations, Third World governments could have forced their economies into recession in response to the second oil price rise. By doing so, they too would have avoided balance of payments problems, and there would have been no Third World debt crisis. The human costs, however, would have been severe. (As chapter 4 related, when that did happen in the thirties it led to a global depression from which no nation could escape.) Instead, most Third World nations in the eighties struggled to maintain the momentum of their development programs.

This posed serious problems. Demand from the industrialized world slowed sharply, which hurt exports from these countries. Higher oil prices increased import bills, both directly and indirectly, through the higher prices of manufactured goods bought from industrialized countries. As a result, the international payments deficits of the less developed countries doubled between 1979 and 1981: their debts started to look cumulatively alarming. Between 1978 and 1982 the amount of money owed to the banks by the Third World doubled, to more than $200 million. The same thing happened to the debts owed directly to Western governments and to agencies like the World Bank—but since those debts were twice as large as the bank loans, the situation was very dangerous. In 1982 even the countries of the Soviet bloc owed the Western banks $50 billion.[18]

With import bills rising and exports depressed, the Third World countries and the centrally planned economies could not even service, let alone repay, their debts without borrowing more. Equally, however, they could not borrow more without austerity programs that caused great political and social problems in addition to decimating investment plans and long-term growth prospects. Their problems were acute. In Latin America and Africa national incomes fell by one fifth. The banks meanwhile had their own agony: they could threaten that unless borrowers repaid some money, they would make no more loans. Yet they knew that if they carried out such threats, the borrowers would lose any incentive to pay back existing loans. Compounding the problem was the multitude of banks, countries, terms, and conditions involved: each bank, fearing that customers would use its money to pay off other banks, began to negotiate special deals so that they could recover some of their own money at the expense of other banks.

The case for intervention by the American government was obvious. Many of the banks involved were American, and the debt problem might bring many of them to their knees, with consequent huge risks to the American economy. Meanwhile, American companies suffered from the absence of any market growth in the Third World. Furthermore, the debts of the debtor nations were almost all dollar denominated; because the dollar was rising, the benefit of exporting to Europe or elsewhere was declining, so Third World nations concentrated their export drives on the United States. Legal exports damaged the American trade balance, while illegal exports (drugs) damaged the American economy in ways that, although indirect, were even more potent.[19]

Ideologically, it was very difficult for the Reagan government to admit that laissez-faire policies had created a dangerous situation. Since the crisis was not actually manifest, it was easy to deny its very existence, especially since some of the evidence seemed to support a sanguine view of the situation. Back in 1978, before the second oil price shock, the Third World had devoted 12 percent of its export earnings to repaying debt, whereas by 1981 the figure was down to 9 percent—suggesting that the situation had improved, not worsened.[20] Furthermore, the flow of net lending from the banks to the Third World was increasing, not declining. In 1978 it had been $33 billion, but by 1981 it was $78 billion, a large increase even after allowing for inflation. And although there were problems caused by a downturn in the world economy, it seemed likely that the downturn would quickly reverse itself. As growth resumed the Third World countries would gradually share in the benefits; meanwhile, the IMF could deal with particular problems that individual countries might face.

Admittedly, most of the IMF's resources came from the American government. American taxpayers, and those Japanese and OPEC institutions which funded the federal deficit, thus subsidized the American banking system. In that sense the American government was acting, but covertly—and very inadequately. With limited resources, though, the IMF could in practice do little: it confined itself to leading a creditor's cartel, lending money to the Third World with which to repay bank debts.[21]

Then in 1982 hopes of a recovery in the world economy evaporated, as did the flow of bank lending to the Third World, which almost halved to $43 billion. Third World trade dwindled: whereas in 1981 the volume of Third World exports had increased by over 10 percent and their prices had risen marginally, in 1982 volumes fell about 4 percent and export prices declined more than 5 percent. As a direct result, the Third World's ability to service its debts disintegrated.

Through the first half of the year Mexico's finance minister, Jesus Silva Herzog, made repeated trips to Washington to warn that the problems of the world's second-largest debtor were becoming unmanageable. The Treasury made no reply, other than that the alleged Third World debt crisis was not the government's concern, a view that American banks led by Citicorp had repeatedly asserted.

Although the official American policy was that there was still no need for an official American policy, Paul Volcker at the Federal Reserve took a different view in private. He realized that to prevent the American banking system falling to its knees, he had to act: in

July 1982 the Federal Reserve lent Mexico $700 million to tide it over until a deal could be struck with the IMF.[22] A month later the money was all gone, and Mexico could no longer pay the interest on its bank loans. The day before the news reached Volcker, he had been told by the chairman of the Continental Illinois Bank that the latter would go bust without Federal Reserve support. Although the two events were not directly related, they gave Volcker the leverage that he needed to persuade the government to act. Still, however, the Treasury stalled, confining itself to persuading the Energy Department to offer Mexico $1 billion of advance payment on oil sales—at a usurious rate of interest.

Volcker got much more cooperation from other central bankers, and he managed to put together a package of temporary assistance for Brazil valued at $1.85 billion.[23] The managing director of the IMF, Jacques de Larosiere, then persuaded the American and European commercial banks to continue lending to Mexico. Most important of all, the Federal Reserve cut interest rates. Lower borrowing costs and faster economic growth averted the threatened catastrophe, not only in Mexico but elsewhere too.

As a result of the Fed's relaxation the banks were able to provide their customers with cheaper finance. They did so for domestic customers but not, unfortunately, for the Third World. Having realized that lending to the Third World was risky after all, they now wanted high interest payments to protect themselves from the risks. Although Third World countries made major efforts to increase exports and reduce imports, by 1985 the industrialized economies were again in disarray. Third World export volumes hardly grew, and their export prices began to fall; their imports had almost halved since the start of the decade, and there was little room for any further cuts. Bank lending dried to a trickle—indeed, the flow practically reversed, as the Third World doggedly struggled to maintain interest payments. Meanwhile, wealthy residents in Third World countries began to send their capital abroad, even in defiance of government controls on capital outflows. Thus the Third World had addressed its problems, but the necessary adjustment was just

too fast and too severe to be sustainable: the only way forward for
the developing nations was to reduce debt-servicing costs. American banks were still in danger.

Meanwhile the American trade deficit was rising at an alarming
rate, and Congress was threatening to introduce drastic protectionist
legislation. American politicians seemed quite willing to repeat the
global crisis of the thirties. Ronald Reagan, wearing his best Herbert Hoover clothes, showed no alarm about the possibility of a
global slump; having declared that government was the problem
not the answer, govern was what he would not do.

Then came the Baker coup. The new treasury secretary recognized that, whatever the fantasies of his leader and the court
sycophants, the United States was in a vulnerable position. Collectively the Third World countries could bring down the American
banks. The consequence would be a massive American recession,
or a huge increase in the federal deficit as Washington bailed out
the banks, or both. While the developing nations stood alone, that
did not matter too much. Then, in the spring of 1985, the leaders
of eleven Latin American debtor nations met together in Cartagena,
Colombia, to develop a concerted policy regarding debt repayment.
The plan they offered was not particularly threatening: each nation's
total interest payments would be limited to a percentage of its
export earnings. However, Baker felt a danger implicit in debtor
countries banding together—a debtors' cartel—so he launched his
Baker Plan on debt management.

Baker offered to secure an extra $20 billion of bank financing
over three years, with further amounts to come from international
agencies and other sources. The finance would go to fifteen hard-
hit but strategically important debtors; in return they would agree
to "liberalize" their economies by removing regulations and pri-
vatizing companies. Supposedly this would make it easier for the
countries to develop and prosper. Most important of all, Baker
made it clear that negotiations over debt problems would proceed
only on a case-by-case basis, and not collectively with the debtor

nations; he wanted no Cartagena Group.[24] Critics were quick to point out that all nations wanted equal treatment. Thus in practice case-by-case meant treating everybody the same; however, that did not matter to Baker, so long as the debtor nations saw themselves as competing for funds, rather than collaborating against the banks.

There was a deeper point. Each bank was trying to reduce its exposure to Third World debt, very much like savers in 1929 individually trying to reduce their exposure to the New York stock market. In 1929 the collective impact of everybody trying to protect themselves had been a market collapse, and everybody had suffered. The 1985 banking version was much slower and more ponderous, but the effect was the same—only far more serious. Each time one bank refused a loan, it became harder for another bank to get its loan repaid, so there was a powerful need for coordination by creditors. However, such a development might provoke the debtors to set up a matching cartel. The dynamics were, to put it politely, more challenging than crude free market philosophy admitted.

Although the Baker Plan represented the least possible action on the part of the American government, it nevertheless averted an emerging crisis of confidence in the world economy and headed off the threat of American protectionism. It also had an important psychological impact: it created the sensation that the debt problem was containable, and that life could go on without too much change. If everybody believed this to be true, then it was broadly correct. Unfortunately, the plan allowed little scope for improvements in Third World living standards.

In 1989 Nicholas Brady, treasury secretary in the Bush administration, introduced his "Brady Plan," which like the Baker Plan ducked the issue of genuine Third World development. It included some obligatory rhetoric about free market policies solving all the problems of the debtor countries, but little more. Admittedly, the plan did include a degree of debt forgiveness, and it promised $35 billion of new lending. However, since Third World debt was about fifteen times that amount, the finance represented little more than crisis aversion, and certainly not a new direction. Mexico alone needed debt relief of $40 billion just to pay its debt servicing out of export earnings; the Mexican government asked for half that, and received just $7 billion.

To some—that is, to the major banks—the Baker and Brady plans were triumphs. If the Third World countries had repudiated all their debts in 1985, all the American banks and most of their European rivals would have lost all of their capital. Over the next half decade the banks set about raising more capital from equity markets, while promising never again to lend to the Third World. Every deal that they cut reduced their exposure slightly. Thus they turned their backs on the Third World with little fear of being stabbed, and instead turned their attention to domestic loans. By then, though, the American economy was firmly in recession, and domestic loans were in trouble too.

## Taming the Currency Markets

While Japan contributed little to dealing with the problems of Third World debt, it contributed mightily to funding the American government deficit—not surprisingly, since that deficit contributed so much to the American current account balance of payments deficit and hence, indirectly, to the rise in Japan's prosperity during the eighties.

The American authorities increased the budget deficit and so generated a rapid rise in domestic demand. Washington also kept the dollar high so that foreign companies inevitably would meet much of the demand. Thus Congress and the president provided a banquet of sales for the Japanese, the Federal Reserve opened wide the front door, and Japanese industry came in and feasted. When, in the seventies, Japan's companies had geared themselves up to fight their American and European rivals, they greatly overestimated the strength of the competition they would face from those companies. Japan's products sold abroad with unexpected ease, and by the eighties Japan had a large current account surplus while the United States had a matching current account deficit. Since the situation was bound to end in crisis, the Japanese were as alarmed as many Americans. Japan's economy, which had once been purely reliant on the growth of domestic demand, became dependent on exports to the United States—$50 billion of them, net, in 1984. These exports were, however, contingent upon the American authorities persevering with a set of macroeconomic policies that neither they nor anybody else could justify.

The American government had difficulty financing its deficit from domestic financial flows, so the cash had to come in from abroad. The nation ran a current account balance of payments deficit and thus was bound to be a net importer of funds. Had Congress cut the budget deficit, the eighties would have been a decade of deep recession. Instead, the balance of payments took the strain, and the Japanese in particular financed rising American living standards—at least for a while.

By 1985, however, the dollar's overvaluation was becoming far too great for anybody to ignore. Although some politicians reckoned that a strong dollar kept pressure on Congress and the president to tackle the budget deficit, others feared that unless the authorities allowed the currency to slip, American trade policy would become massively protectionist.

Reagan's response to the developing crisis was characteristic: in 1985 he vetoed deficit reduction measures agreed by Republicans and Democrats, and in the same year he allowed Japan's voluntary limits on car exports to the United States to lapse. For three months, as Robert Kuttner points out, the president did not even bother to have a U.S. trade representative in his cabinet. When challenged about the dollar, Reagan continued to protest that a strong currency signified a strong nation. Benign neglect was now just neglect, pure and simple.

In the first quarter of 1985 the dollar at last fell. By the summer it had steadied and was climbing again, but without much confidence. Washington lobbyists argued that the currency was now poised on the edge of a massive fall. The only sensible policy was to try to control the impending decline in an orderly way. At first the administration refused, until James Baker shifted to the Treasury. The power vacuum at the White House remained, but the

Treasury now had grander ambitions than merely helping Wall Street to make quick profits.

Baker could do nothing directly to cut the budget deficit, nor could he dictate trade legislation. He had no control over interest rates, which were the preserve of the Federal Reserve. However, he could act on the value of the dollar, especially since he had a powerful ally—the Japanese government.

Prime Minister Yasuhiro Nakasone was ambitious that Japan should assume a much enhanced global economic and political role. He wanted to see Japan in a class above Germany—perhaps even in a class above the United States. Nakasone had always believed in a strong yen as a symbol of national pride, a policy that received considerable support from his many friends among Japanese bankers and financiers. After his appointment as prime minister in 1982, Nakasone commissioned a confidential report on how to achieve that aim. The advice was to end the nation's reliance on export-led growth and to stimulate domestic demand. The report also advised Nakasone to enlist the assistance of the United States in managing the dollar-yen exchange rate. In 1985 Nakasone moved forward on both fronts. More than that, he ordered the Japanese ministry of finance to draw up a plan: he wanted a new arrangement of managed exchange rates and favored a massive multinational intervention fund, and an international monetary conference akin to that held in Bretton Woods in 1944. He was attempting to place on Japanese shoulders the cloak cast off by the Americans, that of global economic leader.

The ministry of finance had little truck with such ambitions. Although Nakasone fancied himself a world leader, few Japanese officials, let alone politicians, wanted their nation to assume a major international role. Equally, the conservative finance ministry was as reluctant as ever to sanction higher government borrowing. With its domestic policies constrained, Japan was not yet ready for global leadership. A currency appreciation was a better policy.

From the time of Baker's appointment onward, Tokyo lobbied repeatedly for a lower dollar. While Americans did not like the damage to their domestic industry caused by the high dollar, the

Japanese worried about the damage to their inflation rates caused by the corresponding weakness of the yen. More than that, they feared the protectionism that Congress might unleash if the dollar did not fall. Lastly, they worried about the instability that might result from an unmanaged collapse.

Don Regan had always responded to foreign demands for a lower dollar by telling the Japanese and the Europeans to get their own houses in order. He had a point: if the American budget deficit was too large, then German and Japanese deficits were proportionally too small. Tight fiscal policies in Europe and Japan helped to generate large current account surpluses, and an equivalent current account deficit for the United States. Less plausibly, Regan criticized both Germany and Japan for being insufficiently open to imports of American goods, and for setting barriers against capital inflows.

Japan's financial deregulation occurred partly in response to such pressure. In May 1984 Don Regan negotiated with the Japanese government for the removal of restrictions that prevented Japanese residents from buying American assets. Regan's aim was to make it easier for the Reagan government to borrow from Japan.[25] The federal deficit was rising, and the government was unwilling either to reduce the deficits or to reduce the dollar exchange rate. American domestic policies were increasingly contingent on foreigners being willing to lend to the United States.

From Japan's point of view, reform was needed anyway. Until the seventies Japan's tightly controlled financial system had worked well enough; however, when Japan's current account went into surplus, the difficulty faced by Japanese institutions wishing to lend abroad put upward pressure on both the yen and domestic asset prices. The government felt obliged to take the pressure off by removing various restrictions on capital outflows.[26] New laws made it much easier for banks and institutions to lend abroad, by means of conventional loans as well as the purchase of bonds such as American government Treasury bills. The Tokyo Stock Exchange opened for membership to foreigners and Japanese institutional investors, who could buy increasing amounts of foreign assets.

The alternative would have been to restrict outflows of Japanese goods, which hardly seemed sensible. On the contrary: significant trade liberalization also took place, and in the eighties Japan removed almost all the remaining explicit trade barriers. (Imports of rice were one exception.)

During 1985 Japan slightly relaxed its budget policies in response to American criticisms. The Germans, however, stood firm: the Bundesbank in particular was frightened that any fiscal boost would simply generate more domestic inflation, which would invite a still weaker deutschemark and a stronger dollar, compounding the problem. The Germans also worried that intervention in currency markets might trigger an uncontrolled collapse in the dollar. Nevertheless, when word reached them that American and Japanese officials were about to strike an agreement to intervene, even the German authorities fell into line. A bilateral relationship between Japan and the United States was not a development that the Germans could accept with any happiness.

Baker chose the September meeting of G5—the finance ministers of the five largest industrialized economies—for the announcement. The finance ministers declared that "some further orderly appreciation of the main nondollar currencies against the dollar is desirable." Since the currency markets were unsure about where the dollar ought to be going, a lead from the world's leading finance ministers had an impact quite out of proportion to its actual importance. Nevertheless, it seemed to many that the announcement, made at New York's Plaza Hotel and hence known as the Plaza Accord, forged a new relationship between the United States and Japan. A joint communique of all the participants, the statement promised a new era of international policy cooperation, going beyond a merely technical commitment on currency management. It seemed clear that five central banks all cooperating to manage the currency markets would have more success than any one on its own, even if the one was the mighty Federal Reserve. However, the political significance of the Plaza Accord was far deeper: the U.S. Treasury secretary had made a deal with the Japanese because deals within Washington were either impossible to strike or impossible to implement. Whereas in 1971 John Connolly had consulted colleagues but kept other finance ministers in the dark, Baker did the reverse: although Volcker knew what was pending, Regan did not.

For a year, the dollar fell and central banks managed the currency downward on the foreign exchange markets, using coordinated cuts in interest rates to manage the descent. During 1986 growth slowed in all three major economies. By the end of 1986 the dollar fall seemed to have gone far enough: the American authorities were intervening to support the dollar. The Germans and the Japanese agreed that the depreciation had gone as far as it should. Now the question was what to do about ending the fall.

In late 1986 the Germans insisted that the Americans should raise interest rates. James Baker countered that the Germans and the Japanese should reduce their rates; he even threatened that the American government would allow a further dollar fall unless the other two governments relaxed their monetary policies. However, the Japanese and the Germans suspected that Baker was bluffing. They knew that the Federal Reserve had become very anxious that the low-dollar policy might have gone too far. If Paul Volcker ordered a rise in American interest rates to prevent an increase in inflation, as he might, Baker would look very silly. Baker became conciliatory.

Now it was time for the Germans to act tough and to refuse to negotiate. Privately they had never liked the Plaza Accord. Karl Otto Pohl, the Bundesbank president, had tried to call a halt to the depreciation before even three weeks were up. In October 1986, Baker signed a bilateral currency agreement with the Japanese finance minister, Kiichi Miyazawa: the two governments announced that they would act in concert to stabilize the dollar against the yen at the rate then prevailing. The Japanese committed themselves to cut interest rates, reform taxes, and raise government spending; Baker made no corresponding commitments, though, since he lacked the necessary power.[27]

Even this modest international package may have been over-ambitious: first the Japanese finance ministry and then the American

Treasury sought to break the spirit of the currency pact. Apparently, international coordination had to be wholehearted or abandoned altogether. In February 1987 the G5 ministers met in Paris to try to put together a new currency pact; rather surprisingly, they succeeded. The Louvre Accord involved spending boosts or tax cuts in both Japan and Germany, while the Americans promised to keep the budget deficit under control. All three nations publicly agreed to intervene in order to stabilize currencies; privately they set very tight bands within which they would not allow currencies to move. As a result, 1987 was a year of remarkable currency stability.

## Problems at Home

Still, something was seriously wrong: although the big three finance ministers had decided that their currencies looked fairly valued at prevailing rates, the currency markets did not agree. They were waiting for the dollar to fall. Those who still held dollars in 1987 mostly sold them: they wanted to buy back later at a lower price. The Bank of Japan and the Bundesbank thus spent 1987 buying dollars to prevent the American currency from collapsing. The more dollars they bought, the more convinced the markets became that the eventual crash would be spectacular.

The currency markets' conviction that the dollar was about to fall was in stark contrast to the view taken earlier in the decade. The dollar's inexplicable rise had been treated without any skepticism at all. Apparently, old-fashioned economics was back in fashion. By the autumn everybody knew that the Bank of Japan and the Bundesbank had spent $120 billion in support of the American currency—there seemed a good chance that 1988's bill would be even higher. Would the Germans and Japanese be willing to pay more? In September came the answer: *No.* The month before, Paul Volcker had been replaced at the Fed by the less experienced Alan Greenspan, who promptly raised interest rates. To his surprise, both the Japanese and the Germans also raised their interest rates, in defiance of the consequence for the dollar. A G7 communique (Canada and Italy had been let into the former G5) was conspicuously empty of content, suggesting no agreement. The various central bankers denounced each other in public. Accordingly, on October 19, 1987, with international cooperation in disarray, the market crashed.

Bizarrely, the wrong market fell: it was the dollar that was in trouble, but it was the American equity market which collapsed. The logic involved was rather tortuous. The 1987 current account of the balance of payments was $157 billion in deficit, and a larger figure seemed in prospect for 1988. Americans either had to find a way to finance their current account or they had to reduce the deficit. There had been no private capital flows in 1987, and so central banks had financed the deficit by intervention. However, the Bundesbank and the Bank of Japan were no longer willing to do the financing, and private investors would not come back into the market until after the dollar fell. That left two options: either the dollar had to collapse, or the American economy had to go into recession to reduce imports, stimulate exports, and thus reduce the current account deficit.

Prompted in part by Greenspan's interest rate rise, the financial markets believed that rather than allowing the dollar to fall, policymakers would push the economy into recession. That left American equities looking significantly overvalued. If the domestic economy slowed and output declined, companies would not achieve the profits growth that Wall Street was expecting—so stock prices were too high and needed to fall. According to such reasoning, the dollar looked fine, but equities were vulnerable. On October 19, Wall Street cut itself down to size.

What happened over the next year, though, was that the recession did not come but the dollar *did* fall. Many assume that the absence of recession was a consequence of the Fed's reduction of interest rates in the wake of the equity crash. This suggestion, although partially true, presents its own puzzles: Why did the Fed (and almost everybody else) imagine that lower equity prices would cause a recession? If lower prices caused recession, what caused the lower prices? Perhaps the equity market believed that the government's failure to reduce the federal deficit would cause a recession.

But why should low taxes and rising spending cause a recession? The only explanation is that the markets expected the Fed to raise interest rates: higher interest rates would support the dollar and spite the politicians for failing to come to grips with the deficit problem. This suggests that the failure of the Louvre Accord was a major setback for the United States, for it forced the Federal Reserve to be much tougher than it might have been under a cooperative arrangement. Yet the Louvre Accord had, indirectly, caused the second Wall Street Crash. But the crash itself was, in retrospect, unnecessary: there was no immediate recession, and the dollar did fall. It was all rather a mess.

All but the most diehard conservatives, such as several elected to Congress in 1994, now agree that the economic policies of the Reagan years were a failure. George Bush, an early critic of what he called Ronald Reagan's "voodoo economics," first became a convert to, and then a victim of, Reaganomics. During the Bush presidency Americans faced the consequences of the public and private profligacy of the eighties: the large budget deficits meant that Bush had to cut government employment (and the employment generated by government contracts) while the fallout from the speculative building boom of the eighties meant that construction employment stayed depressed in the run-up to the election. Encouraged by the collapse of the Soviet empire, Bush instigated a long overdue program of cuts in military and naval spending. He also, quite rightly, raised taxes.

President Bush's opportunity to reassert American military leadership came in August 1990, when Iraq invaded Kuwait. With Saudi Arabia a logical next target, Iraq seemed poised to corner the global oil market. Oil prices surged, and business confidence plunged, not least in the United States. To restore the situation Bush dispatched an army to the desert, and the Federal Reserve along with other central banks cut interest rates. Meanwhile, Saudi Arabia and the other oil-producing nations pumped more oil onto world markets, thereby pushing prices back down.

Nevertheless, the American economy slipped into recession, as did economies abroad. Part of the problem was that Operation Desert Shield—the preparation for war—seemed horribly protracted, which kept both business confidence and consumer confidence depressed. In contrast, the war itself—Operation Desert Storm—was brief and decisive, and it led to revivals of confidence both in the United States and elsewhere. In the spring of 1991 the American economy seemed poised for recovery. Consumer spending increased, housing starts resumed, Wall Street rallied, and output climbed.

Employment, however, increased only slowly. Consumer confidence faded and consumer spending leveled off. Business investment remained subdued and the Federal Reserve, which had briefly raised interest rates, felt obliged to cut them again. That kept the recovery going, but did little either to make Americans feel prosperous and secure or to restore confidence in the president. In 1992 the American electorate voted George Bush out of office, replacing him with a leader who professed to be more willing than his predecessors to face the truth about the American economy, better able to learn from the nation's history, and eager to tackle problems that had been long in the making. Three years on, however, such promises remain largely unfulfilled, and the need for a new direction is greater than ever.

*Chapter Nine*

# CONCLUSION: JAPAN TO THE RESCUE?

## Clinton's Problems

The basic problem facing the American economy, and one that President Clinton barely began to address following his election, is its poor productivity performance. Although American labor is still the most productive in the world, other nations are catching up; some will probably overtake the United States early in the next century. Obviously, this will have severe consequences for the American economy as it becomes ever more difficult for American products to compete in terms of price in world markets. So either American firms must perpetually raise the quality and design of their products or jobs will shift abroad. Nor is that all: as Paul Krugman has argued, trade problems are just a small part of the reason why poor productivity growth limits economic performance—without productivity gains it is impossible for real incomes to rise over the long term.[1]

Some people say this is too gloomy and derive comfort from the fact that American manufacturing productivity has been rising much faster than productivity in the economy as a whole.[2] American factories have boosted their output per worker at about the same rate as factories in Japan and Europe (but still not as fast as in Korea, Taiwan, or China). Nevertheless, it is the growth in productivity in the economy as a whole that largely decides how fast average real incomes can rise: without faster productivity growth, Americans may soon see average living standards in many other nations surpassing their own.

So far, Americans have found ways to make their incomes rise faster than would normally be expected, given their relatively poor productivity performance. Sometimes that has meant encouraging the growth of overseas markets. Now that American competitiveness is under such threat, however, export-led growth is a hard road for the United States to tread. Instead, Americans have expanded their domestic market by spending and borrowing more and saving less. As part of that, the American government has since the early eighties increased its spending by more than it has increased its tax revenues, with a short-term result of higher income and employment levels.[3] In the long term, though, debt-servicing burdens rise, the balance of payments suffers, and the inflation rate may well rise along with (not unreasonable) conservative demands that the government curb the excessive growth in its own and other people's spending.

Indeed, the problem with demand-led growth of the sort that President Reagan in particular pursued is that in the long run it may be self-defeating. Americans save less to allow themselves to spend more, reducing the nation's capacity to invest unless it borrows more from abroad. Without new machinery and equipment American industry has difficulty raising its productivity and improving its product design and quality. That reduces the long-term growth rate. So, to feed the habit of real income growth, the nation saves still less and borrows more. However, the rest of the world is bound to become wary of perpetually lending to the United States simply so that Americans can live beyond their means. American dependency on other nations is in consequence higher now than it has been for a century.

There are other problems that are probably related to poor American productivity performance. Earlier chapters have discussed low American spending on research and development in the sixties and seventies, a pattern that became even more pronounced during the Reagan and Bush presidencies. Meanwhile, infrastructure investment halved as a share of American gross national product between the sixties and eighties, leaving roads in disrepair, airways chronically congested, and many pollution and garbage problems untackled.

Perhaps most important are the problems with the American education system. On average, the American labor force has more educational credentials than almost any other. There are more than three thousand institutions of higher education in the United States, including universities, colleges, professional schools, and junior and teaching colleges; between them they have almost nine million enrolled students. The most prestigious private universities attract high-caliber postgraduate students and researchers from Japan and Europe.

However, not all American colleges and universities are the equal of Harvard or Yale. American undergraduate degrees are generally of a lower standard than those of the major European nations. Like-for-like tests suggest that average American students are undereducated, and that below-average students are profoundly so. The United States spends less on education per head than its major competitors, once adjustment is made for the extra cost of educating young people from severely disadvantaged minority groups. A socially divided and wounded society is more expensive to educate, and the failure to educate the disadvantaged (the high school dropout rate for Hispanic Americans is 33 percent) is very expensive in terms of lost human potential and civic disintegration.[4] As a result, many Americans receive levels of educational provision that are quite inadequate to meet their needs.

The same is true of health and welfare provision. A baby born in Harlem has lower life expectancy than one born in many parts of the Third World. For the nation as a whole, infant mortality is just over ten deaths for every thousand live births—only Italy fares worse among the major industrialized nations—even though Americans spend more on health per person than the people of almost any other nation.

Some people may doubt whether any of this matters. American inequalities generate little organized opposition, and many Americans believe that large social divisions are a good thing, since they make people more self-reliant and more enterprising. Americans often say that the welfare systems that the Europeans constructed to relieve extremes of poverty "emasculated" those nations. Even liberal Americans sometimes suppose that their system derives legitimacy from a high degree of equality of opportunity. In the United States, the story goes, the poor can escape their poverty more easily than elsewhere.

This may have been true a century ago, but today equality of opportunity in the United States is probably no higher than in other leading industrialized nations. An American born into a family from the bottom decile of earners is scarcely more likely to enter the top decile of earners than somebody in Germany or France. In both of those nations the state spreads its educational, health, and welfare benefits much more evenly than does the United States, and both are steadily catching up to the United States in the prosperity league.

Meanwhile, the poverty and squalor within the United States may be eroding the nation's political stability and civic cohesion. The haves care little for the have-nots, who are too likely to be black or Hispanic; often they do not share a common language with the majority. Poor Americans are frequently either participants in, or the victims of, serious crime. All of this has economic consequences, as Bill Clinton rightly said in his 1992 presidential campaign.

These circumstances, plus the American public's rejection of the policies of Presidents Reagan and Bush, should have presented Bill Clinton with the justification to strike out in new directions. His economic agenda needed little research: strengthen government and industry, improve health, education, and investment, weaken the financial markets, and instigate coordinated policymaking at the international level, encompassing trade policies but also policies regarding growth and inflation. Unfortunately, less has happened than was promised.

In 1993 the newly elected president announced a number of approaches to help restore American competitiveness.[5] He proposed, for example, to double the budget spent by the National Institute of Standards Technology on generic high-technology research. Generic research, embarked upon without any specific product in mind, is the kind of research that a laissez-faire economy is likely to ignore, in contrast to the corporatist economies of Japan and Germany. President Clinton also proposed to make permanent the existing temporary tax breaks on companies' research spending. He proposed a range of other initiatives in the research area, including regional technology alliances, local enterprise zones, and targeted assistance for the automobile industry to help it develop environmentally friendly products. Furthermore, the president also announced plans to improve the nation's infrastructure, including its highways.

On a much larger scale, the Clinton administration also planned to strengthen the American education and training systems by means of a wide range of measures. These included an extension to the availability of the Head Start scheme, the provision of extra cash to fund public school reforms, college finance for young people in return for community work, and programs to retrain the unemployed. His intention was both to raise American competitiveness and to spread the provision of education more widely within the nation. Finally and obviously, the administration intended that its health care reforms would give poor Americans the access to health care that low-income people in most other industrialized nations have long enjoyed.

When set against the nation's economic condition, President Clinton's inauguration plans were almost certainly far too modest, and the bowdlerized policies that have been implemented (or merely debated) even more so. In all cases, an unwillingness to raise taxes sharply suggests that the government may not achieve very much and does not expect to do so. Americans are reluctant to pay the taxes necessary to generate long-term gains in their nation's income; this puts a severe brake on the prospects for economic and social advance in the United States.

The problem, as Labor Secretary Robert Reich sees it, is that for the last couple of decades the blurring of the nation's boundaries has eroded people's sense of communal responsibility.[6] Reich and others invoke a past when the United States was more self-sufficient than it is today, when most goods and services consumed within the United States were produced there and when American firms sold most of their output to American consumers. Almost all Americans worked for employers who were themselves American, and most Americans reinvested their savings in the American economy; there was economic cohesion, and with that came social cohesion. Today the situation is, according to Reich, very different: there are no ties between the prosperity of a Wall Street banker and that of Detroit car workers. If the latter lose their jobs because of foreign competition, why should the banker care? He or she drives a German or a Japanese car. The last thing the banker wants is to have his or her living standards eroded by paying high taxes to support unemployed autoworkers in Michigan.

However, as earlier chapters have suggested, that vision of the past is a myth, and the distinction drawn between it and the present is an exaggeration. For decades, succeeding administrations and Congresses have ducked many of their responsibilities, and in doing so they have increasingly abdicated their right to tax, leaving them unable to meet even their reduced commitments. The inability of modern American governments to raise taxes more than marginally is, therefore, a reflection of their lost legitimacy.

## The Case for Keynes

An alternative view, associated with Lester Thurow among others, is that the American economy suffers primarily because it lacks the strong managerial capitalism that characterizes the economies of Japan, Germany, and the emerging economies of East and Southeast Asia. According to this account, which gains some credence from the history set forth here, no amount of extra investment in education or the infrastructure will improve the performance of the American economy unless Americans also make other changes.[7] Americans, it is said, must stop worshiping the paradigm of perfect competition, since in an economy made up of perfectly competitive companies, there are no economies of scale and there is not enough profit to fund research, development, and innovation. Thus every extra bit of investment brings a slightly smaller bit of extra output than its predecessor; so that eventually there is no point in investing, and growth dries up. In these circumstances real living standards tend not to rise, except in short periods—and then thanks to unsustainable trickery.

There is a lot to be said in favor of this view. Admittedly, it is true that much of the American economy is dominated by large firms, but thanks largely to the banking system they are as wary of innovation and investment, as if they were the small, weak firms of the competitive paradigm. All companies live in a constant struggle to appease their bankers, but since American lenders are allowed to know very little about, and hence do not trust, the firms to which they lend, American banks and brokers only want quick financial returns: this means high dividend payments and high bond-servicing costs, which in turn means low investment and slow growth. In the United States, the financial system appropriates the benefits of economies of scale in industry and commerce as well as the advantages accruing from better-educated workers and more infrastructure.

According to Thurow's view, Wall Street ruins everything, and American companies fight with their hands tied behind their backs by their bankers. Japanese companies, on the other hand, fight with their bankers by their sides. The United States is not enough like Japan, and not enough like it was before the Great Depression. In Japan, and in Germany, the banks and their client companies look after each other, as happened once in the United States, before the reforms of the thirties. American prosperity in the Gilded Age did not come from a multitude of small firms competing fiercely for every inch of market space. It depended instead on a small number of very large companies creating, manipulating, and managing their markets, with the backing of the great Wall Street banks. Managers, not market forces, made the United States an economic success— the visible hand, not the invisible one.

It should not be surprising that some Americans such as Thurow want to return to managerial capitalism and allow American companies the freedom of pillowtalk with their banks and brokers. However, such a change is not likely: fundamental shifts in economic institutions do not normally occur without some precipitating crisis, and since American economic decline is so glacial, it seems unlikely that the financial system will change to become more like that of Japan or Germany. Thurow's advice, however sensible, is just not likely to be followed.

Fortunately, there is another possibility which offers the long termism of managerial capitalism without first needing a revolution in the American economic order—the strategy once advocated by Keynes.

In the late forties and fifties, governments in Japan and Europe convinced firms that rapid wartime growth could be replicated in peacetime. By restoring confidence in the economy, governments persuaded firms to invest more, creating the growth, which in turn kept public finances under control.[8] The beauty of the policy was that, having succeeded in changing psychology, there was little more for governments to do. They neither had to raise demand nor support the supply side; the economy took care of itself. The policy was similar to, but much grander than, President Roosevelt's realization in 1933 that if he restored confidence in the banks then he would not have to bail them out. And indeed American governments from Truman to Kennedy did the same, but with less conviction than their European and Japanese contemporaries and, therefore, with less success.

This strategy also has a problem, however. It was suggested in earlier chapters that, by the time that American governments were ready to embrace Keynesian ideas, years of dollar overvaluation had worsened American competitiveness and the nation was becoming involved in the Vietnam War. Although initially the war boosted business confidence, by the late sixties American firms feared for their future as the nation entangled itself ever more tightly in a war that it seemed unable to win. While the United States was losing the war in Vietnam, no economic policies—not price control, monetary control, wage control, deflation, high interest rates, whatever—could possibly win credibility.

Even before the election of the 1994 Congress, it seemed very unlikely that Keynesian policies could be introduced within the United States today. The Reagan government pursued expansionary policies in the eighties that went far beyond the bounds of good sense. Perversely, therefore, the arch anti-Keynesian government of Ronald Reagan, by adopting excessively Keynesian policies, may have queered the pitch for genuine Keynesianism today. That is in part why Clinton has not presented himself as a Keynesian: he fears, probably rightly, that American firms will not have any confidence in such policies. Without such confidence, Keynesianism is sunk. Without Keynesianism, however, the American economy will continue to drift.

Thus what the United States needs are Keynesian policies applied at the *international* level, not at the *domestic* level. For any national government, the essential Keynesian policy advice is to cut taxes or raise government spending in times when the economy is slipping into recession, and to raise taxes or cut spending when the economy is expanding rapidly. The idea is to stabilize the economy and steer a middle path between high inflation and high unemployment. However, governments are often more constrained than Keynes expected, not least by the present American crisis of confidence in such policies themselves. The solution is for governments in different countries to act together, both to reduce the amount that each individually has to do, and to ensure that the policies of one country do not accidentally undermine the policies of another.


The need for international Keynesian policies is made all the more apparent by the failure of policymakers to achieve faster economic growth by means of trade liberalization. The latest round of GATT talks, the Uruguay Round, and the subsequent arguments over the International Trade Organization (ITO), slated to succeed GATT, illustrate how little liking there is for free trade. Even when the Uruguay Round opened in Punta del Este in 1986 there was scant enthusiasm for the negotiations, which were promoted almost exclusively by the Reagan government. Washington had decided that the United States had a comparative advantage in services, and so wanted to see trade in services liberalized around the world. The same was thought to be true for agriculture—although just to make sure, the Reagan government increased its powers to subsidize American farmers while it pushed for reductions in farm subsidies elsewhere. The administration also insisted on keeping the notorious Multi Fiber Agreement that protected the textile industries of the industrialized nations against Third World competition and, in addition, began the process that would soon lead to the North American Free Trade Agreement— a policy that provides open trade for some but high trade barriers for others.

Bill Clinton came into office believing that the free trade route was unobtainable and perhaps undesirable. His administration has found comfort in the writings of the "new trade" theorists, who echo Hamilton when they suggest that there may be nothing natural or inevitable about the distribution of comparative advantages among nations. Conventional trade theory suggests that nations should specialize in the production and export of those items for which they have a comparative advantage. All other items should be imported from abroad. The theory also suggests that free market economies will tend to adopt such structures naturally of their own accord. Trade barriers that hinder or prevent the adjustment process are as injurious to the nations that erect them as to the nations against which the barriers are raised.

The new trade theorists suggest, on the contrary, that comparative advantages are the consequences, not the causes, of specialization.[9] Those countries which specialize in the production and export of, for example, aircraft acquire special knowledge and skills; these, together with straightforward economies of scale, allow them to outcompete other countries. Although leadership may be the result of natural factors (South Africa simply has vast amounts of gold), it is usually the result of human effort (the Prairies first had to be cleared). Government policy can either undermine or reinforce such effort: in the United States it has tended to undermine, whereas in Japan and elsewhere it has tended to reinforce.

A leader of the new trade theory, Paul Krugman, once remarked that because of increasing returns to scale, aircraft production had to be concentrated somewhere. "Seattle just happens to be where the roulette wheel came to stop." To which the economic journalist Robert Kuttner responded that Boeing in Seattle would never have been a success without military contracts.[10] If the air force had been free to buy at the lowest price from foreign aircraft manufacturers, the American aircraft industry would never have been so strong.

As Kuttner notes, new trade theory removes the laissez-faire presumption that nations like Japan, which practice strategic trade policy, cannot be improving their welfare. The implication is that the United States might reasonably consider doing the same, especially since there is a domestic precedent to build upon. Large chunks of American industry and agriculture have been the recipients of protectionist policies for years.

The policy goal for governments is thus to help indigenous industries capture some comparative advantages. According to this view, governments must make sure that their national economies develop and exploit various types of specialization. Governments also need to help firms hang on to their advantages in the face of attacks from foreign rivals. Hamilton argued in the eighteenth century that tariffs should play a role in supporting the growth of certain infant American industries; there may be a similar role for tariffs today in helping the nation to develop the new industries on which its future will depend.

That is the theory—but as Krugman himself has said, it is a theory that probably will not work, and one that is no substitute for Keynesian policies at the international level. One problem, often remarked upon, is that the industries chosen may not be the right ones.[11] Much more serious is the uncomfortable aspect to strategic trade policy which its advocates tend not to mention: the essence of the policy is not just that individual governments should promote some of their own industries, but that they should also sacrifice other industries to the damage inflicted by the policies of governments elsewhere. It is not enough for nations to pursue their own strategic trade policies. They must acknowledge the right of other nations to do likewise. That obviously implies some difficult domestic policy decisions—of the sort the American political system seems particularly poorly equipped to make. Even the Japanese will find these questions harder in the future.

This also implies a major challenge at the international level. If the strategic trade game is to be worth playing, countries will need to consult and cooperate with one another, and to abide by the rules of the game, whatever those rules turn out to be. Yet the experience of the GATT system suggests that international cooperation on trade issues is not easy to achieve, and the result could, therefore, be a shambles. When the overall direction was toward reducing trade barriers it did not matter if the process was "shambolic"; when the direction is toward new barriers, though, it matters rather a lot.

Rather than expecting trade policies to generate rapid growth, governments should pursue faster growth to make sensible trade policies easier to achieve. If economies grow rapidly, helped by Keynesian policies, then governments have little need to pick fights with one another over trade issues. Trade wars are most likely when world economic growth is slow. Trade barriers and deflationary government policies are indeed just alternative solutions to acute balance of payments problems. When growth is rapid, current account deficits are easy to finance; whereas slow growth makes lenders nervous, and financing dries up. Without a foreign government willing to help, countries then have no choice but to cut their deficits. As more and more governments respond to their balance of payments problems by deflating their economies, the slower becomes the growth rate of the world overall. That means unemployment, and political pressure for protectionism. The dangers are familiar, and it is easy to show why beggar-my-neighbor trade restrictions are "wrong," but sometimes governments have no other choice.

So one way to avoid protectionism is to expand the world economy at a higher rate. If the world economy grows under the guidance of Keynesian demand management, much of the financing of balance of payments deficits will be provided by private sector markets and will be self-sustaining. Achieving the growth is an intellectual and a political challenge; it is not, however, particularly expensive, since everything depends on one or more governments simply acting as the manager of the global marketplace by providing both plentiful exports of capital and an open market for imports—Adam Smith's invisible hand made visible.

## International Economic Leadership— Some Lessons

The argument for Keynesian policymaking at the global level is closely linked to the view that the world needs a hegemonic leader. Many people assume that because the American economy is still so large, and American power so mighty, the United States is simply "bound to lead." However, previous hegemonic powers—Britain, and the United States after World War II—were major net exporters of capital and major net importers of goods. That was a very special combination: it depended on the country concerned being able to live off the income of its overseas wealth (acquired, in both cases, by war). Japan today is globally wealthy, but it is not a major net importer. The United States is no longer wealthy, since it borrows rather than lends, although it is a heavy importer. This difference is fundamental. As importers of goods and exporters of financial capital, Britain and then the United States were able to set the rules of the game: they had the markets everybody else wanted, and they had the capital which other nations wanted too. Japan now has the capital but not the domestic markets.

Because the United States was a reluctant superpower, there was no leader in the thirties, and so the major deficit nations, especially Germany, found themselves unable to borrow from the American and British banks. The trade war developed because both private capital markets and national governments turned their backs on the problems of the international economy. The thirties also illustrate another vital point: the need for global economic management is especially large if the world goes into recession, since the whole world can no more compete its way out of a slump than it can use trade barriers to create jobs all around. If growth is to happen, then it must not be stifled by financial policies that focus only on short-term balance of payments problems, since such policies all involve struggling to get the world back into equilibrium by lowering aspirations, achievements, and living standards. Worse still, in pursuing such policies, each deficit country is in competition with each other. They cannot all succeed—indeed, by competing they will all fail.[12]

This is why a global leader is needed: to say that governments should not pursue such mutually defeating policies. Keynes gave precisely that advice at Bretton Woods, where he predicted that large balance of payments deficits would be a feature of the postwar world. But Harry Dexter White, leader of the American delegation to the conference, refused to tolerate the idea of nations running balance of payments deficits for several years. He rejected Keynes's ambitious plans in favor of more conservative proposals that stressed the priority of financial orthodoxy. Those policies failed in 1947 and were replaced by the Marshall Plan, providing the kind of government intervention at the international macroeconomic level that Keynes thought was required, albeit through a mechanism that was much cruder and much more interventionist than any he had envisaged.

Marshall aid bolstered the confidence of the financial markets and private sector banks provided large flows of finance into Western Europe, enabling Europe to grow rapidly. Since the funds were mostly spent on American goods, the American economy expanded rapidly too, allowing the United States to hold down its trade barriers against Western Europe. The boom was also sustained by a climate of expectations in which companies felt able to invest on the assumption that growth would last.

The success of Marshall aid is analogous to the possibility of stimulating growth in the Third World. In the eighties the American authorities tried to develop policies to deal with Third World debt, and the Baker Plan of 1985 seemed on the surface to be a reassertion of American imagination and ambition. The basic assumption of the plan was the Keynesian insight that the only way for the debt problem to decline in importance was for the world economy, and especially the economies of the debtor nations, to grow. Yet the Baker Plan offered no mechanism that would make that happen, other than a rather woolly hope that privatization and supply-side measures in the debtor countries would stimulate output and activity. There was no stimulus to global demand, no cut in interest rates, no debt writeoff. And if the American authorities were right to reason that the world economy was in no shape to cope with any such Keynesian reflation—which is itself debatable —then that itself implied that the Americans had allowed the global system to develop in such a way that neither they nor anybody else could offer it leadership.

During the Reagan years the orthodox line was that all governments ought to struggle to reduce their deficits. The consequence was a period of slow growth. Individual governments tended to blame the world recession for high domestic unemployment rates while denying that they were contributing to the world recession through their own policies. It was Herbert Hoover in the Great Depression all over again. What the revised story lacked in depth, it made up for in breadth. Unemployment in the United States was not so high in the eighties, but in the world as a whole unemployment, destitution, and famine reached levels never before recorded.

The problems of the developing world have rebounded on the industrialized nations. The friction today between Japan and the United States is partly the indirect result of the poor state of the economies of the Third World. For both nations, the other is about their most important trading partner and their most important investment partner. Japan has financed American political hegemony in return for access to American markets. Had the Americans been more successful in the previous decades at stimulating the markets of the Third World, then the American balance of payments would have been stronger and its need for Japanese capital inflows would have been smaller; equally the Japanese would have had other export markets to attack and would not have needed to export so heavily to the United States.

Many economists argue that Keynesian global economic leadership is dangerous because it is inflationary, and unnecessary because the financial markets will always be willing to finance a current account deficit, if the loans are economically viable. Inflation is indeed sometimes a danger, though not seriously so in the late 1990s. As far as the efficiency of financial markets is concerned, banks, brokers, and institutions lack the information needed for the efficient allocation of resources. Those who borrow know better than those who lend the chances of the loan going sour. So the risk of the lender being taken for a ride, deliberately or otherwise, is high. One supposed solution, rejected in this book, is the laissez-faire method—lend only short-term, to low-risk borrowers.[13] Another solution is the managerial capitalism approach—buy a stake in the firm to which you lend, get a seat on the board, give seats to others whom you trust, become privy to inside information, talk softly, and carry a big stick. The third solution is the Keynesian approach—governments accept responsibility for maintaining decent growth in market demand, and banks then lend with the confidence that most of their customers will benefit from such favorable conditions.

As far as the management of the world economy is concerned, it is clearly the third of these which is most relevant and creates the case for a global leader or manager. That is especially clear in light of the fact that the problems of financial markets are largest where international transactions are concerned. The difficulty of financing the revival of Eastern Europe is a case in point: if reconstruction is to happen, then either private sector banks will need to lend Eastern Europe cash with which to buy American, Japanese, and European capital goods, or governments will need to do so. Either way, the countries of Eastern Europe will run large deficits on their balance of payments. That in itself will make banks reluctant to lend; however, if Western governments are unwilling to borrow in order to reduce unemployment in their economies, it seems unlikely that they will borrow to reduce unemployment abroad.

## Who Will Lead the World Economy?

It is easier to say that the world needs an economic leader than to say who that should be. However, it has to be faced that the United States is probably not a candidate. Given the injuries that the American economy sustained in the thirties, the large role that the United States played in the world economy after 1945 was probably too great a burden, right from the start. Vietnam was the final expression of that burden—economic retreat in 1971 was wholly appropriate and should have been accepted by the American government and people.[14] However, although the war deeply damaged American economic leadership, it did not provide a new global political leader in the way that earlier great wars did. Instead, we have seen a series of ad hoc adjustments that have left the United States nominally in charge but practically constrained.

It is equally clear that there is no obvious mechanism for transferring the remains of American hegemonic leadership away from the United States. Thankfully, there seems to be no taste for a major war. So long as nuclear weapons exist, wars are kept local and so do not alter the balance of power. But there is a basic question, unasked by most of the pundits who claim that the United States is bound to lead: What can Americans actually do to reassert their leadership?

It has been argued above that improving competitiveness alone will not increase American economic power. In any event, it is unlikely that Americans will come to grips with their trade and balance of payments problems—nations rarely do. Over the last decade the international economy has grown accustomed to the fact that the United States is a massive net importer of goods. This state of affairs is now treated either as if it is normal and sustainable, or as if it is Japan's fault, although it is neither. Meanwhile, the response of economists to the problem is that if a trade war is to be avoided and a domestic recession is not wanted, then a large dollar devaluation in order to restore competitiveness and achieve some years of trade surpluses is essential.[15] However, British experience suggests that there is no simple or quick policy adjustment available to correct years of trade deficit. The return of the American economy to competitiveness is unlikely to occur within a couple of decades, and certainly not without an intervening period of austerity.

Although the United States is distinctly ambivalent about whether it wishes to be the world's true economic leader, Washington officials are clearly reluctant to subordinate their policy decisions to those of any international agencies, to allow other nations such as Japan to increase their participation in such bodies as the IMF, or to allow other nations to lead directly. Meanwhile, it will be difficult for the United States to maintain a commitment to a liberal international economic order when the American economy is in relative decline. Indeed, repeated American criticisms of Japan for mercantilism can be read as Americans themselves toying with the idea of adopting such policies. Americans are correct that Japan (and Europe) do not "play fair," but the ability to accommodate such behavior is the sign of a genuine leader. In the field of trade policy, most favored nation clauses are the clearest expression of that, and the willingness to replace such clauses with reciprocity policies thus marks a further abdication by the United States of the leadership role.

One possibility would be a new peace between the United States and Japan. If Americans do not want to trim their living standards, then it certainly seems sensible that they should be nice to the Japanese and find common ground with them. As the world's major exporter of capital, self-interest obliges Japan to take some responsibility for the world economy or suffer as a result. The United States, which is an importer of both goods and capital, can do little on its own apart from threaten the kind of trade wars that in the thirties hurt everybody, including the United States itself. But it can guide Japanese policymaking in a benign direction, and help the American economy in the process.

Unfortunately there is no political will to carry out such a course. On the contrary, the American nightmare is that the United States will shortly be supplanted by Japan as the world's richest and most powerful nation. More tactful ways can be found to express those anxieties, but Japan's success seems to pose a peculiarly painful threat to American citizens. One reason is, of course, that the memory of the Pacific War, and especially of Pearl Harbor, still hurts: the suspicion is that the Japanese have consciously refought the war by out-manufacturing and out-trading the United States. Making matters worse, Japan's postwar expansion was clearly achieved with help from the United States. American taxpayers subsidized the Japanese economy in the late forties, and until the mid-eighties Americans tolerated an international trading regime under which the American market was left wide open to imports from Japan. Meanwhile, the Japanese market was largely closed to American imports. Now that the Japanese people have grown rich on American help, what do they do to repay their former benefactors? The answer seems to be that they create unemployment in smokestack America, while refusing to share responsibility for the maintenance of peace and prosperity in the world at large.

Such common sentiments represent a real barrier to any transfer of leadership. Admittedly the European experience shows that former enemies can soon become close collaborators, but that probably requires very different domestic political institutions than those of either Japan or the United States.

Furthermore, Japan has so far lacked the global political and military aspirations that were the major driving forces behind American leadership. The post of global hegemonic leader has its perks, but it also has its duties. In Japan objections to assuming the mantle of leadership are often made on moral and/or pacifist grounds, but they also come from the ministry of finance on grounds of cost. As global leader, even on a shared basis with the United States, Japan might have to do a great deal: offer a New Deal for the United States, a Marshall Plan for Eastern Europe and the Third World, and a new Bretton Woods strategy for managing the world economy. In fact, such policies need not be too onerous: as was suggested earlier, if the world economy grows under the guidance of Keynesian demand management, the bulk of the financing will be provided by private sector markets and should be self-sustaining. The Japanese government's job would simply be to create confidence that the world economy would grow, and that Japan would be the guarantor of that growth. Nevertheless that is not a view to which conservative administrations tend to subscribe, as the record of successive American administrations, sketched out in this book, illustrates. It is clear that American governments delayed for as long as they could becoming the world's economic leader. Eventually they faced a stark choice, between the option of keeping the global system going and the lack of any global system at all. Between 1941 and 1945 the United States took over the world. It was all or nothing. In contrast, the options facing Japan and the world today more closely resemble those of 1918–21, or indeed 1967–71. Muddling along is an available, if uninspiring, option—so why should Japan or any other nation take upon itself the burdens of the age?

## Japan—Another Reluctant Superpower

The one possibility is that political and economic change *within* Japan will lead to a major change in that nation's role within the global economy, and hence precipitate the kind of changes that American leaders, not surprisingly, are themselves reluctant to provoke. Thanks in large part to the industrial restructuring of the seventies, Japan weathered the recession of the early eighties better than most industrialized economies did. It experienced stronger growth and lower inflation than most of its competitors, and only a modest rise in unemployment. However, half the rise in Japan's gross domestic product between 1979 and 1983 was accounted for by an improvement in the trade account, and in the first half of the eighties exports rose by 50 percent whereas domestic demand increased by just 15 percent. Not only did that alarm Japan's trading partners in Europe and the United States but it also worried the Japanese themselves, who feared such heavy dependency on overseas markets. In 1986 the government-commissioned Maekawa Report recommended a large expansion in domestic demand, heavy infrastructure spending, financial liberalization and the removal of trade controls, and the encouragement of investment abroad. Before the report had been fully implemented, however, the European and American economies had moved into recession, dragging Japan with them.

In late 1986 recovery got underway, stimulated by the implementation of Maekawa's advice and hence by rapid growth in domestic, not overseas, demand. Meanwhile the yen strengthened, severely undermining the competitiveness of Japanese industry. As a result, between 1986 and 1990, Japan's imports consistently grew faster than exports. Even so, Japanese manufacturers clearly struggled to maintain their presence in export markets, sacrificing margins to avoid losing sales—behavior perhaps characteristic of a broader commitment to their markets, but also partly a reflection of the increasing pressure being placed on Japanese firms by American and European insistence on supposedly voluntary export restraints and on unusually strict adherence to GATT trading rules.[16]

In the five years from 1985 to 1990, against this background of liberalization and rising demand, real incomes in Japan rose as the economy expanded. However, Japanese land prices nearly tripled, while stock prices doubled. Other asset prices joined in, and as a result many Japanese became, at least on paper, hugely wealthy. They bought rare paintings and rare cars, sending prices spiraling on world markets.

Much of the rise in the Tokyo stock market and in land prices reflected purchases by banks and industrial companies rather than by private individuals. With the stock market rising and land prices soaring, banks and corporations could make large financial gains, boosting their total profits. The increases masked from shareholders any problems in the underlying trading performance of the companies concerned. As prices rose still further, so companies felt justified in their behavior. They bought more land and more equities, and pushed the market higher still. Bank assets rose by three quarters between 1985 and 1989, and in 1989 Japan's biggest bank, Daiichi Kangyo, made two thirds of its profits from share dealing. Then, suddenly, the markets collapsed. Land prices fell to a third of their peak value.[17] Equity prices had a similar experience.

There were obvious comparisons with the Wall Street Crash of 1929. And there is another similarity: in the run-up to the Wall Street Crash, American banks had been reluctant to lend abroad because of worries over slow growth in the world economy. That forced cash to stay within the United States. The consequence should have been a dollar appreciation, but the gold standard prevented that. Instead, domestic U.S. asset prices rose. In the recent Japanese case, the exchange rate policy was much less explicit but it was nevertheless there. In the second half of the eighties the yen did not rise as it should have done because neither the Japanese, nor the American government, allowed that to happen. That transferred instability to domestic financial systems, especially Japan's.

Some writers believe that the recent financial dislocation will produce long-term economic problems. If that is true, and if it includes a shift in the nation's economy toward becoming a net *importer* of goods but still an *exporter* of capital, then Japan will be placed to become the new economic superpower. But will it? It is encouraging that, faced with the worst recession since World War II, Japan's government increased spending and restricted tax increases. Japan thus had a Keynesian reflation, rather than implementing the type of conservative policies that Roosevelt pursued in the thirties under similar circumstances. Because of that, Japan's economy was soon on the mend.

Despite this, the problems are substantial, even if they do not compare with those of the United States in the 1930s. The collapse in asset prices hurt both companies and banks. Japanese companies retrenched in the early 1990s, cutting jobs and investment and shifting production abroad, especially to neighboring nations such as China, Thailand, and Vietnam, a process that intensified as the yen continued to strengthen in the currency markets. Meanwhile the banks are desperate to rebuild their capital but cannot do so unless either the corporate sector or the personal sector is willing to borrow heavily and at expensive rates.

Since many Japanese households were also hit by the collapse in asset prices, they too are reluctant to take risks. Nevertheless, over the longer term a real possibility is that the Japanese people demand, and get, a much larger share of the proceeds of success than in the past half century. Because they are at heart rather like the Americans (and the Italians, and the British, and everybody else) many ordinary Japanese have come to think that it is they who, for decades, have been cheated. Japan has been economically successful partly because the people have made sacrifices: six long working days a week, living conditions that are frequently cramped, poor sanitation, overcrowded transport, negligible public pensions, widespread corruption politics and business, environmental depletion and pollution that, especially in Osaka, almost rivals the standards of the old Eastern Europe. Although the Japanese have long put up with it all and just carried on working, perhaps they will no longer continue doing so.

Giving credence to this is the enormous effort that Japanese employers devote to instilling loyalty—testifying that such loyalty is far from automatic. Furthermore, the loyal job-for-life worker is the exception, not the rule. Ties of mutual obligation bind many Japanese workers to well-managed paternalistic companies that grow in size, year after year and decade after decade, and more than half Japan's workforce is employed in small companies. Those people have little or no job security. They receive few benefits such as sickness pay, and they experience periodic redundancies or dismissals. Their grip on prosperity is tenuous. In hard times Japan's larger companies squeeze this reserve army of disaffiliated workers and small-businesses. That allows the big firms to be commercially successful and generous employers simultaneously. Their presence has in the past made the economic system more successful but less fair—and if it is less fair then it is potentially less stable. The household saving rate has already fallen, and productivity growth may slow. New behavior patterns may turn Japan's large firms from an asset into a liability. Resources are shifting at the margin, away from investment with a direct commercial return and toward more socially minded objectives. So economic growth may slow.

That is very much what happened in Europe and the United States in the sixties and seventies. The end of European colonialism culminated in the Vietnam War. That contributed to the slowdown in economic growth, and provoked a sharp scramble over scarce resources. Unions fought with managers, workers fought against each other, young people and minorities fought with authority figures. The political consensus fell apart and economic growth, once fallen, became enormously difficult to resurrect. Had the total cake continued growing rapidly then the conflicts might have remained in check. It did not, and rapid inflation was just part of the ensuring dislocation.

Japan may be set for the same experience.[18] Essentially Japan is now a mature economy. Wages are high, the population is aging and finance is becoming an increasingly important part of the national economy. Japan is moving toward being a rentier economy, and thus economic policy will gradually shift away from manufacturing interests. A high-yen policy will gradually erode Japanese competitiveness. Partly for this reason and partly because the personal sector saving rate has fallen, on some measures the trade surpluses are declining in real terms.

At first sight, all these developments seem clearly undesirable. A massive slowdown in economic performance, for whatever reason, could, for example, undermine Japanese unity and common purpose. Conflicts beneath Japan's placid surface might become unmanageable if economic difficulties ever become severe. Periodic youth unrest in Japan is a sign that the future could be rougher than the past. Admittedly the same has been said about the young in every culture in every age in history. Usually they have proved themselves willing to be bought off by jobs, homes, spending money, and marriage. But what if the jobs are no longer there?

It is also possible that rising public cynicism over the honesty of politicians and business leaders will make for a less pliable electorate and workforce. Here too, the evidence of past episodes suggests that the scandals of the early nineties may have little long term impact, providing that the government can buy off the people with rising living standards. If standards do not rise, there might be problems.

The collapse in asset prices has also drawn attention to the corruption endemic in Japanese government, starting with the Recruit scandal, which gradually engulfed the then-ruling Liberal Democratic Party (LDP), eventually disgracing both its elder statesman, Shin Kanemaru, and Prime Minister Miyazawa. So long as the politicians were delivering full employment and jobs for life for Japan's salarymen, the scandals were not too threatening, but when the economy moved back into recession, dissatisfaction with the LDP became intense. For a while the LDP clung to power, but on June 18, 1993, Tsutsomu Hata, a leading member of the party, together with other members of the LDP, voted against the Miyazawa government in a Diet motion of no confidence. After thirty-eight years the LDP was out of office, only to be replaced by a coalition government.

It seemed a monumental break. Within months, however, allegations emerged that the new prime minister, Morihiro Hosokawa, was also guilty of financial impropriety; when he resigned, Hata took over. Then in June 1994 Hata's coalition government fell apart, and he too resigned as prime minister. Hata had proved himself popular, capable, and relatively immune to corruption charges, despite having once been close to Kanemaru and to another arch fixer, Ichiro Ozawa. However, Hata was dependent for support on the former Socialist Party, as much dominated by conservatives who opposed reform as the LDP. When it became clear that the Hata government would push through political reforms, the former Socialists, now styling themselves as the Social Democratic Party, left Hata's coalition and made a deal instead with their old enemies the LDP. So, on June 30, 1994, the onetime Socialist Tomiichi Murayama became prime minister of a new coalition government in which the LDP was the leading party.

To most outsiders this chain of events merely confirmed the unfathomability and unchangeability of the Japanese system. Nevertheless, it has become apparent that Japan's traditional institutions only really work when financial markets are rising and growth is strong. When the markets crashed, it became clear that endemic corruption permeated Japan's system. In the future if there is to be a new political move against corruption, corporatism may fall too, for it is corruption's bedfellow.

It is possible that the events of the last decade have terminally weakened Japan's economic and financial systems. That system has in the past been propped up by ministry of finance "administrative guidance" to Japanese banks and financial institutions, about their lending and trading activities. Another prop has been the close inside knowledge that Japanese banks possess about the firms to whom they lend, and a third is the ability of the banks to control the management of those companies when necessary. Clearly, further liberalization and greater transparency may make it difficult for Japan's system to function in this way. Yet that is precisely the direction in which Japanese governments say they want to move, implementing the ideas contained in the 1993 Hiraiwa Report, a semiofficial declaration that Japan should move to American-style openness, with heavy reliance on market relationships rather than traditional relationships of trust.

In this respect Japan today looks a lot like the United States in the late nineteenth and early twentieth centuries. Japan is a nation beginning to question whether it wishes to be run under the managerial capitalist or corporatist system which has long delivered rapid growth. The United States faced the same choices in the thirties, and rejected the old arrangements. Although there is no sign that Japanese political leaders are completely ready to do the same, the pace of change may yet quicken.

Of significant importance to Japan's global economic role will be what that means for Japan's balance of payments. In recent years Japan has boasted large trade surpluses, marginally offset by small deficits in services such as insurance and transport and by small net outflows of interest profits and dividends. The overall surpluses have allowed Japan to invest heavily abroad. As a result, Japanese industry abroad is now nearly one fifth the size of its domestic manufacturing industry, with the automobile sector in the lead; for the United States the equivalent figure is one quarter—not so very different. Partly because Japanese industry has shifted abroad, the trade surpluses now look as if they might diminish, as the Japanese import goods that they can no longer afford to manufacture at home. Meanwhile, services have moved into surplus, soon to be followed by interest profits and dividends—again a reflection of several years of investment abroad. A strong currency reinforces these developments, and whereas Japanese manufacturers might once have lobbied hard for a devaluation, nowadays they feel ambivalent, since their own overseas factories benefit from the strong yen. This is the path followed long ago by the Netherlands, then Britain, and most recently by the United States; if further liberalization at home weakens Japan's industrial base, it too will continue along the path. That will be bad news for manufacturing job prospects in Japan, as the nation becomes the world's favorite market and the world's banker; whether it is good news or bad for the rest of us, and for Japan as a whole, depends on how the Japanese government responds.

For under these circumstances of economic and political change, it cannot be assumed that Japan's political leaders will continue to take a back seat in global economic policymaking. The paradox is that if Japan is indeed moving toward becoming a net importer of goods while continuing to be a net exporter of capital, then its leverage over the world economy will grow sharply. It has been suggested in this book that, from the late nineteenth century onward, the United States, when it was in a similar position, displayed great reluctance to assume the global economic leadership that seemed to be its due. Even when World War II precluded any further prevarication, American policymakers still tried to set up a free market world economy that could run on automatic pilot, with little need for ongoing direct intervention from the American government. The failure of that attempt gave back influence to European and Japanese governments, probably to everybody's mutual benefit. As a result, the United States provided the world with capital and with markets, but made up fewer of the rules of the international game than is generally supposed. For most of us it remains to be seen what, if anything, Japan will do. For the government of the United States, there is a powerful case for trying to guide Japan toward the role of benign global leader—for that is a role the United States itself can no longer credibly fill.

# NOTES

## One: Building the American Economy

1. Colonial defense costs had risen fivefold in the previous fifteen years, and although the 1763 proclamation was intended as a temporary measure, the British were nevertheless keen to fix the border at what they regarded as a manageable length. The British government had also decided to station an army of ten thousand in the colonies to defend against French attack, and intended to get the colonists (whose incomes were apparently higher on average than those who lived in Britain) to pay some of the cost of that defense. See M. A. Jones, *The Limits of Liberty* (Oxford, Eng.: Oxford University Press, 1983), p. 38, and J. Brewer, *The Sinews of Power* (London: Unwin Hyman, 1989), p. 176.

2. The dichotomy between western rural agriculture and eastern urban industry

is clearly an oversimplification. Even in the middle of the nineteenth century the United States was everywhere mostly rural, and frontier towns were frequently established far in advance of the most pioneering farms.

3. In the middle years of the nineteenth century, however, wagon trains obviously worked well enough as transport for migrants. In peak periods the trails became almost overcrowded with travelers, whose well-organized if temporary societies enabled them to make the long crossing of what used to be called the Great American Desert. See J. D. Unruh, *The Plains Across* (London: Pimlico, 1992), esp. ch. 11.

4. See P. Temin, *Causal Factors in American Economic Growth in the Nineteenth Century* (Basingstoke, Eng.: Macmillan, 1975), ch. 5, for a summary of this thesis.

5. At the outbreak of World War I, Russia had just 46,000 miles of railroad compared with 250,000 miles in the United States—a powerful element in Russian backwardness. Even today, a poor transport infrastructure is among the greatest structural problems of the former Soviet Union.

6. See M. A. Jones, *The Limits of Liberty*, p. 289.

7. It has been argued by H. J. Habbakuk, *American and British Technology in the Nineteenth Century* (Cambridge, Eng.: Cambridge University Press, 1962), that because of the high cost of American labor, American companies tended to invest in specifically labor-saving technology. Such a view is no longer generally accepted—it fits neither the facts nor the strict theory. See J. Mokyr, *The Lever of Riches* (Oxford, Eng.: Oxford University Press, 1990), pp. 165–67.

8. See P. N. Carroll and D. W. Noble, *The Free and the Unfree* (Harmondsworth, Eng.: Penguin, 1988), p. 151.

9. Whitney's reputation has, however, been rather undermined by historical research. Simeon North may have been more important in the story of the American system of manufactures: see D. A. Hounshell, *From the American System to Mass Production, 1800–1932* (Baltimore: Johns Hopkins University Press, 1985), pp. 28–32.

10. The idea of interchangeability had been pioneered in Europe but it was the Americans who first exploited it: see Mokyr, *The Lever of Riches*, p. 136. The transmission of interchangeability from industry to industry is discussed in N. Rosenberg, "Technological Change in the Machine Tool Industry, 1840–1910," *Journal of Economic History* 23 (1963), pp. 414–43.

11. See Mokyr, *The Lever of Riches*, pp. 141–42.

12. It is possible, however, that the American market was more willing to accept new designs than was the British market, and for that reason American workers had less attachment to preserving traditional working methods (partly because unemployment was less of a threat than in Europe).

**13.** J. Agnew, *The United States in the World Economy* (Cambridge, Eng.: Cambridge University Press, 1987), ch. 2, describes the growing links between the United States and other economies.

**14.** See A. Sampson, *The Money Lenders* (Sevenoaks, Eng.: Coronet, 1982), p. 54.

**15.** Jefferson is quoted in A. M. Schlesinger, *The Cycles of American History* (London: Penguin, 1989), p. 221.

**16.** Monroe is quoted in Schlesinger, *The Cycles of American History*, pp. 223–24.

**17.** This anecdote is taken from R. Chernow, *The House of Morgan* (New York: Touchstone, 1990), p. 31.

**18.** The purely economic arguments are summarized in S. P. Lee and P. Passell, *A New Economic View of American History* (New York: Norton, 1979), pp. 309–18.

**19.** The South was also hurt by developments in the world economy; for a summary see Lee and Passell, ibid., ch. 12.

**20.** See Schlesinger, *The Cycles of American History*, p. 233, and P. Gates, *Agriculture and the Civil War* (New York: Knopf, 1965).

**21.** See Patrick O'Brien, *The Economic Effects of the American Civil War* (Basingstoke, Eng.: Macmillan, 1988), p. 58.

**22.** J. Bowman and R. Keehn, "Agricultural Terms of Trade in Four Midwestern States, 1870–1900," *Journal of Economic History* 34 (Sept. 1974), demonstrate that in real terms midwestern farm incomes rose in the final quarter of the century.

**23.** Bryan's promise of higher farm prices was implicit in his commitment to tie the dollar to silver, which was plentiful, and not to gold, which was scarce. The use of silver coins had declined decades earlier and been legally ended in 1873; after that year, American silver miners agitated for a commitment from the Treasury to buy all they could mine. They won this under the 1890 Sherman Silver Purchase Act, which Cleveland later revoked.

**24.** The fact that there is a *potential* role for government intervention does not imply that government should always intervene. Government failure may sometimes be worse than market failure. For discussions of the issues, see P. Stoneman and J. Vickers, "The Economics of Technology Policy," and P. Dasgupta, "The Welfare Economics of Knowledge Production," both in *Oxford Review of Economic Policy* 4.4 (Winter 1988).

**25.** See M. G. Blackford, *The Rise of Modern Business in Great Britain, the United States, and Japan* (London: University of North Carolina Press, 1988), p. 53. It is not clear whether this includes the early railroad companies. C. J. Schmitz, *The Growth of Big Business in the United States and Western Europe, 1850–1939* (London: Macmillan, 1993), p. 20, suggests that in 1850 there were seven railroad companies capitalized between $10 million and $35 million.

**26.** See Blackford, *The Growth of Big Business*, p. 55. It is striking that before these mergers, most American firms outside the railroad sector were family owned.

**27.** Duke is quoted in Blackford, ibid., p. 59.

**28.** See Chernow, *The House of Morgan*, p. 84.

**29.** For a discussion, see J. B. de Long, "Did J. P. Morgan's Men Add Value?," in P. Temin, ed., *Inside the Business Enterprise* (Chicago: University of Chicago Press, 1991), pp. 225–26.

**30.** See T. K. McCraw, "Rethinking the Trust Question," in T. K. McCann, ed., *Regulation in Perspective* (Cambridge, Mass.: Harvard University Press, 1981).

**31.** Adam Smith, *An Inquiry into the Nature and Causes of the Wealth of Nations* (New York: Modern Library, 1937), p. 128.

**32.** Britain's Duke of Marlborough did especially well by marrying not one but two American heiresses: Consuelo Vanderbilt in 1895 and Gladys Deacon some years later (although by Vanderbilt standards Gladys Deacon was almost a pauper). See H. Vickers, *Gladys, Duchess of Marlborough* (London: Hamish Hamilton, 1987).

**33.** Much of Alfred Chandler's writing, but especially his *The Visible Hand* (Cambridge, Mass.: Belknap, 1977), sets out why size sometimes succeeds and sometimes does not.

**34.** See Schmitz, *The Growth of Big Business*, pp. 18–22, for a brief discussion; the classic statement is A. D. Chandler, *Strategy and Structure* (Cambridge, Mass.: MIT, 1962).

**35.** Chapter 3 returns to this subject. Chandler, *The Visible Hand*, is, again, the classic text. A striking feature of the nineteenth-century American economy is that although it was less industrialized than much of Europe, it nevertheless went further in the development of big business.

## Two: The Global Background to American Expansion

**1.** In *Phases of Capitalist Development* (Oxford, Eng.: Oxford University Press, 1982), A. Maddison suggests that in 1700 income per head in the Netherlands was 50 percent higher than in Britain, its nearest rival (p. 29).

**2.** Fokkens is quoted in S. Schama, *The Embarrassment of Riches* (London: Colins, 1987), p. 130, as well as on pp. 301–4.

**3.** Maddison, *Phases of Capitalist Development*, p. 33.

**4.** The British colonial markets were generally the largest, and Britons were most adept at illegally penetrating other countries' markets while defending their own: see Immanuel Wallerstein, *The Modern World System III* (San Diego: Academic Press, 1989), pp. 68 and 212.

**5.** See Paul Kennedy, *The Rise and Fall of the Great Powers: Economic Change and Military Conflict from 1500 to 2000* (London: Unwin Hyman, 1988), p. 87.

6. Schama, *The Embarrassment of Riches*, p. 293.

7. Ibid., p. 294.

8. Maddison, *Phases of Capitalist Development*, p. 33.

9. J. Brewer, *The Sinews of Power* (London: Unwin Hyman, 1989), p. 184.

10. J. Miller, *The Glorious Revolution* (London: Longman, 1983), discusses the revolution that put William and Mary on the throne; see also H. Roseveare, *The Financial Revolution, 1660–1760* (London: Longman, 1991).

11. See P. J. Cain and A. G. Hopkins, *British Imperialism: Innovation and Expansion, 1688–1914* (London: Longman, 1993), p. 59.

12. Brewer, *The Sinews of Power*, p. 79, suggests that in the eighteenth century the British excise department more closely resembled Weber's ideal bureaucracy than did any other government agency in Europe.

13. Newcomen's pump was a development of one invented in 1698 by Thomas Savery that had proved to be rather prone to exploding, thereby causing as much harm as good. Newcomen's machine was the first to turn thermal energy or heat into kinetic energy or work—although its fuel efficiency was distinctly limited. See J. Mokyr, *The Lever of Riches* (Oxford, Eng.: Oxford University Press, 1990), p. 85.

14. Ibid., p. 88.

15. A number of improvements to hydrotechnology meant that water power was probably as efficient as steam power, but much less convenient.

16. There has been much debate why it was cotton textiles and not the more important woollen textiles that attracted the technological innovations; Wallerstein, *The Modern World System III*, pp. 24–25, summarizes.

17. Kay's shuttle was probably not quite the threat that British weavers feared, although some weavers certainly became unemployed, including Andrew Carnegie's father, who in 1848 left Scotland for the United States in search of work. See Mokyr, *The Lever of Riches*, p. 179, and M. G. Blackford, *The Rise of Modern Business in Great Britain, the United States, and Japan* (London: University of North Carolina Press, 1988), p. 45.

18. It may be significant that British inventors were mostly concerned with improving the efficiency and hence the commercial value of existing devices. It is also possible that inventors in continental European countries were distracted or censored by the political upheavals in their countries: see Mokyr, *The Lever of Riches*, pp. 240 and 252.

19. See Wallerstein, *The Modern World System III*, pp. 87–90, and, on the role of government, Cain and Hopkins, *British Imperialism*, p. 79.

20. Ricardo's law of comparative advantage suggests that even if one nation has an absolute advantage in the production of everything relative to another nation, it should still specialize in the production of those things in which its

advantage is greatest while importing the other items from the other nation in return for its own specialized exports.

21. C. P. Kindleberger, *Manias, Panics, and Crashes* (New York: Basic Books, 1978), includes an account of the repeal of the Corn Laws.

22. See R. Cameron, *A Concise Economic History of the World* (New York: Oxford University Press, 1989), pp. 273–78, and the sources cited therein.

23. The workings of the gold standard is a controversial matter. B. Eichengreen, "International Policy Coordination in Historical Perspective," in *International Economic Policy Coordination*, W. H. Buiter and R. C. Marston, eds. (Cambridge, Eng.: Cambridge University Press, 1985), contains a short description; see also the various articles in Eichengreen, *The Gold Standard in Theory and History* (New York: Methuen, 1985), and in S. N. Broadberry and N. F. R. Crafts, eds., *Britain in the International Economy, 1870–1939* (Cambridge, Eng.: Cambridge University Press, 1992).

24. The classic discussion is W. A. Lewis, *Growth and Fluctuations, 1870–1913* (London: George Allen and Unwin, 1978), but see also N. Blake, "Import Prices, Economic Activity, and the General Price Level in the UK, 1870–1913," in Broadberry and Crafts, eds., *Britain in the International Economy*.

25. Cain and Hopkins, *British Imperialism*, p. 151.

26. The Germans were also much helped by the massive tributes they extracted from France at the end of the Franco-Prussian War.

27. See D. S. Landes, *The Unbound Prometheus* (Cambridge, Eng.: Cambridge University Press, 1969).

28. For examples, see C. Wilson, "Economy and Society in Late Victorian Britain," *Economic History Review* 2d ser., 17 (1965); D. N. McCloskey, *Economic Maturity and Entrepreneurial Decline* (Cambridge, Mass.: Harvard University Press, 1973).

29. See M. Abramovitz and P. A. David, "Reinterpreting Economic Growth," *American Economic Review* 63, papers and proceedings (1973), pp. 428–39.

30. The expression is that of T. G. Orsagh, "Progress in Iron and Steel, 1870–1913," in *Comparative Studies in Society and History* 3 (1960), pp. 421–60.

31. See D. N. McCloskey, "Did Victorian Britain Fall?" *Economic History Review* 23 (1970), pp. 446–59.

32. See M. G. Blackford, *The Rise of Modern Business*, p. 68.

33. See C. J. Schmitz, *The Growth of Big Business in the United States and Western Europe, 1850–1939* (London: Macmillan, 1993), ch. 3.

34. See Cain and Hopkins, *British Imperialism*, pp. 125–28.

35. Ibid., p. 84; see also M. Collins, *Banks and Industrial Finance in Britain, 1800–1939* (Basingstoke, Eng: Macmillan, 1991).

36. McCloskey, "Did Victorian Britain Fall?," and W. P. Kennedy, *Industrial Markets, Capital Structure, and the Origins of Economic Decline* (Cambridge, Eng.:

Cambridge University Press, 1987), held opposing positions in a famous debate on this subject, which is summarized in Collins, *Banks and Industrial Finance*.

**37.** See, for example, P. L. Payne, *British Entrepreneurship in the Nineteenth Century* (Basingstoke, Eng.: Macmillan, 1974), p. 55; N. F. R. Crafts, *British Economic Growth during the Industrial Revolution* (Oxford, Eng.: Clarendon, 1985), p. 159; Cameron, *A Concise Economic History*, p. 225; and M. Sanderson, "Technical Education and Economic Decline, 1890–1980's," *Oxford Review of Economic Policy* 4.1 (1988), and *Education, Economic Change, and Society in England, 1780–1870* (London: Macmillan, 1983).

**38.** See Mokyr, *The Lever of Riches*, p. 241.

**39.** See D. C. Coleman, "Gentleman and Players," *Economic History Review* 2d ser., 26 (1973), and Landes, *The Unbound Prometheus*.

**40.** It used to be thought that the global economic slowdown of the 1880s was comparable to that of the 1930s; however, more accurate data now shows that not to be true. See S. B. Saul, *The Myth of the Great Depression, 1873–1896* (Basingstoke, Eng.: Macmillan, 1985).

**41.** For discussions, see P. Kennedy, *Strategy and Diplomacy, 1870–1945* (London: Fontana, 1989), ch. 8, and Cain and Hopkins, *British Imperialism*, pp. 456–65.

**42.** See Cain and Hopkins, *British Imperialism*, p. 461.

**43.** According to P. Kennedy, *The Rise and Fall of the Great Powers*, p. 154. However, the same author argues that Tirpitz may have been planning a fleet to rival Britain's when World War I broke out. See P. Kennedy, *Strategy and Diplomacy*, ch. 8.

**44.** Princip is quoted in T. Aronson, *Crowns in Conflict* (London: John Murray, 1986), p. 108. A distinguished account of Germany's move toward war is Paul Kennedy's *The Rise of the Anglo-German Antagonism* (London: Allen and Unwin, 1980).

## Three: From the Great War to the Great Crash

**1.** See P. Fearon, *War, Prosperity, and Depression: The U.S. Economy, 1917–45* (Oxford, Eng.: Philip Allan, 1987), p. 3. P. Kennedy, *The Rise and Fall of the Great Powers: Economic Change and Military Conflict from 1500 to 2000* (London: Unwin Hyman, 1988), pp. 242–44, summarizes information on American industrial strength.

**2.** Kennedy, *The Rise and Fall of the Great Powers*, p. 248.

**3.** See R. Chernow, *The House of Morgan* (New York: Touchstone, 1990), p. 188, or for more detail, K. Burk, *Britain, America, and the Sinews of War, 1914–1918* (London: Allen and Unwin, 1985).

4. For sources and further discussion, see D. C. Watt, *Succeeding John Bull* (Cambridge, Eng.: Cambridge University Press, 1984), p. 32.

5. Germany, however, was more self-sufficient than the British supposed: see Kennedy, *The Rise and Fall of the Great Powers*, p. 259.

6. See P. J. Cain and A. G. Hopkins, *British Imperialism: Innovation and Expansion, 1688–1914* (London: Longman, 1993), pp. 59–60.

7. Quoted in M. A. Jones, *The Limits of Liberty: American History, 1607–1980* (Oxford, Eng.: Oxford University Press, 1983), p. 422. Since the Allies spent more on American food than on American munitions, the populist complaint seems misplaced.

8. See Cain and Hopkins, *British Imperialism*, p. 61, and Watt, *Succeeding John Bull*, p. 33; for the economic context, see A. S. Milward, *The Economic Effects of the Two World Wars on Britain* (Basingstoke, Eng.: Macmillan, 1984), p. 51.

9. Wilson is quoted in Watt, *Succeeding John Bull*, p. 32.

10. The growth of consumer credit made individuals more vulnerable than they previously had been to increases in interest rates. This development had enormous consequences in the thirties, when wages fell, real interest rates rose, and people found themselves unable to meet their obligations.

11. Initially the production line was used only for assembling the flywheel for the car's magneto, but soon the whole transmission mechanism and then the engine were being similarly assembled, and eventually entire cars were built on production lines. See D. A. Hounshell, *From the American System to Mass Production, 1800–1932* (Baltimore: Johns Hopkins University Press, 1985), ch. 6.

12. Ibid., pp. 263–64.

13. The most famous contributor to this endeavor was Frederick Taylor; see his *The Principles of Scientific Management* (New York: Harper and Bros., 1947). As Hounshell observes, Taylor's attempts to analyze workers as if they were machines was a very old-fashioned nineteenth-century mistake which had little influence on the changes actually taking place in firms like Ford. See Hounshell, *From the American System to Mass Production*, pp. 249–53.

14. H. T. Johnson, "Managing by Remote Control: Recent Management Accounting Practice in Industrial Practice in Historical Perspective," in P. Temin, ed., *Inside the Business Enterprise* (Chicago: University of Chicago Press, 1991), argues that the accounting systems used in monitoring business performance influence the objectives and behavior of corporations.

15. This is discussed in Bernstein, *The Great Depression* (Cambridge, Eng.: Cambridge University Press, 1987); see Fearon, *War, Prosperity, and Depression*, ch. 3, or T. Kemp, *The Climax of Capitalism* (London: Longman, 1990), ch. 2, for summaries.

16. Both comments are taken from D. Yergin, *The Prize: The Epic Quest for Oil, Money, and Power* (London: Simon and Schuster, 1991), p. 108.

17. Part of the opinion delivered by the Chief Justice with regard to Standard Oil's appeal is quoted in Yergin, *The Prize*, p. 109.

18. See Chernow, *The House of Morgan*, p. 151.

19. The main factors behind falling prices were the arrival of new suppliers and the impact of new technology, both in agriculture and in mineral extraction. A. S. Kenwood and A. L. Lougheed, *The Growth of the International Economy, 1820–1980* (London: Unwin Hyman, 1983), pp. 176–78, summarize the issue.

20. See D. H. Aldcroft, *From Versailles to Wall Street, 1919–1929* (Harmondsworth, Eng.: Penguin, 1987), pp. 13–17. Allowing for the fall in the birthrate, Aldcroft estimates that the total loss of life was more than sixty million.

21. One of the main sources of information on Versailles is Keynes's own highly readable account, which became an instant best-seller (it has been criticized, though more on grounds of cruelty than inaccuracy). See J. M. Keynes, *The Economic Consequences of the Peace* (London and Basingstoke, Eng.: Macmillan, 1971 [1919]).

22. The expression is that of Cain and Hopkins, *British Imperialism*, p. 61, but see also F. Costigliola, *Awkward Dominion: American Political, Economic, and Cultural Relations with Europe, 1913–1933* (Ithaca, N.Y.: Cornell University Press, 1985).

23. Quoted in R. Skidelsky, *John Maynard Keynes: Hopes Betrayed, 1883–1920* (London: Macmillan, 1983), p. 374.

24. See Costigliola, *Awkward Dominion*.

25. The Genoa Conference is described in Cain and Hopkins, *British Imperialism*, pp. 63–65.

26. For a discussion of Anglo-American rivalries at Genoa, see Costigliola, *Awkward Dominion*, pp. 107–8.

27. See C. P. Kindleberger, *The World in Depression, 1929–1939* (Berkeley: University of California Press, 1973), ch. 5, which gives a full account of the Great Crash.

28. A myth has developed that the market "correction" turned into a rout because, in the heady atmosphere of the twenties, gullible "nonprofessional" investors who had been drawn into the rising market failed to notice when stock prices lost touch with underlying values—and supposedly panicked as soon as the market dipped. This rather patronizing view was originally propagated by the economist Irving Fisher. However, very little of the market's rise was due to such buyers, who were also usually the last to sell.

**29.** This is set out in Keynes, *General Theory of Employment, Interest, and Money* (London: Macmillan, 1936), ch. 12.

## Four: The World in Danger

**1.** See R. Chernow, *The House of Morgan* (New York: Touchstone, 1990), p. 348.

**2.** P. Fearon, *War, Prosperity, and Depression: The U.S. Economy, 1917–45* (Oxford, Eng.: Philip Allan, 1987), is an up-to-date discussion of the Great Depression and the surrounding period. See also M. A. Bernstein, *The Great Depression* (Cambridge, Eng.: Cambridge University Press, 1987).

**3.** See M. Friedman and A. Schwartz, *A Monetary History of the United States, 1867–1960* (Princeton: Princeton University Press, 1963). The implication of this analysis was that the New Deal approach of dealing with the recession by more government spending and more regulation was misguided. Significantly, Friedman and Schwartz published their work just when Kennedy and Johnson seemed to be reviving New Deal ideas. P. Temin, *Causal Factors in American Economic Growth in the Nineteenth Century* (Basingstoke, Eng.: Macmillan, 1976), emphasizes that the monetary policy of the Federal Reserve may have been to blame for prolonging the recession past 1931, but not for instigating the downturn.

**4.** P. Temin, *Did Monetary Forces Cause the Great Depression?* (New York: W. W. Norton, 1976), is the classic critique of the Friedman view, while K. Brunner and A. H. Meltzer, "What Did We Learn from the Monetary Experience of the United States in the Great Depression?" *Canadian Journal of Economics* 1 (1980), exposes the Fed's confusions.

**5.** The Federal Reserve believed that, because nominal interest rates were low, monetary policy was loose; however, inflation was negative so real interest rates were high, and bank reserves were being kept tight by the Fed's open market operations.

**6.** Given Hoover's policy of nonintervention, any activist policy on the part of the Federal Reserve would have meant that the central bank was effectively performing the function of the government.

**7.** The description is that of M. A. Jones, *The Limits of Liberty* (Oxford, Eng.: Oxford University Press, 1983), p. 455.

**8.** The career of the Van Sweringen brothers is described in Chernow, *The House of Morgan*.

**9.** See N. Spulber, *Managing the American Economy from Roosevelt to Reagan* (Bloomington: Indiana University Press, 1989), pp. 11–12, for a fuller discussion.

**10.** See A. H. Hansen, *Full Recovery or Stagnation* (New York: Norton, 1938), and also Spulber, *Managing the American Economy*, pp. 8–9, 11. Hansen's description of the United States as a mature economy in which the rate of return on new investment is very low because so much investment has already taken place is similar to the Marxist notion of the accumulation crisis that sooner or later must affect every capitalist economy. Hansen subsequently revised his views and became a leading proponent of Keynesian economics.

11. R. Skidelsky, *John Maynard Keynes: The Economist as Saviour, 1920–1937* (London: Macmillan, 1992), describes this period in Keynes's life. See also G. K. Peden, *Keynes, the Treasury, and British Economic Policy* (Basingstoke, Eng.: Macmillan, 1988).

12. See Skidelsky, *John Maynard Keynes: The Economist as Saviour*, pp. 492–93.

13. Ibid., p. 506. Apparently Keynes often judged people by their hands.

14. See Jones, *The Limits of Liberty*, p. 458, and Fearon, *War, Prosperity, and Depression*, p. 218. Schlesinger writes that "Roosevelt's own heart belonged—and would belong for several years—to fiscal orthodoxy"; see A. M. Schlesinger, *The Age of Roosevelt: The Politics of Upheaval* (Boston: Houghton Mifflin, 1960), pp. 407–8.

15. Roosevelt is quoted in P. N. Carroll and D. W. Noble, *The Free and the Unfree* (Harmondsworth, Eng.: Penguin, 1977), p. 339.

16. Roosevelt is quoted in A. Sampson, *The Arms Bazaar* (Sevenoaks, Eng.: Coronet, 1981), p. 67.

17. Roosevelt is quoted in A. M. Schlesinger, *The Age of Roosevelt: The Coming of the New Deal* (Boston: Houghton Mifflin, 1958), p. 182.

18. Ibid., p. 183.

19. See E. Hawley, *The New Deal and the Problem of Monopoly* (Princeton: Princeton University Press, 1966). Roosevelt did not devise a planning regime and then call it the New Deal—he offered a "new deal" and then later decided that planning would be needed in order to deliver his pledge.

20. This implies, amongst other things, that white farmers gained at the expense of blacks.

21. See Hawley, *The New Deal and the Problem of Monopoly*. Roosevelt's grand coalition, and his image of being above mere politics, reflected his conjuring trick of appearing to give special status to everybody—farmers, workers, and capitalists. Unfortunately, that made it rather difficult to be politically truthful or politically rational.

22. This description is quoted in Schlesinger, *The Age of Roosevelt: The Coming of the New Deal*, p. 286.

23. Other aspects of the Second New Deal continued initiatives already under consideration during the First New Deal. W. E. Leuchtenberg, *Franklin Roosevelt and the New Deal, 1932–1940* (New York: Harper, 1963), emphasises the continuity between the First and Second New Deals.

**24.** Frankfurter is quoted in Chernow, *The House of Morgan*, pp. 410–11.

**25.** Keynes is quoted in A. M. Schlesinger, *The Age of Roosevelt: The Politics of Upheaval*, p. 401.

**26.** See J. A. Schwarz, *The New Dealers: Power Politics in the Age of Roosevelt* (New York: Knopf, 1993), as well as Schlesinger, *The Age of Roosevelt: The Politics of Upheaval*, p. 411.

**27.** T. Huertas and H. Van B. Cleveland, *Citibank* (Cambridge, Mass.: Harvard University Press, 1987), note that the committee was never able to discover any illegal collusion. They add that there were no barriers to entry and, thus, that Morgan could not have achieved excess profits; they fail to see that Morgan's formidable reputation was itself an effective entry barrier for others. See J. P. de Long, "Did J. P. Morgan's Men Add Value?," in P. Temin, ed., *Inside the Business Enterprise* (Chicago: University of Chicago Press, 1991).

**28.** See Chernow, *The House of Morgan*, p. 371.

**29.** The word "investing" was used by Congress to mean savers and those who lent, rather than the companies that borrowed the funds and bought plant or machinery. Keynes argued strongly that "saving" and "investment" were not synonymous, and that policies that promoted saving might have no effect on investment or even reduce it.

**30.** See de Long, "Did J. P. Morgan's Men Add Value?," for a full presentation of this view.

**31.** C. P. Kindleberger, *The World in Depression, 1929–1939* (Berkeley: University of California Press, 1973), ch. 4, discusses the world agricultural depression in detail.

**32.** Chernow, *The House of Morgan*, pp. 332–34 points out that the cable was much more benign than the British Cabinet perceived.

**33.** R. Skidelsky, *Interests and Obsessions* (London: Macmillan, 1993), ch. 25, argues that MacDonald was outmaneuvered by the Conservative Party.

**34.** See B. Eichengreen, *Elusive Stability* (Cambridge, Eng.: Cambridge University Press, 1990), and P. J. Cain and H. G. Hopkins, *British Imperialism: Innovation and Expansion, 1688–1914* (London: Longman, 1993), p. 77.

**35.** See M. E. Falkus, "The German Business Cycle in the 1920s," *Economic History Review* 28 (Aug. 1975), pp. 451–65.

**36.** Offering to pay a higher interest rate may make it more difficult, not less, for a borrower to obtain funds; interest rates, then, do not necessarily clear credit markets, and rationing may thus occur, even in an apparently free market. See J. E. Stiglitz and A. Weiss, "A Credit Rationing in Markets with Imperfect Information," *American Economic Review* (1981).

**37.** R. J. Overy, *The Nazi Recovery, 1932–1938* (Basingstoke, Eng.: Macmillan, 1982), discusses the period in detail, as does H. James, *The German Slump* (Oxford, Eng.: Oxford University Press, 1986).

38. See Chalmers Johnson, *MITI and the Japanese Miracle* (Stanford, Calif.: Stanford University Press, 1982), and W. J. MacPherson, *The Economic Development of Japan, c. 1868–1941* (Basingstoke, Eng.: Macmillan, 1987).

39. See Richard Storry, *Japan and the Decline of the West in Asia, 1894–1943* (London: Macmillan, 1979).

40. W. Carr, *Poland to Pearl Harbor* (London: Edward Arnold, 1985), describes Japan's journey to war.

41. A. S. Milward writes that Japan's original war aims were a "positive and realistic attempt at the reconstruction of her own economic area": see *War, Economy, and Society, 1939–1945* (Harmondsworth, Eng.: Penguin, 1987).

## Five: Reconstruction

1. See G. D. A. MacDougall, *Don and Mandarin* (London: John Murray, 1987), p. 47. MacDougall later became the first economics director of the Organization for European Economic Cooperation.

2. See S. M. Black, *A Levite Among the Priests* (Boulder, Colo.: Westview, 1991), ch. 3.

3. For further details see Milward, *War, Economy, and Society, 1939–1945* (Harmondsworth, Eng.: Penguin, 1987), p. 335.

4. See MacDougall, *Don and Mandarin*, p. 37.

5. Black, *A Levite Among the Priests*, pp. 35–38, sets out White's thinking.

6. See, for example, R. Kuttner, *The End of Laissez Faire* (New York: Knopf, 1991), p. 25.

7. Bernstein is quoted in Black, *A Levite Among the Priests*, p. 40.

8. White is quoted in ibid., p. 38.

9. See K. H. Hennings, "West Germany," in A. Boltho, ed., *The European Economy: Growth and Crisis* (Oxford, Eng.: Oxford University Press, 1982), pp. 476–77.

10. A. S. Milward, *The Reconstruction of Western Europe, 1945–1951* (London: Methuen, 1984), p. 8, provides details.

11. Before the war Britain was a poor second place in quantitative terms and also in qualitative terms, the latter related to the fact that its products were sold mostly to the colonies rather than within Europe.

12. "The European Crisis—Memorandum by William Clayton," May 27, 1947, is quoted in Milward, *The Reconstruction of Western Europe*, p. 2.

13. It should not be forgotten in this context that the Cold War was still some way away.

14. See J. L. Gaddis, *The Long Peace* (New York: Oxford University Press, 1987), p. 42.

**15.** The significance of Marshall aid as a mechanism of American political leverage is discussed in Milward, *The Reconstruction of Western Europe*, pp. 113–25.

**16.** The expression is taken from ibid., p. 321.

**17.** The IMF recognized this before the British authorities would accept the fact: see Black, *A Levite Among the Priests*, pp. 65–68.

**18.** See Milward, *The Reconstruction of Western Europe*, p. 217.

**19.** A. S. Milward, *The Reconstruction of Western Europe*, ch. 12, discusses the Schuman Plan in detail.

**20.** Ibid., pp. 353–54.

**21.** A. K. Sen, *Poverty and Famines* (Oxford, Eng.: Oxford University Press, 1981), ch. 6, contains an important discussion of the famine.

**22.** D. Reynolds, "Roosevelt, Churchill, and the Wartime Anglo-American Alliance, 1939–45," in W. M. Louis and H. Bull, eds., *The 'Special Relationship'* (Oxford, Eng.: Clarendon, 1989), discusses the contrasting wartime policies of the American and British governments, while B. Perkins, "Unequal Partners: The Truman Administration and Great Britain," in ibid., looks at the Truman government. See also W. R. Louis's "American Anti-colonialism and the Dissolution of the British Empire," in the same volume.

**23.** H. Van der Wee, *Prosperity and Upheaval* (Harmondsworth, Eng.: Penguin, 1986), ch. 9, discusses postwar trade policy in more detail.

**24.** For this view see M. Beloff, "The End of the British Empire and the Assumption of World Wide Commitments by the United States," in Louis and Bull, *The 'Special Relationship.'*

**25.** A skeptical view from the fifties of the value of trade to developing countries is provided in Gunnar Myrdal, "Development and Underdevelopment," National Bank of Egypt Fiftieth Anniversary Commemoration Lectures, reprinted in G. M. Meir, ed., *Leading Issues in Economic Development* (New York: Oxford University Press, 1976). A. K. Cairncross, *Factors in Economic Development* (London: George Allen and Unwin, 1962), provides the contrary argument from much the same period.

**26.** See M. Schaller, *The American Occupation of Japan* (New York: Oxford University Press, 1985), p. 11.

**27.** It is uncertain how effective Japanese resistance would have been. A plan by the Japanese government to martial almost the entire Japanese population to rebel an invasion was dogged by rivalries between the various armed services and government departments: see Ben Ami Shillony, *Politics and Culture in Wartime Japan* (Oxford, Eng.: Clarendon, 1991), ch. 3.

**28.** The atom bomb avoided the risk of heavy loss of American life. Nevertheless, the haste with which Truman used the weapon suggests that he was very much motivated by a desire to preempt—and perhaps warn off—the Soviet

Union. See T. E. Vadney, *The World Since 1945* (Harmondsworth, Eng.: Penguin, 1987), pp. 42–47, for a summary of the issue.

29. For details see Schaller, *The American Occupation of Japan*, pp. 37–38.

30. MacArthur is quoted in ibid., p. 49.

31. The military was also given scope to use more of its existing EROA budget on Japanese reconstruction: see ibid., pp. 131–32.

32. W. S. Borden, *The Pacific Alliance* (Madison: University of Wisconsin Press, 1984), emphasizes the contribution of American expenditure on the Korean War to Japan's economic recovery.

33. In contrast Britain received many orders for highly sophisticated military weapons, thereby furthering the bias that already existed in British industry toward products with low peacetime commercial potential.

34. See Schaller, *The American Occupation of Japan*, pp. 297–98.

35. Bisson is quoted in ibid., p. 32.

36. Kennan is quoted in ibid., p. 113.

37. T. Yamashita, *The Panasonic Way* (Tokyo: Kodansha, 1987), A. Alletzhauser, *The House of Nomura* (London: Bloomsbury, 1990), and T. Toyoda, *Toyota: Fifty Years in Motion* (Tokyo: Kodansha, 1987), offer contrasting accounts of life inside the *keiretsu*.

38. See A. Boltho and C. J. M. Hardie, "The Japanese Economy," in D. Morris, ed., *The Economic System in the UK* (Oxford, Eng.: Oxford University Press, 1985).

39. See Toyoda, *Toyota*, pp. 106–12.

40. See J. P. Womack, D. T. Jones, and D. Roos, *The Machine That Changed the World* (New York: Rawson, 1990), ch. 3, for a full account, as well as Toyoda, *Toyota*.

41. See Toyoda, *Toyota*, pp. 57–59.

## Six: *The Golden Age Reassessed*

1. W. H. Whyte, *The Organization Man* (New York: Simon and Schuster, 1956); J. K. Galbraith, *The Affluent Society* (Boston: Houghton Mifflin, 1958); V. O. Packard, *The Hidden Persuaders* (New York: McKay, 1957).

2. A. Sampson, *The Money Lenders* (Sevenoaks, Eng.: Coronet, 1982), ch. 5, contains brief histories of the American "superbanks" up until the late seventies.

3. Sampson writes of Boeing in the late fifties that "the commercial aircraft still could not be viable on their own, and the military programmes were carrying the commercial on their shoulders": see A. Sampson, *The Arms Bazaar* (Sevenoaks, Eng.: Coronet, 1977), p. 113.

4. Quoted in Sampson, *The Arms Bazaar*, p. 115.

5. The statistics are from T. Kemp, *The Climax of Capitalism* (London: Longman, 1990), p. 135.

6. The period is discussed in N. Spulber, *Managing the American Economy from Roosevelt to Reagan* (Bloomington: Indiana University Press, 1989), ch. 2, esp. pp. 24–27.

7. This is discussed in R. J. Gordon, "Postwar Macroeconomics," in M. Feldstein, ed., *The American Economy in Transition* (Chicago: University of Chicago Press, 1980), pp. 124–25, and in Spulber, *Managing the American Economy*, ch. 3.

8. See P. Volcker and T. Gyohten, *Changing Fortunes* (New York: Times Books, 1992), p. 21.

9. Quoted in R. Chernow, *The House of Morgan* (New York: Touchstone, 1990), p. 356.

10. See Spulber, *Managing the American Economy*, p. 62. The quotation is from a report of a presidential task force chaired by Nobel Laureate Paul Samuelson.

11. For this and other details of Kennedy's budgetary policies see J. D. Savage, *Balanced Budgets and American Politics* (Ithaca, N.Y.: Cornell University Press, 1988) pp. 175–79.

12. Kennedy did, however, ask for standby presidential powers to alter taxes or spending programs temporarily without reference to Congress—a request that received a predictably cool reception.

13. Kennedy is quoted in Spulber, *Managing the American Economy*, p. 68.

14. See P. N. Carroll and D. W. Noble, *The Free and the Unfree* (Harmondsworth, Eng.: Penguin, 1977), p. 392.

15. K. Sale, *Power Shift* (New York: Random House, 1975), describes the rising importance of the Sunbelt.

16. Savage, *Balanced Budgets and American Politics*, pp. 179–82, summarizes the budgetary policies of President Johnson.

17. Survey evidence suggests that the Great Society was not associated with any increased public willingness to fund welfare provisions; it was not until the late sixties that public opinion turned decisively against high military spending. See W. G. Mayer, *The Changing American Mind* (Ann Arbor: University of Michigan Press, 1992), pp. 122–23 and 246–47.

18. See W. H. Branson, "Trends in United States International Trade and Investment since World War II," in Feldstein, ed., *The American Economy in Transition*, p. 188, table 3.3.

19. See ibid., esp. table 3.19 on pp. 208–11 for details.

20. Again, ibid. summarizes the data: see esp. table 3.12 on p. 195.

21. For evidence on this see S. Dowrick and D.-T. Nguyen, "OECD Comparative Economic Growth, 1950–85: Catch up and Convergence," *American Economic Review* 79 (1989), and R. Marris, "How Much of the Slowdown

Was Catch-up?" in R. C. O. Mathews, ed., *Slower Growth in the Western World* (London: Heinemann, 1982).

22. The classic exposition of this is E. F. Denison, *Why Growth Rates Differ* (Washington, D.C.: Brookings Institution, 1967).

23. National Science Foundation, *Science Indicators, 1976* (Washington, D.C.: Government Printing Office, 1977).

24. E. Mansfield, "Technology and Productivity in the United States," in Feldstein, ed., *The American Economy in Transition*, provides a comprehensive account of trends in innovation, research, and development.

25. Organization for Economic Cooperation and Development (OECD), *Gaps in Technology* (Paris: OECD, 1968).

26. See Mansfield, "Technology and Productivity in the United States," p. 594.

27. National Science Foundation (NSF), *National Patterns of R&D Resources, 1953–76* (Washington, D.C.: Government Printing Office, 1986).

28. Mansfield, "Technology and Productivity in the United States," pp. 572–73.

29. See H. Nason, J. Stegers, and G. Manners, *Support of Basic Research by Industry* (Washington, D.C.: National Science Foundation, 1978).

30. M. Casson, ed., *The Growth of International Business* (London: George Allen and Unwin, 1983), is an extensive discussion of this subject.

31. The details are from M. G. Blackford, *The Rise of Modern Business in Great Britain, the United States, and Japan* (London: University of North Carolina Press, 1988), pp. 119–22.

32. See L. Galambos and J. Pratt, *The Corporate Commonwealth* (New York: Basic Books, 1988), p. 167.

33. See S. Burman, *America in the Modern World* (London: Harvester Wheatsheaf, 1991), p. 30, and sources quoted therein for details.

34. D. M. Meerschwam, "Breaking Relationships," in S. L. Hayes, ed., *Wall Street and Regulation* (Boston: Harvard Business School Press, 1987), describes the origins and uses of CDs and Eurodollars, while B. M. Friedman, "Postwar Changes in the American Financial Markets," in Feldstein, ed., *The American Economy in Transition*, provides a fuller context.

35. See H. Van der Wee, *Prosperity and Upheaval* (Harmondsworth, Eng.: Penguin, 1987), pp. 380–82, for further details.

36. Ibid., p. 382.

37. See W. M. Scammell, *The International Economy Since 1945* (London: Macmillan, 1983). Van der Wee, *Prosperity and Upheaval*, p. 385, describes the Kennedy round as a failure.

38. Japan's low reliance in this period on exports to generate growth is emphasized in K. Ohkawa and H. Rosovsky, *Japanese Economic Growth* (Stanford, Calif.: Stanford University Press, 1973). A. Boltho and C. J. M. Hardie, "The Japanese Economy," in D. Morris, ed., *The Economic System in the UK* (Oxford,

Eng.: Oxford University Press, 1985), provides a slightly more recent summary.

39. D. A. Hay, "International Trade and Development," in D. Morris, ed., *The Economic System in the UK*, p. 487, and S. A. B. Page, "The Management of International Trade," in R. Major, ed., *Britain's Trade and Exchange Rate Policy* (London: Heinemann, 1979), provide details.

40. See R. Prebisch, *Towards a New Trade Policy for Development* (United Nations Conference on Trade and Development, 1964); he originally set out his view in "Commercial Policy in the Underdeveloped Countries," *American Economic Review* 49 (May 1959). R. Gilpin, *The Political Economy of International Relations* (Princeton: Princeton University Press, 1987), pp. 274–81 summarizes the thesis, often known as structuralism.

41. There are many ambiguities associated with the measurement of relative prices (or the terms of trade) between industrialized and less developed economies: see R. Findlay, "The Fundamental Determinants of the Terms of Trade," in S. Grassman and E. Lundberg, eds., *The World Economic Order* (London: Macmillan, 1981), for a summary.

42. Gilpin, in *The Political Economy of International Relations*, p. 235, notes that multinational corporations have emerged in response to "the relatively more open world economy produced by the several rounds of trade barriers." This is true as far as trade in components is concerned, but, for trade in finished manufactures, higher trade barriers may encourage multinationals to locate abroad—witness Japanese car firms in the United States.

43. See T. E. Vadney, *The World Since 1945* (Harmondsworth, Eng.: Penguin, 1987), p. 280.

44. The fortunes of UNCTAD and the NIEO are summarized in Van der Wee, *Prosperity and Upheaval*, pp. 403–7.

45. See Gilpin, *The Political Economy of International Relations*, p. 295, for a brief discussion.

46. B. Tew describes this as the binary phase: see Tew, *The Evolution of the International Monetary System, 1945–1981* (London: Hutchinson, 1982), ch. 2.

47. This is discussed by R. Kuttner, *The End of Laissez Faire* (New York: Knopf, 1991), pp. 60–61.

48. This is an underlying theme of Paul Volcker's account in P. Volcker and T. Gyohten, *Changing Fortunes* (New York: Times Books, 1992).

49. H. R. Nau, *The Myth of America's Decline* (New York: Oxford University Press, 1990), p. 150, says that SDRs were championed by the American government against European government opposition. In R. Kuttner, *The End of Laissez Faire*, p. 63, Kuttner says the opposite.

50. The case for an earlier depreciation is usually presented in highly eliptical

terms: see, for example, Nau, *The Myth of America's Decline* (New York: Oxford University Press, 1990), pp. 138–39.

51. Quoted in Spulber, *Managing the American Economy*, p. 74. The power to do this had been bequeathed to the president by Congress the previous year. At the time Nixon had said that he could not imagine ever needing such powers—as if Congress was keener on the imperial presidency than the president. Perhaps the point was that Congress did not want a repetition of the thirties, when President Hoover claimed he had no power to act.

52. The administration also hoped that price and wage controls would bolster its anti-inflationary credentials in the currency markets and prevent the dollar fall from becoming a rout.

53. See Volcker and Gyohten, *Changing Fortunes*, p. 95.

54. See D. Marsh, *The Bundesbank* (London: Mandarin, 1992), pp. 189–90.

## Seven: Crises in the Seventies

1. This is described in D. Yergin, *The Prize* (London: Simon and Schuster, 1991), pp. 515–16.

2. See P. R. Odell, *Oil and World Power* (Harmondsworth, Eng.: Penguin, 1986), ch. 6, for a description of the rising importance of Japan in the oil market.

3. The policy problem is set out fully in C. J. Allsopp, "Inflation," in A. Boltho, ed., *The European Economy* (Oxford, Eng.: Oxford University Press, 1985), pp. 589–90.

4. For a much fuller discussion see ibid.

5. For further details see N. Spulber, *Managing the American Economy from Roosevelt to Reagan* (Bloomington: Indiana University Press, 1989), pp. 109–10.

6. This is quoted in ibid., p. 111.

7. For a brief description of Japan's response to higher oil prices see J. E. Hunter, *The Emergence of Modern Japan* (London: Longman, 1989), pp. 315–19.

8. This is discussed in A. Boltho and C. J. M. Hardie, "The Japanese Economy," in D. Morris, ed., *The Economic System in the UK* (Oxford, Eng.: Oxford University Press, 1985), pp. 533–38.

9. T. Sakaiya, *Honda Motor* (Tokyo: Kodansha, 1982), ch. 9, describes Honda's management approach in the decade after the oil price hike.

10. Allsopp, "Inflation," and A. Budd and G. Dicks, "Inflation: A Monetarist Interpretation," in Boltho, ed., *The European Economy*, discuss this from contrasting perspectives.

11. This is described in A. Sampson, *The Money Lenders* (Sevenoaks, Eng.: Coronet, 1981), ch. 20.

12. Some believe that these efforts were genuine and important: see S. Burman, *America in the Modern World* (Hemel Hemptead: Harvester Wheatsheaf, 1991),

pp. 144–46. After the usual lag they prompted a flurry of academic interest in the theoretical issues of policy coordination, little of which provided much illumination: see W. H. Buiter and R. C. Marston, eds., *International Economic Policy Co-ordination* (Cambridge, Eng.: Cambridge University Press, 1985).

13. The quotation, and the opinion, are from R. Kuttner, *The End of Laissez Faire* (New York: Knopf, 1991), p. 73.

14. For a less jaundiced view see J. Llewellyn, S. Potter, and L. Samuelson, *Economic Forecasting and Policy* (London: Routledge and Kegan Paul, 1985), ch. 12.

15. The deal is described in P. Volcker and T. Gyohten, *Changing Fortunes* (New York: Times Books, 1992), pp. 158–59.

16. See Yergin, *The Prize*, ch. 33, for a full account.

17. See M. J. Boskin, *Reagan and the Economy* (San Francisco: Institute for Contemporary Studies, 1987), p. 11.

18. Corporate taxes did rise rather faster, however; the taxation policies of the period are discussed in J. D. Savage, *Balanced Budgets and American Politics* (Ithaca, N.Y.: Cornell University Press, 1988), pp. 175–95.

19. Quoted by W. Niskanen, *Reaganomics* (New York: Oxford University Press, 1988), p. 158.

20. This involved setting short-term targets for bank reserves, specifically non-borrowed reserves, rather than for interest rates: see W. C. Melton, *Inside the Fed* (Homewood, Ill.: Drew Jones-Irwin, 1985) for an explanation. It is not clear whether the techniques adopted by the Fed in 1979 really did represent a fundamental improvement in monetary control.

21. The official is quoted in Niskanen, *Reaganomics*, p. 165.

22. For further details see I. M. Destler and C. R. Hennings, *Dollar Politics* (Washington, D.C.: Institute for International Economics, 1989), esp. pp. 20–21.

## Eight: A Decade of Neglect

1. See C. J. Bliss, "The Rise and Fall of the Dollar," *Oxford Review of Economic Policies* 2.1 (Winter 1985), p. 8.

2. He has since expressed these in P. Volcker and T. Gyohten, *Changing Fortunes* (New York: Times Books, 1992), p. 179.

3. The clashes are not mentioned by Volcker in his account of the period but are referred to by others. Compare ibid. with W. Niskanen, *Reaganomics* (New York: Oxford University Press, 1988). The Treasury argument that lower monetary growth would lead to lower interest rates completely ignored Volcker's problem—that to achieve lower monetary growth he needed *higher* interest rates.

4. These quotations are from, respectively: Niskanen, *Reaganomics*, p. 292; D. A. Stockman, *The Triumph of Politics* (London: The Bodley Head, 1981), p. 258 (Stockman does not substantiate the curious suggestion that temper tantrums are characteristic of the Irish); and Edwin Gray, chairman of the Federal Home Loan Bank board, as quoted in J. O'Shea, *The Daisy Chain* (London: Simon and Schuster, 1991), p. 42.

5. The administration did not, however, explicitly subscribe to the view that the tax cut would be costless. It was expected that more activity would in time tend to bring with it more tax revenue, so the final cost to the Treasury would be less than the initial cost (as the Kennedy administration discovered when it cut taxes), but there was no suggestion that the net cost would be zero. See P. C. Roberts, "Supply Side Economics," in J. M. Buchanan et al., *Reaganomics and After* (London: Institute of Economic Affairs, 1989).

6. See Stockman, *The Triumph of Politics*.

7. In 1982 the deficit of the federal government was 4.6 percent of GNP; the average for the major seven economies was 4.7 percent. The equivalent figures for 1985 were 4.5 percent and 4.5 percent; for 1990 they were 2.7 percent and 2.5 percent. See OECD, *Economic Survey: The United States* (Paris: OECD, 1989), table 12, p. 51.

8. D. Regan, *For the Record* (New York: Harcourt Brace Jovanovich, 1988), p. 142.

9. See OECD, *Economic Survey: The United States*, table 27, p. 75.

10. New technology made this possible. As information technology found its way into the branches and onto the dealing floors, banking soon became one of the most technologically intensive sectors. See E. J. Kane, "Accelerating Inflation, Technological Innovation, and the Decreasing Effectiveness of Banking Regulation," *Journal of Finance* 36 (May 1981).

11. See J. B. Stewart, *Den of Thieves* (New York: Touchstone, 1992), p. 54.

12. Stewart, *Den of Thieves*, and D. A. Vise and S. Coll, *Eagle on the Street* (New York: Collier, 1991), both record these events.

13. Even the OECD, in its annual reports on the American economy, felt obliged to spin this line, despite an evident lack of conviction: see OECD, *Economic Survey: The United States*, p. 85.

14. See O'Shea, *The Daisy Chain*.

15. A large proportion of the failures occurred in such key electoral states as California and Texas, a consideration that motivated the Reagan administration to avert any collapse in confidence until after the 1988 election.

16. For accounts see O'Shea, *The Daisy Chain*, and P. Z. Pilzer and R. Dietz, *Other People's Money* (New York: Simon and Schuster, 1990).

17. The ratio of intermediated to total financial assets also rose, even if more gradually: see OECD, *Economies in Transition* (Paris: OECD, 1989), table 3.3, p. 90.

**18.** H. Lever and C. Huhne, *Debt and Danger* (Harmondsworth, Eng.: Penguin, 1985), records the early period of the debt crisis.

**19.** S. George, *The Debt Boomerang* (London: Pluto Press, 1992), ch. 2, sets out this point in detail.

**20.** See International Monetary Fund (IMF), *World Economic Outlook* (Washington, D.C.: IMF, Oct. 1984), for this and subsequent data.

**21.** See R. Kuttner, *The End of Laissez Faire* (New York: Knopf, 1991), p. 248, for a fuller discussion.

**22.** Although technically a swap arrangement, the loan was genuine enough: see Volcker and Gyohten, *Changing Fortunes*, p. 199.

**23.** Ibid., p. 201.

**24.** This was completely different from the American attitude toward European postwar reconstruction when the United States had been keen to see a united Europe and had resisted (unsuccessfully) allocating Marshall aid on a case-by-case basis.

**25.** See I. M. Destler and C. R. Henning, *Dollar Politics* (Washington, D.C.: Institute for International Economics, 1989), chs. 3 and 8, for full discussions.

**26.** Another possible reason for Japan's policy was that strategic advantages, both commercial and political, accrued to the nation from its capital flowing into the United States: see Kuttner, *The End of Laissez Faire*.

**27.** Y. Funabashi, *Managing the Dollar* (Washington, D.C.: Institute for International Economics, 1988), discusses this and other aspects of the Plaza and Louvre deals.

## *Nine: Conclusion*

**1.** See P. Krugman, "Proving My Point," and C. V. Prestowitz et al., "The Fight over Competitiveness," both in *Foreign Affairs* (July/Aug. 1994), pp. 186–202.

**2.** See, for example, J. S. Nye, *Bound to Lead* (New York: Basic Books, 1990), p. 210.

**3.** S. Marris, *Deficits and the Dollar* (Washington, D.C.: Institute for International Economics, 1987), sets out the relationship between the federal deficit, the decline in personal saving, and the decline in the balance of payments on current account.

**4.** Organization for Economic Corporation and Development (OECD), *Economic Survey: The United States* (Paris: OECD, 1993), p. 79.

**5.** Ibid. provides an independent assessment of the original Clinton policy program.

**6.** See Robert Reich, *The Work of Nations* (London: Simon and Schuster, 1991), ch. 4, for a full presentation of this argument.

7. Lester Thurow calls this "producer economics" in *Head to Head* (New York: Morrow, 1992).

8. The view that managerial capitalism and Keynesianism are alternative approaches to the same problem—the failure of a purely free market economy—is implicit in R. Skidelsky, "Keynes and the State," and C. J. Allsopp, "The Macroeconomic Role of the State," both in D. Helm, ed., *The Economic Borders of the State* (Oxford, Eng.: Oxford University Press, 1989).

9. See J. Brander and B. Spencer, "Export Rivalries and International Market Share Rivalry," *Journal of International Economics* (Feb. 1985), and P. Krugman, ed., *Strategic Trade Policy and the New International Economics* (Cambridge, Mass.: MIT Press, 1986).

10. See Kuttner, *The End of Laissez Faire*, p. 120.

11. See, for example, P. Krugman and A. Smith, eds., *Empirical Studies of Strategic Trade Policy* (Chicago: University of Chicago Press, 1994).

12. This point is made strongly in Allsopp, "The Macroeconomic Role of the State," in Helm, ed., *The Economic Borders of the State*.

13. There are two variants: one is to regard as low risk those who do not innovate (the American error in the fifties and sixties); the other is to regard as low risk any loans provided via supposedly liquid assets (the error of the seventies, and especially the eighties).

14. See K. Oye, R. J. Lieber, and D. Rothchild, eds., *Eagle Defiant* (Boston: Little, Brown, 1983).

15. See esp. Marris, *Deficits and the Dollar*.

16. See Organization for Economic Cooperation and Development (OECD), *Economic Survey: Japan* (Paris: OECD, 1991), pp. 56–59.

17. See International Monetary Fund (IMF), *World Economic Outlook* (Washington, D.C.: IMF, 1993), p. 35.

18. Japanese universities were not immune to student unrest, but the long-term implications were much more limited—witness the lack of consequent institutional reform along the European, let alone the American line.

# BIBLIOGRAPHY

Abramovitz, M. "Catching Up, Forging Ahead, and Falling Behind." *Journal of Economic History* 46 (June 1986): 385–406.

Abramovitz, M., and P. A. David. "Reinterpreting Economic Growth: Parables and Realities." *American Economic Review* 63. Papers and Proceedings (1973): 428–39.

Agnew, J. *The United States in the World Economy.* Cambridge, Eng.: Cambridge University Press, 1987.

Aldcroft, D. H. *From Versailles to Wall Street, 1919–1929.* Harmondsworth, Eng.: Penguin Books, 1977.

Alletzhauser, A. *The House of Nomura.* London: Bloomsbury, 1990.

Allsopp, C. J. "Inflation." In *The European Economy: Growth and Crisis.* Edited by A. Boltho. Oxford, Eng.: Oxford University Press, 1982.

————. "International Macroeconomic Policy." In *The Economic System in the UK*. Edited by D. Morris. Oxford, Eng.: Oxford University Press, 1985.

————. "The Macroeconomic Role of the State." In *The Economic Borders of the State*. Edited by D. Helm. Oxford, Eng.: Oxford University Press, 1989.

Aronson, T. *Crowns in Conflict*. London: John Murray, 1986.

Bauer, P. T. "Foreign Aid Forever?" *Encounter* (March 1974): 18–25.

Beloff, M. "The End of the British Empire and the Assumption of World Wide Commitments by the United States." In *The 'Special Relationship.'* Edited by W. M. Louis and H. Bull. Oxford, Eng.: Clarendon Press, 1989.

Benston, G. J. "Interest Payments on Demand Deposits and Bank Investment Behaviour." *Journal of Political Economy* 72 (Oct. 1964): 431–39.

Bergsten, C. F. *America in the World Economy: A Strategy for the 1990's*. Washington, D.C.: Institute of International Economies, 1988.

Bernanke, B. S. "Nonmonetary Effects of the Financial Crisis in the Propagation of the Great Depression." *American Economic Review* 73 (June 1993): 257–76.

Berndt, E., and D. Wood. "Energy Price Shocks and Productivity Growth in US and UK Manufacturing." *Oxford Review of Economic Policy* 2.3 (Autumn 1986).

Bernstein, M. A. *The Great Depression*. Cambridge, Eng.: Cambridge University Press, 1987.

Bisson, T. A. *Zaibatsu Dissolution in Japan*. Berkeley: University of California Press, 1954.

Black, S. M. *A Levite Among the Priests*. Boulder, Colo.: Westview, 1991.

Blackford, M. G. *The Rise of Modern Business in Great Britain, the United States, and Japan*. London: University of North Carolina Press, 1988.

Blake, N. "Import Prices, Economic Activity, and the General Price Level in the UK, 1870–1913." In *Britain in the International Economy, 1870–1939*. Edited by S. N. Broadberry and N. F. R. Crafts. Cambridge, Eng.: Cambridge University Press, 1992.

Bliss, C. J. "The Rise and Fall of the Dollar." *Oxford Review of Economic Policies* 2.1 (Winter 1985): 7–24.

Boltho, A., and C. J. M. Hardie. "The Japanese Economy." In *The Economic System in the UK*. Edited by D. Morris. 3d ed. Oxford, Eng.: Oxford University Press, 1985.

Borden, W. S. *The Pacific Alliance: United States Foreign Economic Policy and Japanese Trade Recovery, 1947–1955*. Madison: University of Wisconsin Press, 1984.

Boskin, M. J. *Reagan and the Economy*. San Francisco: Institute for Contemporary Studies, 1987.

Bowman, J., and R. Keehn. "Agricultural Terms of Trade in Four Midwestern States, 1870–1900." *Journal of Economic History* 34 (Sept. 1974).

Brander, J., and B. Spencer. "Export Subsidies and International Market Share Rivalry." *Journal of International Economics* (Feb. 1985): 83–100.

Branson, W. H. "Trends in United States International Trade and Investment Since World War II." In *The American Economy in Transition.* Edited by M. Feldstein. Chicago: University of Chicago Press, 1980.

Brewer, J. *The Sinews of Power: War, Money, and the English State, 1688–1783.* London: Unwin Hyman, 1989.

Broadberry, S. N., and N. F. R. Crafts. *Britain in the International Economy, 1870–1939.* Cambridge, Eng.: Cambridge University Press, 1992.

Broeze, F. J. A. "The New Economic History, the Navigation Acts, and the Continental Tobacco Market, 1770–90." *Economic History Review* (1973): 668–78.

Brunner, K., and A. H. Meltzer. "What Did We Learn from the Monetary Experience of the United States in the Great Depression?" *Canadian Journal of Economics* 1 (1980).

Budd, A., and G. Dicks. "Inflation: A Monetarist Interpretation." In *The European Economy: Growth and Crisis.* Edited by A. Boltho. Oxford, Eng.: Oxford University Press, 1982.

Buiter, W. H., and R. C. Marston, eds. *International Economic Policy Co-ordination.* Cambridge, Eng.: Cambridge University Press, 1985.

Burk, K. *Britain, America, and the Sinews of War, 1914–1918.* London: George Allen and Unwin, 1985.

Burman, S. *America in the Modern World: The Transcendence of United States Hegemony.* London: Harvester Wheatsheaf, 1991.

Burrough, B., and J. Helyar. *Barbarians at the Gate: The Fall of NJR Nabisco.* New York: Harper and Row, 1990.

Cain, P. J., and A. G. Hopkins. *British Imperialism: Innovation and Expansion, 1688–1914.* London: Longman, 1993.

———. *British Imperialism: Crisis and Deconstruction, 1914–1990.* London: Longman, 1993.

Cairncross, A. K. *Factors in Economic Development.* London: George Allen and Unwin, 1962.

Cameron, R. *A Concise Economic History of the World.* New York: Oxford University Press, 1989.

Carr, W. *Poland to Pearl Harbor: The Making of the Second World War.* London: Edward Arnold, 1985.

Carroll, P. N., and D. W. Noble. *The Free and the Unfree.* Harmondsworth, Eng.: Penguin, 1988.

Casson, M., ed. *The Growth of International Business.* London: George Allen and Unwin, 1983.

Chandler, A. D. *The Visible Hand.* Cambridge, Mass.: Belknap, 1977.

———. *Strategy and Structure: Chapters in the History of American Industrial Enterprise.* Cambridge, Mass.: MIT Press, 1962.

Chernow, R. *The House of Morgan*. New York: Touchstone, 1990.

Cohen, S., and J. Zysman. *Manufacturing Matters*. New York: Basic Books, 1987.

Coleman, D. C. "Gentlemen and Players." *Economic History Review* 2d ser., 26 (1973).

Collins, M. *Banks and Industrial Finance in Britain, 1800–1939*. Basingstoke, Eng.: Macmillan, 1991.

Corbett, J. "International Perspectives on Financing: Evidence From Japan." *Oxford Review of Economic Policy* 3.4 (Winter 1987): 30–55.

Costigliola, F. "Anglo-American Financial Rivalry in the 1920's." *Journal of Economic History* 37 (1977): 911–34.

————. *Awkward Dominion: American Political, Economic and Cultural Relations with Europe, 1913–1933*. Ithaca, N.Y.: Cornell University Press, 1985.

Crafts, N. F. R. "The Eighteenth Century: A Survey." In *The Economic History of Britain Since 1700*. Vol 1. Edited by R. C. Floud and D. N. McCloskey. Cambridge, Eng.: Cambridge University Press, 1981.

————. *British Economic Growth during the Industrial Revolution*. Oxford, Eng.: Clarendon, 1985.

Cumings, B., ed. *Child of Conflict: The Korean-American Relationship, 1943–53*. Seattle: University of Washington Press, 1983.

Dasgupta, P. "The Welfare Economics of Knowledge Production." *Oxford Review of Economic Policy* 4.4 (Winter 1988).

David, P. *Technical Change, Innovation, and Economic Growth*. Cambridge, Eng.: Cambridge University Press, 1975.

de Long, J. B. "Did J. P. Morgan's Men Add Value? An Economist's Perspective on Financial Capitalism." In *Inside the Business Enterprise*. Edited by P. Temin. Chicago: University of Chicago Press, 1991.

Denison, E. F. *Why Growth Rates Differ*. Washington, D.C.: Brookings Institution, 1967.

Destler, I. M., and C. R. Henning. *Dollar Politics: Exchange Rate Policy Making in the United States*. Washington, D.C.: Institute for International Economics, 1989.

Dowrick, S., and D.-T. Nguyen. "OECD Comparative Economic Growth 1950–85: Catch Up and Convergence." *American Economic Review* 79 (1989): 1010–1030.

Egnal, M., and J. A. Ernest, "An Economic Interpretation of the American Revolution." *William and Mary Quarterly* (1972): 3–32.

Eichengreen, B., ed. *The Gold Standard in Theory and History*. New York: Methuen, 1985.

————. "International Policy Coordination in Historical Perspective: A View From the Interwar Years." In *International Economic Policy Coordination*. Edited by W. H. Buiter and R. C. Marston. Cambridge, Eng.: Cambridge University Press, 1985.

―――. *Elusive Stability: Essays in the History of International Finance.* Cambridge, Eng.: Cambridge University Press, 1990.

Falkus, M. E. "The German Business Cycle in the 1920s." *Economic History Review* 28 (1975): 451–65.

Fazzari, S. M., R. G. Hubbard, and B. C. Petersen. "Financing Constraints and Corporate Investment." *Brooking Papers on Economic Activity* 1 (1988): 141–206.

Fearon, P. *The Origins and Nature of the Great Slump, 1929–1932.* Basingstoke, Eng.: Macmillan, 1979.

―――. *War, Prosperity, and Depression: The US Economy, 1917–45.* Oxford, Eng.: Philip Allan, 1987.

Findlay, R. "The Fundamental Determinants of the Terms of Trade." In *The World Economic Order: Past and Prospects.* Edited by S. Grassman and E. Lundberg. London: Macmillan, 1981.

Fogel, R. W. *Railroads and American Economic Growth: Essays in Econometric History.* Baltimore: Johns Hopkins University Press, 1964.

Fremdling, R. "Railroads and German Economic Growth: A Leading Sector Analysis with a Comparison to the United States and Great Britain." *Journal of Economic History* 37 (Sept. 1977): 583–604.

Friedman, B. M. "Postwar Changes in the American Financial Markets." In *The American Economy in Transition.* Edited by M. Feldstein. Chicago: University of Chicago Press, 1980.

Friedman, M. "The Demand For Money: Some Theoretical and Empirical Results." *Journal of Political Economy* 67 (1959): 327–51.

Friedman, M., and A. Schwartz. *A Monetary History of the United States, 1867–1960.* Princeton: Princeton University Press, 1963.

Funabashi, Y. *Managing the Dollar: From the Plaza to the Lourve.* Washington, D.C.: Institute for International Economics, 1988.

Gaddis, J. L. *The Long Peace.* New York: Oxford University Press, 1987.

Galambos, L., and J. Pratt. *The Corporate Commonwealth.* New York: Basic Books, 1988.

Galbraith, J. K. *The Affluent Society.* Boston: Houghton Mifflin, 1958.

―――. *The New Industrial State.* 2d ed. Harmondsworth, Eng.: Penguin, 1972.

Gates, P. *Agriculture and the Civil War.* New York: Knopf, 1965.

George, S. *The Debt Boomerang.* London: Pluto Press, 1992.

Gilpin, R. *The Political Economy of International Relations.* Princeton: Princeton University Press, 1987.

Gordon, R. J. "Postwar Macroeconomics: The Evolution of Events and Ideas."

In *The American Economy in Transition*. Edited by M. Feldstein. Chicago: University of Chicago Press, 1980.

Gurley, J. G. "The Radcliffe Report and Evidence." *American Economic Review* 50 (1960): 672–700.

Habbakuk, H. J. *American and British Technology in the Nineteenth Century*. Cambridge, Eng.: Cambridge University Press, 1962.

Hamilton, A. *A Report on the Subject of Manufactures*. Presented to the House of Representatives, 1791.

Hansen, A. H. *Full Recovery or Stagnation*. New York: W. W. Norton, 1938.

Hardach, G. *The First World War, 1914–1918*. Harmondsworth, Eng.: Penguin, 1987.

Hawley, E. *The New Deal and the Problem of Monopoly*. Princeton: Princeton University Press, 1966.

Hay, D. A. "International Trade and Development." In *The Economic System in the UK*. Edited by D. Morris. Oxford, Eng.: Oxford University Press, 1985.

Hennings, K. H. "West Germany." In *The European Economy: Growth and Crisis*. Edited by A. Boltho. Oxford, Eng.: Oxford University Press, 1982.

Hogan, H. *The Marshall Plan*. Cambridge, Eng.: Cambridge University Press, 1987.

Hounshell, D. A. *From the American System to Mass Production, 1800–1932*. Baltimore: Johns Hopkins University Press, 1985.

Huertas, T. F. "The Regulation of Financial Institutions: A Historical Perspective on Current Issues." In *Financial Services: the Changing Institutions and Government Policy*. Englewood Cliffs, N.J.: Prentice-Hall, 1983.

Huertas, T. F., and H. Van B. Cleveland. *Citibank*. Cambridge, Mass.: Harvard University Press, 1987.

Hunter, J. E. *The Emergence of Modern Japan: An Introductory History since 1853*. London: Longman, 1989.

International Monetary Fund (IMF). *World Economic Outlook*. Washington, D.C.: IMF, October 1984.

———. *World Economic Outlook*. Washington, D.C.: IMF, October 1993.

James, H. *The German Slump: Politics and Economics, 1924–1936*. Oxford, Eng.: Oxford University Press, 1986.

Johnson, C. *MITI and the Japanese Miracle: The Growth of Industrial Policy, 1925–1975*. Stanford, Calif.: Stanford University Press, 1982.

Johnson, H. T. "Managing by Remote Control: Recent Management Accounting Practice in Historical Perspective." In *Inside the Business Enterprise*. Edited by P. Temin. Chicago: University of Chicago Press, 1991.

Jones, M. A. *The Limits of Liberty: American History, 1607–1980*. Oxford, Eng.: Oxford University Press, 1983.

Kane, E. J. "Accelerating Inflation, Technological Innovation, and the Decreasing Effectiveness of Banking Regulation." *Journal of Finance* 36 (May 1981): 355–67.

———. "Principal-Agent Problems in Savings and Loans Salvage." *Journal of Finance* 45 (July 1990).

Kemp, T. *The Climax of Capitalism*. London: Longman, 1990.

Kennedy, P. *The Rise and Fall of the Great Powers: Economic Change and Military Conflict from 1500 to 2000*. London: Unwin Hyman, 1988.

———. *The Rise of the Anglo-German Antagonism*. London: George Allen and Unwin, 1980.

———. *Strategy and Diplomacy, 1870–1945*. London: Fontana, 1989.

Kennedy, W. P. *Industrial Structure, Capital Markets, and the Origins of Economic Decline*. Cambridge, Eng.: Cambridge University Press, 1987.

Kenwood, A. S., and A. L. Lougheed. *The Growth of the International Economy, 1820–1980*. London: Unwin Hyman, 1983.

Keynes, J. M. *The General Theory of Employment, Interest, and Money*. London: Macmillan, for the Royal Economic Society, 1936.

———. *The Economic Consequences of the Peace*. London & Basingstoke, Eng.: Macmillan, 1971 [1919].

Kindleberger, C. P. *The World in Depression, 1929–1939*. Berkeley: University of California Press, 1973.

———. *Manias, Panics, and Crashes: A History of Financial Crises*. New York: Basic Books, 1978.

———. *The World in Depression, 1929–1939*. London: Penguin, 1987.

Krause, L. B., and Salant, W. S., eds. *Worldwide Inflation*. Washington, D.C.: Brookings Institution, 1977.

Krugman, P., ed. *Strategic Trade Policy and the New International Economics*. Cambridge, Mass.: MIT Press, 1986.

Krugman, P. "Proving My Point." *Foreign Affairs* (July–Aug. 1994): 198–202.

Krugman, P., and A. Smith, eds. *Empirical Studies of Strategic Trade Policy*. Chicago, University of Chicago Press, 1994.

Kuttner, R. *The End of Laissez Faire: National Purpose and the Global Economy after the Cold War*. New York: Knopf, 1991.

Lamoreaux, N. R. *The Great Merger Movement in American Business, 1895–1904*. Cambridge, Eng.: Cambridge University Press, 1985.

Landes, D. S. *The Unbound Prometheus*. Cambridge, Eng.: Cambridge University Press, 1969.

Lee, S. P., and P. Passell. *A New Economic View of American History*. New York: W. W. Norton, 1979.

Leuchtenberg, W. E. *Franklin Roosevelt and the New Deal, 1932–1940*. New York: Harper, 1963.

Lever, H., and C. Huhne. *Debt and Danger*. Harmondsworth, Eng.: Penguin, 1985.

Lewis, W. A. *Growth and Fluctuations, 1870–1913*. London: George Allen and Unwin, 1978.

Llewellyn, J., S. Potter, and L. Samuelson. *Economic Forecasting and Policy: The International Dimension*. London: Routledge and Kegan Paul, 1985.

Louis, W. R. "American Anti-colonialism and the Dissolution of the British Empire." In *The 'Special Relationship.'* Edited by W. M. Louis and H. Bull. Oxford, Eng.: Clarendon, 1989.

McCloskey, D. N. "Did Victorian Britain Fail?" *Economic History Review* 23 (1970): 446–59.

———. *Economic Maturity and Entrepreneurial Decline: British Iron and Steel, 1870–1913*. Cambridge, Mass.: Harvard University Press, 1973.

McCraw, T. K. "Rethinking the Trust Question." In *Regulation in Perspective*. Edited by T. K. McCann. Cambridge, Mass.: Harvard University Press, 1981.

MacDougall, G. D. A. *The World Dollar Problem: A Study in International Economics*. London: Macmillan, 1957.

———. *Don and Mandarin: Memoirs of an Economist*. London: John Murray, 1987.

Macpherson, W. J. *The Economic Development of Japan, c. 1868–1941*. Basingstoke, Eng.: Macmillan, 1987.

Maddison, A. *Phases of Capitalist Development*. Oxford, Eng.: Oxford University Press, 1982.

Mansfield, E. "Technology and Productivity in the United States." In *The American Economy in Transition*. Edited by M. Feldstein. Chicago: University of Chicago Press, 1980.

Marris, R. "How Much of the Slowdown Was Catch-up?" In *Slower Growth in the Western World*. Edited by R. C. O. Mathews. London: Heinemann, 1982.

Marris, S. *Deficits and the Dollar*. Washington, D.C.: Institute for International Economics, 1987.

Marsh, D. *The Bundesbank: The Bank That Rules Europe*. London: Mandarin, 1992.

Mayer, W. G. *The Changing American Mind*. Ann Arbor: University of Michigan Press, 1992.

Meerschwam, D. M. "Breaking Relationships: The Advent of Price Banking in the United States." In *Wall Street and Regulation*. Edited by S. L. Hayes. Boston: Harvard Business School Press, 1987.

Melton, W. C. *Inside the Fed: Making Monetary Policy*. Homewood, Ill.: Drew Jones-Irwin, 1985.

Miller, J. *The Glorious Revolution*. London: Longman, 1983.

Milward, A. S. *The Reconstruction of Western Europe, 1945–51*. London: Methuen, 1984.

———. *The Economic Effects of the Two World Wars on Britain*. Basingstoke, Eng.: Macmillan, 1984.

————. *War, Economy, and Society, 1939–1945.* Harmondsworth, Eng.: Penguin, 1987.

Mishkin, F. S. "The Household Balance Sheet and the Great Depression." *Journal of Economic History* 38 (Dec. 1978): 918–37.

Mokyr, J. *The Lever of Riches.* Oxford, Eng.: Oxford University Press, 1990.

Myrdal, G. "Development and Underdevelopment." National Bank of Egypt Fiftieth Anniversary Commemoration Lectures. Reprinted in *Leading Issues in Economic Development.* Edited by G. M. Meir. 3d ed. New York: Oxford University Press, 1976.

Nason, H., J. Steger, and G. Manners. *Support of Basic Research by Industry.* Washington, D.C.: National Science Foundation, 1978.

National Science Foundation (NSF). *Science Indicators, 1976.* Washington, D.C.: Government Printing Office, 1977.

————. *National Patterns of R&D Resources, 1953–76.* Washington, D.C.: Government Printing Office, 1986.

Nau, H. R. *The Myth of America's Decline.* New York: Oxford University Press, 1990.

Nester, W. R. *Japan's Growing Power over East Asia and the World Economy.* Basingstoke, Eng.: Macmillan, 1990.

Niskanen, W. *Reaganomics: An Insider's Account of the Policies and the People.* New York: Oxford University Press, 1988.

Nye, J. S. *Bound to Lead: The Changing Nature of American Power.* New York: Basic Books, 1990.

O'Brien, A. P. "Factory Size, Economies of Scale and the Great Merger Wave of 1898–1902." *Journal of Economic History* 48 (Sept. 1988): 639–49.

O'Brien, P. K. *The Economic Effects of the American Civil War.* Basingstoke, Eng.: Macmillan, 1988.

Odell, P. R. *Oil and World Power.* 8th ed. Harmondsworth, Eng.: Penguin, 1986.

Ohkawa, K., and H. Rosovsky. *Japanese Economic Growth: Trend Acceleration in the Twentieth Century.* Stanford, Calif.: Stanford University Press, 1973.

Ohkawa, K., and M. Shinohara, eds. *Patterns of Japanese Economic Development: A Quantitative Appraisal.* Yale: Yale University Press, 1979.

Organization for Economic Cooperation and Development (OECD). *Gaps in Technology.* Paris: OECD, 1968.

————. *Economies in Transition: Structural Adjustment in OECD Countries.* Paris: OECD, 1989.

————. *Economic Survey: Japan.* Paris: OECD, 1991.

————. *Economic Survey: The United States.* Paris: OECD, 1989.

————. *Economic Survey: The United States.* Paris: OECD, 1993.

Orsagh, T. G. "Progress in Iron and Steel: 1870–1913." *Comparative Studies in Society and History* 3 (1960).

O'Shea, J. *The Daisy Chain*. London: Simon and Schuster, 1991.

Overy, R. J. *The Nazi Recovery, 1932–1938*. Basingstoke, Eng.: Macmillan, 1982.

Oye, K., R. J. Lieber, and D. Rothchild, eds. *Eagle Defiant: United States Foreign Policy in the 1980s*. Boston: Little, Brown, 1983.

Packard, V. O. *The Hidden Persuaders*. New York: McKay, 1957.

Page, S. A. B. "The Management of International Trade." In *Britain's Trade and Exchange Rate Policy*. Edited by R. Major. London: Heinemann, 1979.

Payne, P. L. *British Entrepreneurship in the Nineteenth Century*. 2d ed. Basingstoke, Eng.: Macmillan, 1974.

Peden, G. K. *Keynes, the Treasury, and British Economic Policy*. Basingstoke, Eng.: Macmillan, 1988.

Perkins, B. "Unequal Partners: The Truman Administration and Great Britain." In *The 'Special Relationship.'* Edited by W. M. Louis and H. Bull. Oxford, Eng.: Clarendon, 1989.

Pilzer, P. Z., and R. Dietz. *Other People's Money: The Inside Story of the Savings and Loan Mess*. New York: Simon and Schuster, 1990.

Prebisch, R. "Commercial Policy in the Underdeveloped Countries." *American Economic Review* 49 (May 1959): 251–73.

———. *Towards a New Trade Policy for Development*. United Nations Conference on Trade and Development, 1964.

Prestowitz, C. V., et al. "The Fight over Competitiveness." *Foreign Affairs* (July/August 1994): 186–202.

Raaport, A. *Henry L. Stimson and Japan, 1931–33*. Chicago: University of Chicago Press, 1963.

Regan, D. *For the Record: From Wall Street to Washington*. New York: Harcourt Brace Jovanovich, 1988.

Reich, L. S. *The Making of American Industrial Research: Science and Business at GE and Bell, 1876–1926*. Cambridge, Eng.: Cambridge University Press, 1986.

Reich, R. B. *The Work of Nations*. London: Simon and Schuster, 1991.

Reynolds, D. "Roosevelt, Churchill, and the Wartime Anglo-American Alliance, 1939–45: Towards a New Synthesis." In *The 'Special Relationship.'* Edited by W. M. Louis and H. Bull. Oxford, Eng.: Clarendon, 1989.

Roberts, P. C. "Supply Side Economics." In *Reaganomics and After*. J. M. Buchanan et al. London: Institute of Economic Affairs, 1989.

Rosenberg, N. "Technological Change in the Machine Tool Industry, 1840–1910." *Journal of Economic History* 23 (1963): 414–43.

Rosevere, H. *The Financial Revolution, 1660–1760*. London: Longman, 1991.

Rothenberg, W. B. "A Price Index for Rural Massachusetts, 1750–1855." *Journal of Economic History* (1979): 975–1001.

Sakaiya, T. *Honda Motor: The Men, the Management, the Machines*. Tokyo: Kodansha, 1982.

Sale, K. *Power Shift: The Rise of the Southern Rim and Its Challenge to the Eastern Establishment*. New York: Random House, 1975.

Sampson, A. *The Arms Bazaar*. Sevenoaks, Eng.: Coronet, 1977.

————. *The Money Lenders: Bankers in a Dangerous World*. Sevenoaks, Eng.: Coronet, 1982.

Sanderson, M. *Education, Economic Change and Society in England, 1780–1870*. London: Macmillan, 1983.

————. "Technical Education and Economic Decline: 1890–1980's." *Oxford Review of Economic Policy* 4.1 (1988).

Saul, S. B. "The Market and the Development of the Mechanical Engineering Industries in Britain, 1860–1914." *Economic History Review*. 2d ser., 20 (1967): 111–30.

————. *The Myth of the Great Depression, 1873–1896*. 2d ed. Basingstoke, Eng.: Macmillan, 1985.

Savage, J. D. *Balanced Budgets and American Politics*. Ithaca, N.Y.: Cornell University Press, 1988.

Scammell, W. M. *The International Economy Since 1945*. 2d ed. London: Macmillan, 1983.

Schaller, M. *The American Occupation of Japan: The Origins of the Cold War in Asia*. New York: Oxford University Press, 1985.

Schama, S. *The Embarrassment of Riches: An Interpretation of Dutch Culture in the Golden Age*. London: Collins, 1987.

Schlesinger, A. M. *The Age of Roosevelt: The Politics of Upheaval*. Boston: Houghton Mifflin, 1960.

————. *The Age of Roosevelt: The Coming of the New Deal*. Boston: Houghton Mifflin, 1958.

————. *The Cycles of American History*. Harmondsworth, Eng.: Penguin, 1989.

Schmitz, C. J. *The Growth of Big Business in the United States and Western Europe, 1850–1939*. London: Macmillan, 1993.

Schuker, S. A. "American Reparations to Germany, 1919–33: Implications for the Third World Debt Crisis." *Princeton Studies in International Finance* 61 (1988).

Schwarz, J. A. *The New Dealers: Power Politics in the Age of Roosevelt*. New York: Knopf, 1993.

Sen, A. K. *Poverty and Famines: An Essay on Entitlement and Deprivation*. Oxford, Eng.: Oxford University Press, 1981.

Shannon, H. A. "The Sterling Balances of the Sterling Area." *Economic Journal* (1950).

Shillony, B. A. *Politics and Culture in Wartime Japan*. Oxford, Eng.: Clarendon, 1991.

Skidelsky, R. *John Maynard Keynes: Hopes Betrayed, 1883–1920*. London: Macmillan, 1983.

————. "Keynes and the State." In *The Economic Borders of the State*. Edited by D. Helm. Oxford, Eng.: Oxford University Press, 1989.

————. *John Maynard Keynes: The Economist as Saviour, 1920–1937*. London: Macmillan, 1992.

————. *Interests and Obsessions*. London: Macmillan, 1993.

Smith, A. *An Inquiry into the Nature and Causes of the Wealth of Nations*. New York: Modern Library, 1937.

Spulber, N. *Managing the American Economy from Roosevelt to Reagan*. Bloomington: Indiana University Press, 1989.

Stewart, J. B. *Den of Thieves*. New York: Touchstone, 1992.

Stiglitz, J. E., and A. Weiss. "Credit Rationing in Markets with Imperfect Information." *American Economic Review* (1981): 393–410.

Stockman, D. A. *The Triumph of Politics: The Crisis in American Politics and How It Affects the World*. London: The Bodley Head, 1981.

Stockwin, J. A. A. *Japan: Divided Politics in a Growth Economy*. New York: W. W. Norton, 1982.

Stoneman, P., and J. Vickers. "The Economics of Technology Policy." *Oxford Review of Economic Policy* 4.4 (Winter 1988).

Storry, R. *Japan and the Decline of the West in Asia, 1894–1943*. London: Macmillan, 1979.

Suzuki, Y., ed. *The Japanese Financial System*. Rev. ed. Oxford, Eng.: Clarendon, 1990.

Taylor, F. W. *The Principles of Scientific Management*. New York: Harper, 1911.

Temin, P. *Causal Factors in American Economic Growth in the Nineteenth Century*. Basingstoke, Eng.: Macmillan, 1975.

————. *Did Monetary Forces Cause the Great Depression?* New York: W. W. Norton, 1976.

Tew, B. *The Evolution of the International Monetary System, 1945–81*. 2d ed. London: Hutchinson, 1982.

Thomas, R. P. "A Quantitative Approach to the Study of the Effects of British Imperial Policy upon Colonial Welfare: Some Preliminary Findings." *Journal of Economic History* (1965): 615–38.

Thurow, L. *Head to Head*. New York: Morrow, 1992.

Tobin, J. "Monetary Policy and the Management of the Public Debt: The Patman Enquiry." *Review of Economics and Statistics* 35 (1953): 118–27.

Toyoda, T. *Toyota: Fifty Years in Motion*. Tokyo: Kodansha, 1987.

Triffin, R. *Gold and the Dollar Crisis*. New Haven: Yale University Press, 1960.

Unruh, J. D. *The Plains Across*. London: Pimlico, 1992.

Vadney, T. E. *The World Since 1945*. Harmondsworth Eng.: Penguin, 1987.

Van der Wee, H. *Prosperity and Upheaval: The World Economy, 1945–1980*. Harmondsworth, Eng.: Penguin, 1986.

Vickers, H. *Gladys Duchess of Marlborough*. London: Hamish Hamilton, 1987.

Vise, D. A., and S. Coll. *Eagle on the Street*. New York: Collier, 1991.

Volcker, P., and T. Gyohten. *Changing Fortunes: The World's Money and the Threat to American Leadership*. New York: Times Books, 1992.

Wallerstein, I. "The Rise and Future Demise of the World Capitalist System: Concepts for Comparative Analysis." *Comparative Studies in Society and History* (1974): 387–415.

———. *The Modern World System III*. San Diego, Calif.: Academic Press, 1989.

Watt, D. C. *Succeeding John Bull*. Cambridge, Eng.: Cambridge University Press, 1984.

White, E. N. "Before the Glass-Steagall Act: An Analysis of the Investment Banking Activities of National Banks." *Explorations in Economic History* 23 (Jan. 1986): 33–35.

Whyte, W. H. *The Organization Man*. New York: Simon and Schuster, 1956.

Wilson, C. "Economy and Society in Late Victorian Britain." *Economic History Review*. 2d ser., 17 (1965).

Womack, J. P., D. T. Jones, and D. Roos. *The Machine That Changed the World*. New York: Rawson, 1990.

Yamashita, T. *The Panasonic Way*. Tokyo: Kodansha, 1987.

Yergin, D. *The Prize: The Epic Quest for Oil, Money, and Power*. London: Simon and Schuster, 1991.

# INDEX